Limerick County Library
30012 00513488 6

D0298188

NEIL LENNON

Man and Bhoy

NEIL LENNON

Man and Bhoy

HarperSport
An Imprint of HarperCollins*Publishers*

First published in UK in 2006 by
HarperSport
an imprint of HarperCollins*Publishers*
London

1

A CIP catalogue record for this book is
available from the British Library

ISBN-13 978 0 00 723347 2
ISBN-10 0 00 723347 7

Set in Linotype Sabon by
Rowland Phototypesetting Ltd,
Bury St Edmunds, Suffolk

Printed and bound in Great Britain by
Clays Ltd, St Ives plc

The HarperCollins website address is
www.harpercollins.co.uk

To Alisha and Gallagher

Contents

Acknowledgements

First of all I would like to thank everyone at HarperCollins publishers, and especially Michael Doggart, Neil Dowden, Tim Whiting and Andrea Woodman.

My agents Martin Reilly and Mark Donaghy did an excellent job as usual, as did our literary agent Mark Stanton. Thanks, guys.

I am grateful to Martin O'Neill for his kind words and support down the years. My thanks also go to all at Celtic, Leicester and Crewe, and to all my friends and family for their reminiscences as well as their support.

I particularly want to thank my mother and father, Ursula and Gerry, for their advice during the writing, and my mother's many years of maintaining scrapbooks about my career proved absolutely invaluable.

In addition I want to thank Karen, my personal assistant, for all her hard work and help down the years.

It almost goes without saying that I am so very grateful for the love and support of my partner Irene, but I want to place that on record.

Lastly, my thanks go to Martin Hannan, without whom this book would not have been possible.

Foreword

I first met Neil Lennon one lovely summer morning not far from his home town of Lurgan in County Armagh. I was on the first rungs of the management ladder, and he was playing for Crewe Alexandra, trying to rebuild a footballing career that had been threatened by a serious back injury sustained as a young kid at Manchester City. We exchanged pleasantries, I wished him good luck with his life, walked away, and thought little more of Neil Lennon and his problems.

I had absolutely no idea that not many years later, when I was managing Leicester City, my assistant manager John Robertson and I would drive up to Stockport, encamp ourselves in some rundown hovel and try to persuade the occupant of the said hovel to come and help us get promotion at Leicester rather than play for Premiership club Coventry City, where he was bound the following day. I think I remember seeing a couple of mice in the corner of the sitting room, both probably deafened by some early Oasis music and wistfully eyeing the last remnants of a tuna sandwich lying on the sofa. John and I refused to leave until the ginger-haired, stockily built young Irishman gave us his word that he would join us. Whether or not the mice finished off that sandwich

I just don't know, but the lad decided to come to Leicester and save my bacon.

For the next four years he bestrode Filbert Street like a colossus, winning tackles, playing the ball, bawling out instructions, cajoling and generally being brilliant. 'Lenny', as his team-mates named him, had an immediate and lasting impact, not only in the dressing room but also on the field of play where it really mattered. Every Leicester City fan will testify to his excellence. Certainly, the club itself would not have achieved the success that followed had Neil not been there.

I left Leicester in June 2000, because the call of Celtic was too great to withstand. I immediately put in a big money offer to my former club in an attempt to persuade Neil to join me at Celtic. For various reasons, he didn't arrive until December that year, playing his first game for the Hoops one bitterly cold evening at Dundee. We scrambled a late winner, but the following day, some unimpressed reporter wanted to know what was all the fuss about Neil Lennon? I think five-and-a-half years on, he's got the picture. Whatever Neil achieved at Leicester City, he surpassed at his beloved Celtic.

Controversy and Neil seem inextricably linked but I suppose given his background – similar to my own – potential bother in Glasgow is never a million miles away. Just occasionally Neil might not be the innocent party. Nights out with Paul Lambert, Chris Sutton, Alan Thompson, Johann Mjallby and Henrik Larsson did not always pass incident-free. The following day's inquest would always start with, 'Were you involved in any way, Lenny?' 'Absolutely not, gaffer!' was usually followed by 'Well, it wasn't all my fault . . .' It was very sad, however, that death threats prevented him playing more football for Northern Ireland, for whom he did so well.

And now we have had another great season for Neil Lennon, as captain no less. I am genuinely delighted for him, as he is an amazing character and a great, great player – that is stated with almost a decade of knowledge of the man. I also have great regard for his parents, Gerry and Ursula, and I'm sure, like most parents, that they are proud of their boy – almost all of the time!

He has been one of the best footballers I have known, let alone worked with. His ability is unquestioned, but he also possesses something quite rare in human beings – great courage. That is why I hold him in such high esteem.

We have both been part of Celtic Football Club for a brief but memorable time in the club's long history, and we have worked together for a decent period of our lives. Which is why I can say that Neil Lennon is a pretty special man and bhoy.

I wish him all the best with this book and his life to come.

Martin O'Neill

CHAPTER ONE

A Troubled Footballer

The telephone call which changed my life was not even made to me.

It was late in the afternoon of 21 August 2002, when 'he' called the BBC's office at Ormeau Avenue in Belfast. He didn't say his name – they never do – but left enough hints as to his background. His message was brief and to the point. As it was recounted to me, the call went something like this . . .

'This is the LVF. If Neil Lennon takes the field tonight he will get seriously hurt.'

LVF stands for Loyalist Volunteer Force, one of the more extreme terrorist groups in Northern Ireland at that time. They battled in their own way for what they perceived to be the Protestant and Unionist cause. I, on the other hand, was a Roman Catholic from Lurgan in County Armagh, and to them I was guilty of a terrible crime – I played for Glasgow Celtic, the club which, despite being non-sectarian since its foundation, is seen as a totem of Irish Catholic nationalism.

It didn't matter to the caller that I had lived away from Northern Ireland for fourteen years. He didn't know that my family was not associated in any way with political or sectarian groups. My three sisters and I had been brought up with 'the Troubles' all around, but hadn't lost a relative. We were always lectured by our parents that we should avoid being caught up in the madness that had besmirched our country over four decades.

It only mattered to the caller that, for the first time, a Roman Catholic who also played for Celtic would captain Northern Ireland in Belfast that night. It was a 'friendly' match against Cyprus to prepare both sides for the forthcoming qualifying matches for the European Championships. There was nothing remotely friendly in what the caller said.

They say a week is a long time in politics. Well, let me tell you that two hours can be a lifetime in football, and eighteen months can seem an eternity. For the seeds of what happened that night in Belfast were laid on the evening of 28 February 2001, with an event that made headlines in newspapers in Britain, Ireland and further afield.

That was the first time I played for Northern Ireland after joining Celtic, in a friendly match against Norway at Windsor Park. Geography is vitally important in my country, so you should know that the crumbling old stadium is in the heart of East Belfast and is home to Linfield FC, a club traditionally supported by the Protestant and Unionist section of Northern Irish society who predominate in that area.

The events of that night didn't come as a complete surprise to me. When I signed for Celtic a few months earlier I had known that it was highly probable that when I turned out for Northern Ireland I would get some stick and maybe a bit of hassle here and there. It had happened to Celtic players capped by Northern Ireland in the past, such as Anton Rogan and Allan McKnight. A captain of Celtic had actually led Northern Ireland in the past – the late Bertie Peacock, who played thirty-one times for his country and went on to manage the national side, in the fifties and sixties. But he was a Protestant in an era when there was rather more respect around.

I, on the other hand, was the antithesis of what some 'fans' stood for in a sectarian time. There had been warnings in various newspapers that my move to Celtic could earn me some serious grief when I played for Northern Ireland, so I wasn't entirely taken aback, but nothing could have prepared me for the sheer scale of what happened before and during that match against Norway.

A few days before the game, my mother and father at home in Lurgan were appalled to learn from journalists that the words 'Neil Lennon RIP' had been scrawled on a wall in the town of Lisburn. Someone was saying that I was going to be a dead man.

It was a terrible shock to my family who are quiet-living and fundamentally decent Christian people. My father Gerry had not been well and was to suffer a heart attack in August 2001. He, my mother Ursula and the rest of my family were deeply upset by what some moron undoubtedly thought was a sick joke – or maybe in light of subsequent events, he or she meant it as a shot across my bows, a warning of worse to come. And indeed worse, much worse, did come my way as I joined my colleagues of different religions and none at all to play for my country against Norway.

From the moment I went onto that pitch to play in the green and white colours of Northern Ireland I was the target of an unremitting chorus of boos, jeers, catcalls and insults. In a half-empty stadium, the noise seemed to amplify and at times it seemed as though it was the only sound to be heard.

I had anticipated the odd jibe from individuals in the crowd or on the streets, but nothing prepared me for the extent of the hatred I faced. Deep down, it was the sheer scale of things which upset me.

Prior to the game, the graffiti incident became known and there were some rumours about threats to me. The Irish FA and manager Sammy McIlroy appealed for me to be supported, but perhaps that backfired. I myself had spoken of the support and letters of encouragement I had received, but inside I had a justifiable dread of what might happen at Windsor Park. Later, people would try to play down what happened, saying that it was only a minority in the crowd who had hurled abuse. There wasn't a massive crowd at the game, maybe 7,000 or so, and the minority might only have been 500 or 600, but to me the proportion booing me didn't matter – one per cent would have been too much for me.

On the pitch I was only too aware of what was happening off it. Not only could I hear the booing and jeering, but I could also see people in the stands arguing and gesticulating at each other amidst the home support. I could see and hear sections of the Northern Ireland crowd having a go at their fellow supporters who were abusing me – I use the word abuse because that is what such conduct is – and after a while I could clearly see that nobody was paying much attention to proceedings on the pitch.

The focus was no longer on the team as we battled to contain a slick Norway side. Instead the crowd's concentration – and mine too – was almost totally on events off the pitch. And all too obviously, those events were connected to my part in the game. Every time I went near the ball there would be a chorus of boos and jeers, and then a spattering of cheers from fans who were clearly disgusted at what was happening to me.

Now I have been booed and jeered many times – just about every time I play for Celtic away from home in Scotland, and yes, I'll have more to say about that later in this book. I had heard anti-Catholic songs being sung at Windsor Park internationals before but like most Catholic players, played on and ignored them.

This was substantially different, however. The fact is you do not mind being booed by the opposition fans or even your own supporters if you are having a stinker. But this was something else again and was, I believe, completely premeditated by a part of a hard core of the support which could not stomach seeing a Catholic Celtic player turning out for 'their' country. I say it was premeditated and planned because it started with my very first kick of the ball, it emanated from particular groups within the crowd and continued all the way to half-time without letting up. Also, I had played thirty-five times for my country before that night and had a good relationship with most fans who knew I gave my all for Northern Ireland. So what had happened to make things so different? Answer: I now played for Celtic.

It was a totally surreal atmosphere inside Windsor Park that night. God only knows what the small number of Norwegian supporters made of it all. Ole Gunnar Solskjaer of Manchester United was playing for them that night. He was interviewed afterwards and was quite bewildered. He had no idea what it was all about and just couldn't understand why one of Northern Ireland's own players was being booed every time he touched the ball.

Whether the clubs can do anything about it or not, Celtic and Rangers have become identified with the two sides of the sectarian divide in Northern Ireland. Here was I, in my thirty-sixth appearance for my country, never having been singled out before, being roundly abused simply because I was now a Celtic player. In the small minds of some people that fact was sufficient to make me an enemy, someone they could single out for sectarian abuse.

As I have said, I was aware that joining Celtic might give

me problems of this nature. Indeed, I had spoken at length on the subject to my mentor and manager, Martin O'Neill, while we had been discussing my move from Leicester City to Celtic – and who better to talk things over with? He had been the first Catholic to captain Northern Ireland and had been proud to play for and lead his national side. We both knew that anyone signing for Celtic, or indeed Rangers, automatically became a hate figure to one faction or the other in a Northern Ireland divided by religion – it sounds like something out of ancient history, and that's where it all stems from and should have stayed, but it is a modern-day fact.

Martin's attitude was that I should come to Celtic and then we would deal with whatever problems arose. I was happy to go along with that advice, but truthfully, neither of us anticipated the escalation of problems or the lack of support I would get when things boiled over as they duly did in the Norway game.

As we approached half-time with Norway winning 3–0, it was clear that something would have to happen. All of the team had suffered as a result of the abuse – not surprisingly, their concentration was less than total. Opinions differ as to what exactly took place at half-time, but my recollection is that Sammy McIlroy came to me and said that he had spoken to Martin about taking me off at the interval before the game in any case. Given that I was relatively new at Celtic and should not be playing every minute of every game, that sounded plausible.

I have to say that in retrospect, I don't think Sammy handled things very well that night. Martin O'Neill has no memory of such a conversation, and perhaps Sammy said this at the time to cover up the deep embarrassment which he and the Irish Football Association's officials were undoubtedly feeling. I would have preferred him to be up front, to have said 'we're going to take you off for your own sake and we'll deal with this afterwards', but what was happening was completely new to him and being honest, I think he was overwhelmed by it all. My team-mates were also embarrassed and that was understandable – I don't know how I would have reacted had it been someone else in the team getting the jeers. Some people later suggested that they should have shown solidarity and refused to come out for the second half, but I would not have wanted that, not least because it would have worsened the situation with the crowd. In addition, they were getting no lead from the manager or the Irish FA to do something of that nature.

After the match, Sammy tried to play things down and was so blasé in interviews that unfortunately he gave out the wrong message. It was as though he did not understand what lay at the heart of the whole situation. He indicated that everyone got booed at some time or another in their career – a remark that angered my family in particular, as they were the ones who had been forced to live with the appalling graffiti and who would now be the centre of unwanted attention back home in Lurgan.

I know what Martin O'Neill would have done – he would have addressed that section of the crowd who were abusing me and told them to cease their activities forthwith. And I suspect the majority of the crowd would have backed him, though realistically nothing was going to deter the bigoted boo boys.

But Martin wasn't there. Instead, nothing happened at all. Neither Sammy nor anyone from the Irish FA confronted the issue at the time, and there were no warnings to the crowd that I heard, though to be fair the abuse was roundly condemned afterwards. So the minority got their wicked way. The football pitch can be a very lonely place, and I never felt so isolated in a match as I did on that night against Norway.

My substitution led to an even more bizarre event. I got dressed as quickly as possible and then did an interview outside the dressing room in which I gave my response to what had happened to the BBC.

This is what I told them: 'A lot of people got behind me tonight and I was touched by that. There are minorities in all walks of life who make trouble for everyone else. But there are a lot more good people than bad in this country. I hope to be back but first I will talk things over with my club and family and take it from there.' That really was the situation – I didn't want to make a decision immediately.

The Royal Ulster Constabulary then stepped in. Some of the officers were worried about my safety, and I couldn't very well go and sit in the dugout or the stand, could I? They insisted that I miss the rest of the game and go with them in an unmarked car. That's how I found myself making a swift exit from Windsor Park and being whisked through the back streets of East Belfast in the back of a fairly beaten-up car that no one could have mistaken for a police vehicle. Here I was, minutes after playing for my country, getting a police escort through its largest city – it was beyond satire and in the realms of madness. I never did get to see what happened in the second half, though things must have improved as we only conceded one more goal and lost 4–0.

The police took me back to the hotel to fetch my stuff and I returned quickly to Glasgow where the following morning I went to Parkhead, home of Celtic, and discussed what had happened with Martin O'Neill. Some people in the media had already speculated that I might retire from international football, and for once they were close to the mark. I told Martin that I didn't know what to do and really wasn't sure that I should go back and play for Northern Ireland, and certainly not at Windsor Park. He had been as shocked as anyone and could see I was still upset, but his advice was that I should give it another go as I might regret it in the long term, and perhaps miss out on the chance to play in major finals such as the European Championships.

The massive press speculation that I would quit international football continued for days and I decided to speak out. I said truthfully that I was considering standing down from the Northern Ireland squad but needed more time to think things through.

Meanwhile a huge furore had broken out over what had happened to me. The Irish FA's community relations officer Michael Boyd said he would be calling for action: 'The time has come for the IFA to send out a strong message that this sort of behaviour cannot be tolerated. Banning these people is what the majority of decent supporters want.'

He was promptly contradicted by a different IFA spokesman who was quoted as saying: 'Obviously we are very disappointed by the reaction of a section of the crowd. But there is very little we can do about it.

'It is very difficult to counter a small element. We don't even know who they are. It might have been Rangers supporters coming over for the match, because we'd read press reports before this match that Rangers supporters were planning to attend to give Neil Lennon a hard time.'

Talk about living in cloud cuckoo land . . . so hundreds of Rangers fans travelled from Scotland just to boo me? I'm not exactly the Rangers supporters' favourite person but I don't think hundreds of people would go that far just to jeer me.

There were all sorts of mixed messages coming from the Irish FA. Its president Jim Boyce condemned the abuse but said that the majority of the crowd were behind me. He told reporters: 'I have no time for bigotry in any walk of life, let alone football. I have no time for sectarianism and I totally oppose it, as I've always done.

'You had a certain section of people with moronic brains who did boo. But the vast majority of people in the ground were supporting Neil Lennon and it's important not to forget that.'

The press and politicians also weighed in, and I was touched by the many ordinary decent folk who did try to encourage me to play on. But this was not really helping me one bit. I lay awake at night wondering what to do. I spoke to friends and most importantly, to my family, and with their backing I eventually decided that I would carry on playing.

Sammy McIlroy was grateful for my decision and assured me I was very much an important part of his plans. My next game for Northern Ireland was against the Czech Republic. I was nervous beforehand and despite assurances from the Irish FA, who had appealed for decent fans to support me, I was worried about the 'welcome' I would receive. I need not have been so apprehensive. My name was cheered to the echo when it was announced and I was warmly applauded onto the field. I did not kid myself that this show of support was unanimous, but it was incredibly heartening that ordinary football fans were prepared to stand up and be counted on my behalf. Sammy McIlroy would later say that their response had 'drilled it in' that the supporters wanted me in the team.

My own feelings before the match were that I would give it one more go and my continued career for Northern Ireland would depend on the reaction at Windsor Park. There were people within the Irish FA who had wanted my participation to be seen as a statement that the boo boys would not be allowed to win, but I had not been taking that line in public – I just wanted to play football for my country and not be abused.

After another two World Cup qualifiers against Bulgaria, which we lost home and away, I missed three games but was picked to be part of the squad in matches running up to the European Championships. Even though my knee was bothering me, I came on as substitute against Poland in a friendly in Limassol in Cyprus which we lost 1–4. At the start of what would be a momentous season for Celtic and for me personally, Northern Ireland played Cyprus. In view of what transpired, it was interesting that the match was to be co-sponsored by Northern Ireland's Community Relations Council. There were also to be banners saying 'Give Sectarianism The Boot'. You may shortly appreciate the irony . . .

A few hours before the match it was announced that in my forty-first appearance for my country, I would captain the national side. Steve Lomas was injured and Michael Hughes was unavailable while Gerry Taggart, who would probably have been given the armband, was also out with a knee injury. With those players out, I was the most experienced player in the squad and pretty much the obvious choice to lead the side. By default, almost, the captain's armband was passed to me, even though I felt I was not 100 per cent match fit as I had undergone a knee operation during the close season.

It was often forgotten in the aftermath of what transpired that I had actually captained Northern Ireland before. We played the Republic of Ireland in 1999 in a benefit match and at one point in the second half there was a raft of substitutions. The manager at the time, Lawrie McMenemy, was a good and decent man who did what he thought was right rather than convenient. Lawrie would later recall: 'My over-riding memory was when I gave the armband to Neil after I brought off my skipper. He could barely keep his chest inside his shirt and was as proud as punch.'

I was indeed very proud, just as I was thrilled to bits when

Lawrie made me captain from the start in an away match against Finland. But I was still at Leicester then. This time I was a Celtic player and that was to make all the difference.

When Sammy told me early in the week of the Cyprus match that I was going to be captain I was delighted. We were installed as usual in the Hilton hotel in Templepatrick and were doing our routine of training and discussing tactics, but it all took on a different dimension for me on the Monday when I was appointed captain.

Sammy went public with the news the night before the match and all the newspapers carried his statements explaining his reasons.

'He is my sixth captain,' he was quoted as saying. 'With no disrespect to Neil, being the sixth captain shows you the problems we have had. Hopefully, things will change. He is the second most-capped player in the current squad. Being in the engine room he can start us off with his passing and knowledge of the game.

'Neil is a leader; he has been captain for Celtic as well. It's a good honour for him. I hope he enjoys it and that his performance rubs off on the rest of the lads.'

I certainly was honoured, and my family were also proud and delighted for me. At a press conference I emphasized that the unpleasant events of the Norway game were in the past and that I preferred to look forward. I said honestly that it had been difficult for me at the time, but I had put it all behind me, and added the thought that being named captain was a nice way to start the season.

The political situation in Northern Ireland had also changed. It was now more than four years on from the Good Friday Agreement, and I thought there was genuine goodwill on all sides. But one man in a phone box many miles away thought differently.

It all went pear shaped late in the afternoon. We were having our pre-match meal and I had just come down to the tables when Sammy took me to one side. He told me straightforwardly that there were two police officers from the newly named Police Service of Northern Ireland (PSNI) outside wanting to talk to me.

I asked him what it was about, and he told me there had been a phone call and I would have to talk to the officers – one male and one female – about it. I knew immediately what the call was, and my heart sank into my boots. For in the run-up to the match I knew I was 'fair game' for any madman wanting to make a point and I had anticipated someone trying to get publicity for their 'cause', especially after it was announced that I would captain the side. But I had not thought it would go as far as someone threatening my life.

The two police officers – as is the accepted protocol in writing about Northern Ireland, they must remain anonymous – were very matter of fact. They said that there had been a telephone call to the BBC's offices in Belfast by someone who claimed to represent the LVF. The threat was that if I played that night I would get hurt. Without it being needed to be said, we all knew that in all probability 'hurt' meant getting shot.

I asked the officers how genuine the threat was and they said that nine out of ten of these calls prior to sporting events were hoaxes.

They were firm, however, that they could not tell me what to do. That decision would have to be mine and they would react accordingly. I presumed that meant if I decided to play I would get armed police escorts to and from the game etc., but my immediate thought was how would anyone be able to stop someone getting to me in the many public areas I would enter that night, not least the Windsor Park pitch?

My first reaction, nevertheless, was that I should play on.

The percentage bet was that the whole thing was a hoax and I would be safe. But a whole whirlwind of thoughts started coursing through my mind, the vast majority of which centred on my family and their safety. And finally it came down to this – how much of a bet do you take with your life?

This time Sammy McIlroy reacted well and sympathetically. He said that if the call had been about his son, he would want him to go home.

My mind was in turmoil at that second. I really didn't know what to do and I knew I needed advice.

I used my mobile phone to call Celtic's security adviser in Scotland – unfortunately, I knew him only too well as I had had reason to call him previously – and he was adamant that I should take no chances whatsoever and should get back to Glasgow as soon as possible.

I then called my parents. My father said that of course I could not play and he would come and get me. He rushed to the hotel and was angered that no one could tell him where I was. He eventually made his way to my room where I was just finishing packing. A few minutes later I was in his car and on my way home to Lurgan. We had a police escort at first but then some friends met us and we travelled in convoy for the rest of the journey. I have not been back to Windsor Park since . . . and Dad still has his unused complimentary tickets for the match in which I didn't captain Northern Ireland.

Before I left the hotel, I told Sammy that I probably would not be returning to play for the national side ever again. He was entirely understanding but said he hoped I would change my mind. I then spoke to most of the rest of the squad. I learned later that one or two had wanted the Irish FA to pull the team out of the match, but I insisted before the match that they should go on and do their best. My thoughts genuinely were for the team as I knew they had a tough campaign ahead and needed the match practice.

It was agreed that the Irish FA would put out my press statement and that there would be a cover story that I was already on the way back to Glasgow. In reality, there was no way to catch a plane home at that time and I would have to spend a night in Lurgan.

My statement read: 'After close consultation with the footballing authorities and the Police Service of Northern Ireland I will not be participating in this evening's international game.

'I am very disappointed that my desire to play for my country, on my first opportunity to captain my team at home, has been taken away from me.'

In the car on the way to Lurgan, my father and I talked things over. He was very angry, of course, as was I, but funnily enough I was a bit more philosophical.

In a sense there was an inevitability about these events. For better or worse, I had become a controversial figure, both in Scotland and in Northern Ireland. I was a symbol for one side, the epitome of what was wanted in a Celtic man dedicated to the club he loved, whereas for the other side I was something to despise. I could see that the two sides would never meet on common ground, and that there would always be extremists who simply could not tolerate my presence in a Northern Ireland jersey.

My main thoughts were for my family. It was hard enough for them when I joined Celtic, and the graffiti before the Norway game had been an awful experience for them. My father told me that 'a cold chill' had gripped him when he first saw the pictures. So I just could not in all conscience put them through that strain again.

And I had my daughter to think of. We had managed to

shield Alisha – at home in England and just ten years old – from the dreadful facts of her father's life in a divided city and country. How was I now going to explain to her that her daddy's life was under threat because he played football for a certain team?

All these things and more raced through my mind as we hurried back to Lurgan. In retrospect it was then that I finally decided I would not play for Northern Ireland again. Frankly, given my thoughts for my family, the decision was pretty easy for me.

The proof of the effects such happenings can have on family members met me at the door of our house in Lurgan. My mother was very upset, and in turn that affected me. After a brief reunion with the other members of my family, who all backed my decision, it was agreed that I should get away from the house. We knew it would only be a short time before the news broke and then a media scrum would descend on us. As long as I wasn't there, the journalists, photographers and camera crews would go away.

My family were able to say truthfully to callers that I was not at home, for I was in fact at the house of my best friend, Gary McCavigan. We have been mates since schooldays and now, when I needed him most, Gary was there for me, and his presence would lead to the only light-hearted note in this whole symphony of sadness.

As the evening wore on, Gary and I talked and talked but eventually we decided to try to get some sleep. Gary's wife and daughter took one bedroom and we were in the other bedroom. It may not surprise you to learn that I didn't get a wink of sleep that night. Every time a car went by the house I was startled, and I kept imagining that people were out there trying to find me.

And maybe one of them had a gun ... but it wasn't that

fear which stopped my brain from switching off – no, it was Gary's snoring that kept me awake!

In the wee small hours, the ludicrous nature of the situation really struck me and I had a laugh to myself – what else could I do?

The next morning my dad called to say that a journalist who was known and respected by the family, Adrian Logan of Ulster Television, had made contact. I spoke to him and he pointed out that I would get no peace until I had given an interview and made some sort of statement. I could see that was true. He offered to make the proceedings available to other television stations and on that basis I agreed to do a short interview.

The gist of it was my feeling that football had been irrelevant the previous night. I said: 'My parents were pretty distraught really. I've got a ten-year-old daughter who knows nothing about this at the minute and we're going to try to keep her away from it as much as we can. Obviously, I can't put them through this every time, so I've thought long and hard about it and I've decided that I probably won't be going back to play for Northern Ireland.

'It's a decision that I've thought about previously and this time I've come to the conclusion that it's probably for the best for everybody.

'My manager, Sammy McIlroy, was magnificent with me throughout it. He said if it was his son in the same position, he'd do exactly the same thing and he backed me on that and I can't thank him enough for that, because obviously it was difficult for him, but this can't go on.'

With that I jumped in the car and headed for Scotland. It was a relief to get back to Glasgow and the catcalls I get there on a daily basis.

That night Celtic's security team put me up in a hotel as

they feared that I would get no peace at home. I sat there alone in that hotel room making calls to my family and friends and watching the television. I was utterly amazed when the news programmes were completely dominated by what had happened to me. When you have reached a certain level in football, having to watch yourself on television is one of the more unnerving experiences that you go through. I had never quite got used to seeing myself play, never mind being interviewed off the pitch, but here I was now featuring in the headlines and in the main bulletins. It was almost as if I was watching a different person – who was this Neil Lennon they kept referring to along with the words 'death threats'? How could a mere footballer gain such attention? But of course, it wasn't my footballing prowess that was the issue.

As I lay there contemplating my future I couldn't help but think of quitting the game altogether. Only my desire to succeed at Celtic kept me from walking away.

Even so, I had lost something very special. No one except another footballer can really know about the long hard hours of work that go into reaching the top level that is international football. All the other sacrifices such as special diets and the rigours of self-discipline through the years all count towards your achievements, and here was I with the pinnacle of my career to date snatched away from me by a man with a telephone. It seemed for a while that all the hard work had not been worth the candle.

The following day the LVF announced they had nothing to do with the call. That actually made me feel a lot better – it now appeared that it really was a hoax, and the caller would also not want to make enemies of those lads.

But I had made up my mind and before Celtic's weekend match against Partick Thistle I told a press conference of my final and irrevocable decision to quit playing international football.

'It's not a snap decision,' I said. 'I've thought long and hard about it. It would have been nice in a way to turn things right round from that experience in the Norway game, but it has reared its ugly head again. I can't keep putting the people I love most through the wringer yet again. They suffer most.

'Genuine Northern Ireland fans have sent me many letters of support during this whole period. I really feel sorry for everyone associated with the Northern Ireland team but I have to move on from this situation.

'It's not only my parents and the rest of my family. I have to think about Sammy McIlroy and the team as well. It's not right that the focus should be taken away from them for all the wrong reasons. It's also disruptive to what Sammy is trying to do. Just hours before the game he was forced to change his whole plan because of this.

'So I feel it's best for everybody that I make this decision now. The game will go on, it will continue and I hope the lads go on and do really well. But enough is enough. This can't go on. The buck stops with me, and I want to nip it in the bud.'

I then played against Partick at Firhill in something of a strange dream. At the start I was applauded by both sets of supporters – I will always be grateful to the Thistle fans for that gesture. But my mind wasn't really on the game.

I received messages of support from across the world, some of it from most surprising places. There was a letter from leading Unionist politician David Irvine expressing his abhorrence of what had happened and Unionist party leader David Trimble stated his concerns.

Michael Boyd of the Irish FA's Community Relations Department wrote to say: 'The IFA's Community Relations Department is 100 per cent behind you at what must be a very difficult period of your career. In partnership with the supporters we are working hard to eradicate sectarianism from the game in Northern Ireland. Much progress has been made in this area in recent years and that is why it is so disappointing what happened at the Cyprus game. We are all totally gutted and frustrated that the actions of a very small minority have taken away from all the very positive work being carried out by our supporters to make the game more inclusive.'

John McMillan, chairman of the Rangers Supporters Association, told the press that what had happened was 'absolutely disgusting'. He added: 'These are not football fans. I don't care who is involved or which side the threats come from, it is terrible for any person to be treated in that way. It's hard to imagine what it must be like when you're not in Neil Lennon's position, but I would probably feel the same way as he does. I would hope for his own sake that he does continue in international football, but I can understand you have to think about your own safety and that of your family.' Thanks for that, John – I believe that to be an eloquent expression of the feelings of most ordinary decent fans, whatever their club.

Even the British Government got involved. Northern Ireland Deputy First Minister Mark Durkan said: 'The sectarian threats against Neil Lennon are deplorable. Sectarianism and paramilitarism should not intrude into the sporting arena.'

Around the world, it seemed that every major newspaper and broadcaster carried the story – it even made headlines in the USA where soccer is rarely regarded as newsworthy. I suppose that for a short period I was one of the most famous players on the planet, though not for a reason I would ever have wanted.

Some pundits would later say that I had been ill-advised to call for the football teams of Northern Ireland and the Republic to be united, but not for the first or last time, they were misquoting or misunderstanding what I had said in an interview some weeks before the match. I had said that a team drawn from all of Ireland's thirty-two counties would do better than the two separate teams. In saying that I was only recognizing that in rugby union, all Ireland played as one and did so very successfully. But at no point did I say the two countries should unite, in football or politically. In fact, I was only stating the same position as the late George Best, the greatest of all Northern Irish players. But then he didn't play for Celtic.

In the aftermath, much was made of the fact that the call was apparently a hoax. Two detectives from the PSNI came to Glasgow to interview me and said it was probably a hoax, but they had taken it seriously enough to trace the call and found it came from a phone box in Rathcoole in north Belfast. But how does anyone actually know that it was a hoax? How can anyone prove 100 per cent that the caller was not some deranged lunatic with a gun? In Northern Ireland and elsewhere I had seen players assaulted on the pitch by fans – what if one of them had a gun and wanted to make a name for himself?

One English journalist wrote I was a 'big girl's blouse' for not risking death. Funnily enough, he never had the courage to say that to my face . . .

Maybe I could have gone out and played but what kind of focus would I have had? How could anyone perform to their best in such a situation? The fact is that I did not play that night and have never played for Northern Ireland since, and therefore the caller did not need to carry out the threat, so we will never know for certain whether or not it was a hoax.

That reasoning seems to have been lost on the alleged intellect of people like that English journo.

What might have been the most upsetting speculation was that pulling out of the game served some sort of hidden agenda on my part. But I did not let that nonsense upset me because you cannot reason with idiocy like that. It's the sort of biased reasoning which has seen me burned in effigy on the tops of bonfires across Northern Ireland on 12 July, the great Unionist and Protestant day of celebration – I must be rivalling Guy Fawkes for being 'toasted'.

After that weekend, things did die down a little, and I was left to pick up the pieces. I took a long time to recover fully and it did affect my form for Celtic. But in the long run it may have been a blessing as quitting the international game may have prolonged my club career. I long ago concluded that I was correct to make my decision to quit, even though I have had tinges of regret – though I have never missed the exhausting trips to out-of-the-way places like Moldova.

It had been an awful experience, not least because it was my first real contact with the people and issues of 'the Troubles'. I had never made public my political views or my religious leanings, but here was I, a footballer, being treated as some sort of public hate figure, not because I was making statements but because I was a Catholic who wore the green and white hoops of Celtic.

What message did it send to young Catholics in Northern Ireland that they could be singled out for such treatment if they ever played for Celtic? A lot of Catholics will not attend matches at Windsor Park – after what happened to me, can you blame them?

The plan for a new national stadium, principally for football, to be built elsewhere in Northern Ireland could be a good start in uniting the country behind its sportspeople, as used to happen with our football team and individuals like Olympic champion Mary Peters and world champion boxer Barry McGuigan. I think that a new stadium will be a big step forward for sport in Northern Ireland.

In the meantime there is undoubtedly a cancer in the society of Northern Ireland and it will take a long time to excise. But that cancer should not be allowed to infect sport.

You can argue that the Old Firm have profited from being on the two sides of the sectarian divide, and I would not disagree. But events have often been way beyond their control and what happened to me was a wholly different matter – the incidents took place in the international arena while I was playing for my country; they were seen by the whole world as disgraceful; and they damaged me as a person.

I have to confess I was scarred by those events. I will admit now that I really and truly was in fear for my life at times. No one can undergo such an experience and not be affected. And yes, it made me bitter against the 'other side' for a time, something I had never been before. But I have accepted things and in time I have lost that bitterness. I believe it all made me a stronger person in the long run.

I had to be strong, for it was not to be the last time I would be assailed and indeed assaulted because I played for Celtic.

CHAPTER TWO

A Lurgan Bhoy

There is a noise that occasionally haunts me. It is the noise of the Troubles in the 1970s and 1980s, the time when I was growing up in a country that was trying to tear itself apart. The particular sounds I recall are those of whistles blowing, women wailing and metal clashing. It was the noise that signified death, and is one of the strongest memories from my childhood.

I was born in Carlton Home, Portadown, Northern Ireland, on 25 June 1971, the second child of Gerry and Ursula Lennon, née Moore, of Lurgan in County Armagh. I was christened Neil, but it might well have been Cornelius as I was called after my grandfather on my mother's side who owned a grocer's shop in the town. His 'Sunday name' was Cornelius but he was always known as Nealie Moore, so that's how I got my name. I took after him in other ways as he was a talented footballer of the Gaelic variety. My middle name is Francis, after my paternal grandfather.

My elder sister Orla and I were later joined by my sisters Aileen and Jane to complete what has always been a very close and loving family.

Situated in the Craigavon district, roughly halfway between the town of that name and Lisburn, Lurgan at that time had a population in excess of 22,000. A market town that was once a leading player in the linen industry, in the 1970s Lurgan had mainly light engineering, textile and agricultural industries.

The town was founded by the Brownlow family and properly planned and laid out in the seventeenth and eighteenth centuries. The biggest building in the area is Brownlow House, otherwise known as Lurgan Castle. To the north of Lurgan lies Lough Neagh, by area the largest expanse of fresh water in the British Isles. To the south east can be seen the famed Mountains of Mourne, and everywhere south run the roads to the Republic of Ireland. It is a beautiful part of the world, and I remain a frequent visitor despite having lived on mainland Britain for nearly twenty years.

Like many towns in Northern Ireland, Lurgan's population consisted of two distinct sectors, defined by religious and political leanings. No individual should be stereotyped, but across Northern Ireland generally at that time it is safe to say that on one side were Protestants who wanted the country to stay part of the United Kingdom, the Unionists or Loyalists, and on the other side were Roman Catholics who wanted Northern Ireland to be part of a united Ireland, the Republicans or Nationalists. The island of Ireland had experienced civil wars before and in the late 1960s, pressure for social change somehow transformed into the violent era called the Troubles which lasted for more than three decades. Yet thanks to my wonderful parents, I was largely insulated from the horrendous consequences of what was almost another civil war.

Both my parents were warm and sociable people with a wide circle of friends and I am sure that it is from them that I get my love of sharing a good time with family and companions. My mother says I was a brilliant baby who slept and ate well, and was no trouble at all – nice to know I haven't changed . . .

As any man who has been brought up in a household with three sisters will tell you, they spoil you and drive you daft in equal proportions. For instance, I don't think I've ever won an argument with Orla in my life. But then she is a superb debater and orator, and in 1985 she reached the Northern Ireland final of the All-Ireland Public Speaking Championships. When she was fifteen she went on a trip to Bangladesh for three weeks as a prize for winning a speaking contest at school. Orla's feats were reported in all the local newspapers and for a time she got bigger headlines than her wee brother. She later became a very fine teacher and is now married with two boys.

Like many people in Ireland, my dad went over to England to find work in the 1960s. He had a job at the Bedford truck factory in Luton but he came back to Lurgan – just as well he did, for that was when he and my mum encountered each other. The story is always told in our family that my mum met my dad at a dance in the town, and on that very first night she went home and told my grandparents that she had met the man she was going to marry. I am not sure whether or not that was my father's reaction, but knowing my mum's quiet determination, he was a lost cause to bachelorhood from that night on.

Dad worked as a foreman in an electronics factory but had to take premature retirement because he developed a debilitating illness which often leaves him very tired, but by and large he has not allowed it to affect him too much.

My earliest memories are of our house in Edward Street in the middle of Lurgan where we first lived. There was just Orla and me at the time. Between our house and my grandfather's shop across the road, there was a long line of concrete barrels all joined together with metal piping. They were there to stop people parking their cars in the centre of town. In the 1970s, car bombs were a regular feature of life in towns across Northern Ireland, and the barriers were then supposed to prevent the bombers from getting access to the main shopping areas in Lurgan.

The security paraphernalia made life difficult at times, but I suppose that was the price we had to pay in order to live some kind of normal life in relative safety. As a child you do not realize the seriousness of events going on around you, and it is only in recent years, after what has happened to me, that I realize what a strain it must have been for my parents to raise children at such a time and in such a place.

We were constantly being evacuated from the house because of bomb scares which were usually, but not always, hoaxes. I remember one Friday afternoon very vividly. That was the day my mother always made her special stew which I loved and which was a real highlight of the week for me. I was starving that day and could barely wait to start. My sister Orla was carrying the pot from the oven to the dinner table when a huge explosion shook the house. A bomb had gone off somewhere in the town and the noise was absolutely deafening. Orla got a terrible fright, dropped the pot and burst out crying. My mother went over to comfort her but I was more upset that she had spilled the stew all over the floor and gave her pelters!

The local council had plans to develop the area around our house – they finally did it twenty-odd years later, as you can tell by the name Millennium Way – and in 1976 we were moved to a new house at Richmount Gardens on Taghnevan estate on the edge of town. Jane had been born the year before and my youngest sister Aileen arrived in 1978. There were now four Lennon children – I don't know how my mother coped with all of us, but she did so magnificently.

Apart from the occasional inconveniences of life in Ulster at that time in the 1970s, I have to say I had a very happy childhood.

Fortunately for us, no members of my family were killed or injured in the Troubles, but one of my former schoolmates was not so lucky. Dennis Carville was one of the many people who died because they just happened to be of the wrong religion in the wrong place at the wrong time.

It was on 6 October 1990 that he was murdered. By then I was living in Stockport in England. I learned of the tragedy shortly after it happened and immediately recalled from schooldays a decent lad, an ordinary boy who would never have got mixed up in sectarian politics or fighting.

He was in his car with his girlfriend at a nature reserve, Oxford Island, at the south end of Lough Neagh. They had gone for some peace and quiet to a lover's lane which was well known as such in Lurgan. A fortnight previously, a part-time soldier from the Ulster Defence Regiment, Colin McCullough, had been killed by the IRA as he sat in a car with his girlfriend at the same place.

As Dennis sat there, a paramilitary from one of the Loyalist groups came up and knocked on the window. Dressed as a soldier, he asked to see Dennis's driving licence and as soon as he had established that Dennis was a Catholic, the gunman shot him dead in cold blood at a range of only inches. A Loyalist extremist group later let it be known that they had killed my Catholic former schoolmate in revenge for the murder of the Protestant UDR man.

It was one of many tit-for-tat killings during the Troubles, and it could have been any one of us Catholic boys from Lurgan who got the bullet that killed Dennis. He was just nineteen when he died, exactly the same age as myself at the time.

It was the banshee howl of the Troubles that I remember most.

Taghnevan was an almost totally Catholic/Republican/ nationalist estate – for the uninitiated, I should explain that many towns in Northern Ireland have their own system of virtual apartheid, with people from the Protestant/Unionist/ Loyalist tradition and the Catholics/Republicans/Nationalists both occupying their own enclaves and largely keeping themselves to themselves. It came as a shock to me when I moved to mainland Britain to discover that people of different faiths and cultures all lived together, cheek by jowl in the same streets and apartment blocks.

The worst period for tension and violence was undoubtedly the time of the hunger strikes in the early 1980s. The country was on the edge of all-out civil war during that long campaign by the Republican prisoners, led by Bobby Sands who, despite being in prison, had been elected an MP shortly before he died from the effects of self-starvation.

You could always tell when a hunger striker had died. As soon as news of the death broke, no matter whether it was in the dead of night or during the day, people would come out of the houses and would start to bang metal bin lids, either thrashing two together or thumping them off the pavement. Whistles would be blown at the highest possible volume, and men and women would shout the news. The noise would spread through the estate and sometimes there would be women wailing and frightened children screaming. I was only nine or ten at the time, but I can remember that cacophony as if it was yesterday. On one occasion a hunger striker died at about 4 a.m. and the noise of the bin lids and the shouts of protest reverberated around the estate in an unearthly manner. It was as if the banshee of ancient Irish folklore had suddenly come to life in Lurgan. I was truly frightened as I lay in my bed wondering how long the noise would go on for and what would happen the next day – in many places across Northern Ireland there would be riots and shootings. I knew why the noisy protest was taking place, of course, but I had no real concept of the underlying problems which had caused the Troubles to start in the first place.

My parents always did their best to shield us from the Troubles but there were occasions when the grim realities of that time just could not be avoided, as when the hunger strikers died. Mostly, however, we just tried to get on with our lives as normally as possible, which I suspect was the attitude of the vast majority of people in Lurgan and elsewhere in Northern Ireland.

The price of safety was constant vigilance. My mother and father would watch out like hawks for any problems in the streets around our house and at the first sign of any trouble we would be hauled indoors. 'Trouble' usually consisted of gangs of boys taunting the security services or throwing stones at police vehicles. The girls kept out of the road but it was accepted practice for boys of my age and older teenagers to take part in this frequent ritual. I have to confess I got caught up in a couple of episodes of stone-throwing largely because it was second nature to several friends of mine. Peer pressure can be a terrible thing at that age, and it was only later when I had moved to England that I realized that the police had actually been there to protect us. Of course I would later require their services on a couple of occasions in Belfast, as I have already described.

You could try to avoid the Troubles, as we did as a family, but you could never ignore them. One of my uncles on my father's side had been born long before the Beatles came on the scene or else my grandparents might have called him something other than John. He was stopped by the police one night and of course they asked him for his name. 'John Lennon,' was his truthful reply. 'Aye,' said the cop, 'and I'm John Wayne,' before throwing him in the back of the police vehicle.

A real character, my uncle John sadly died three years ago. But then all the Lennons were characters. My father's brother Francie went to a big Gaelic football match at Croke Park in Dublin, and that was the last my grandfather Frank and grandmother Jane saw of him for ten years. He joined the Irish Navy and in 1953, was the wireless operator who intercepted the first distress signal from the Stranraer–Larne ferry *Princess Victoria* which sank in the Irish Sea during a massive storm, with the loss of more than 130 lives. He later went to England and joined the RAF, ending up in Hull.

I have vivid memories of many of the major events of the Troubles when I was growing up, such as the murder of Airey Neave MP, the bombing which killed Earl Mountbatten, and the explosions which killed eighteen soldiers at Warrenpoint. That last incident took place on a bank holiday at a place just down the road from Lurgan, so the whole area was very tense for some time afterwards with police and soldiers everywhere.

As I grew older, I became more aware of the history and tragedies which had led to the Troubles, but I did not let things influence me and was never tempted to get involved in politics. To be truthful, I was just too busy playing football and Gaelic football to get sucked into what was going on around me.

As for religion, I was raised a Catholic. I was baptized in St Peter's Church in Lurgan and made my first Holy Communion and received confirmation in St Paul's Church which served Taghnevan. The influence of my parents was strong – we were taught to live as Christians and show a good example, rather than flaunt our religion ostentatiously.

The people of Lurgan lived for their sport. Football, or rather soccer, was followed avidly in the town, but there was also a great deal of interest in horse racing and boxing, and in the Nationalist areas of the town, Gaelic football was played with a passion. There were about ten Gaelic football clubs and school teams in the town at one time or another. Hurling was nowhere near as popular as football of either variety, and there were quite a few of us who played both Gaelic football and soccer, though in some parts of Ireland that was very much frowned upon – soccer was seen as an alien English game by Irish cultural traditionalists.

Practically since I had learned to walk I had kicked a football around, playing with my mates in the streets or local parks and playgrounds. But it was thanks to the schools and local boys' clubs that I got to play 'proper' organized matches on real pitches.

I attended St Joseph's Primary School in Lurgan, known as the infant school, for the first three years of my education, followed by St Peter's for primary four to seven. The two schools were beside each other and were later amalgamated into St Thomas's.

After St Peter's I attended St Paul's junior high school, where I sat and passed the exams which enabled me to go on to St Michael's Grammar School, which was the senior high school for the Catholic youth of Lurgan.

I think I was a good pupil and tried hard to learn, but in all my schools my main interest was football. We played bounce games in the playground with piles of jerseys for goalposts, after school was finished we would go home for our dinner and then go back out to play more football in the local parks, as long as there was light to play by.

I soon realized that I loved football and was not too bad at it at all. There were other young boys around the town who were pretty good, too, one of them being Gerry Taggart, who you will read more about later.

The only thing that caused more excitement in school than football was a playground scrap. There would be a big circle of us, maybe three or four deep, around the two combatants, and we would egg on the fighters, especially if one of them was a mate. Nobody ever got really badly hurt in those schoolboy battles, and invariably the teachers would arrive to break them up and we would soon get back to playing football.

Despite the Troubles and economic recession, Lurgan's people were very resilient and there was a great determination on the part of many men and women that the children of the town should lead as normal lives as possible.

When I look back and think of all the sacrifices that people made just so we could get a game of football I am in awe of their commitment to the sport. Getting us kit and a place to play, transporting us all over the county and beyond, coaching us, keeping us safe and arranging for some of us to be looked at by senior teams – and all this against a background of the Troubles. Later in life I was able to repay some of my debt to those people in Lurgan by donating some money for training younger children to play football. But it was small change compared to what I and many other players owed for the start we were given.

I will be eternally grateful to Dessie Meginnis in particular. He was the local 'Mr Football' and took me under his wing from the very start when I joined Lurgan Celtic Boys Club at the age of ten. Dessie was the Pied Piper of Lurgan – wherever you saw him he had a bag of footballs and a bunch of kids following him. He had the nickname 'bunker', but I never found out why.

His enthusiasm for football was infectious, and no one

knew more about the schoolboy scene in Northern Ireland than Dessie, who also had good links with Celtic in Glasgow. It's amazing to think that he started the careers of Gerry Taggart and myself on more or less the same day in the same boys' team, and we both went on to play for Northern Ireland. Dessie not only taught you good habits on the field but he also encouraged you to behave well off it. He would say things like 'be first on the training ground and the last off it', and give you a friendly word of encouragement when you needed it. I still call or go to see him for advice to this day.

My dad always supported me in my football ambitions but he tended to stay in the background. Mum and he provided me with my early boots and strips, as I used to beg them for football equipment each Christmas, but Dad rarely came to watch me play, though there was a good reason for that. He had gone to see me a couple times but did not like the comments and the actions of parents on the sidelines. Dad was worried that if he came to a match and somebody criticized me, he would lose his temper and smack them, so he chose to stay away. He was quite right, too, because some of the insults were terrible, and the worst offenders were often women who clearly did not realize the pressure they were putting on young children.

As well as playing the game, we Lurgan boys were also passionate about the teams we supported. Most people I know become football supporters at a young age when they choose their team to follow by some strange process that sometimes defies scientific analysis.

Throughout Ireland, British football is the game of choice for fans. The fortunes of Manchester United, Arsenal, Liverpool and the other big English clubs are followed closely by tens of thousands of people, many of whom rarely see their heroes in the flesh. In Northern Ireland, for not always the best of reasons, the two clubs with the biggest support are Celtic and Rangers. Dozens of buses leave Belfast, Derry and elsewhere for Scotland every weekend of the season, with people travelling on segregated buses and ferries. The colours of the two teams are seen everywhere, though they are never side by side. That's just a fact of life in Northern Ireland.

The dedication of those fans to the Old Firm clubs is unbelievable. It is almost like a pilgrimage for them. Those who come over from Donegal, for instance, have to get up at four in the morning and then after the match they have to leave straight away in order to be on time for the boat home.

For as long as I can remember, my team was Celtic. My dad supported them, most of the rest of the family were fans, and they were very important to us and to many people in our community, as shown by the fact that one of the biggest clubs in the town was called Lurgan Celtic. It just seemed natural to follow Celtic, even if they played many miles away in Scotland, and as a fan, I dreamed of one day playing for them.

Live football was a rare thing on television when I was a boy. We did not have satellite television in those days, and you only got to see European games now and again, but we would avidly watch any scraps of highlights shown.

I actually saw Celtic in the flesh, so to speak, on two occasions as a young boy. They played a friendly match in Dundalk which is not far south of Lurgan, and my dad took me to see them. The second time was as a special treat as I went with Lurgan Celtic Boys Club to see them play Aberdeen in the Scottish Cup semi-final of 1983 when I was not quite twelve years old. It was a tremendous experience, and I was amazed at the sheer number of people all around me. The noise and the colours made it a real adventure, but the ending wasn't so great – the Hoops were beaten 1–0 by

Alex Ferguson's fine side who were then at their peak and went on to win the cup.

I could have gone to more games as there were buses and cars which left from Lurgan and my dad occasionally went to Glasgow where he had friends and relatives. But by the age of ten I was playing every Saturday and I much preferred to play rather than watch. However, I used to love listening to the stories of those who did go over to Parkhead, and I suppose I got a bit jealous of those who had seen my heroes.

My favourite player as a youngster was Kenny Dalglish. He had it all – great skill with either foot, amazing strength in the penalty box, and the vision to make telling passes or take up perfect positions. He had been largely unheralded outside Scotland before his record-breaking move to Liverpool, but it was no surprise to those of us who idolized him that he quickly made his mark in England and Europe, and went on to become a legend at Anfield. In modern times, Kenny is the king of Celtic players as far as I am concerned, and only Henrik Larsson ranks alongside him.

From the outset with Lurgan Celtic's boys' side and with St Peter's primary's team, I was a prolific goalscorer. I played on the right wing for the club but for the school I played at centre-forward and I really did score a barrowload. That may come as something of a shock to those Celtic fans who have seen me score precisely three times in the five-and-a-half seasons that I have been at Parkhead. But as a youngster I scored regularly, almost week in and week out, both for my schools teams and for my clubs, and while still at primary school, a headline appeared in my local newspaper 'Lennon Hits Three'.

At the same time as I was starting out in football, I was also learning the ropes in Gaelic football. While there are similarities between the two sports, the latter involves handling and passing the ball from hand or foot. From the start I loved them both, but soccer – I'll use that term to avoid confusion – was always my preferred version.

Junior soccer was given quite good coverage in the local press, and my family have newspaper clippings to prove that I was something of a goalscoring sensation. I particularly remember playing in five-a-side and indoor tournaments, and I think the first picture of me in a newspaper was when we won the Craigavon Festival Under-11 trophy. Also in that five was Gerry Taggart, who would become a lifelong friend and a very fine professional footballer. Gerry and I also played in the Lurgan Celtic team which was chosen to represent Armagh in the Ulster age group finals at the Community Games in Letterkenny, County Donegal. Gerry scored two as we won the final 6–1 against Monaghan, and I got a hat-trick inside fifteen minutes – a little different to my scoring ratio with Celtic of one goal every two seasons!

The national finals of the All-Ireland Community Games at Butlins' Irish camp at Mosney was a very prestigious tournament, and Gerry Taggart and myself were both picked for the Lurgan area Under-12 side which represented Armagh in the games. Scouts from senior clubs in Britain watched the final in which we beat Galway on penalties thanks largely to goalkeeper Dee Horisk saving three of their spot kicks.

Butlins camp at Mosney would become a regular haunt for me. In September 1983, several of us who had won the soccer trophy returned to contest the Community Games Gaelic football final, which was played for the Charles Haughey Perpetual Cup. Gerry Taggart, Dee Horisk and I all played for the Craigavon select eleven which won this trophy competed for by sides from all over Ireland.

I loved our visits to Butlins, because apart from the football there were all sorts of fun and games for youngsters. There was an amusement park attached to the camp and when we weren't playing matches, we could be found there having a whale of a time.

In my last year at St Peter's, I was selected for the Mid-Ulster District Primary Schools Team to play in various tournaments. It was as a result of playing well for the Mid-Ulster side that I first came to the attention of the Northern Ireland schoolboy team selectors.

The official records showed that in my final year at primary school, I played all five games for Mid-Ulster against the likes of Belfast and East Antrim, scoring five of our fourteen goals as we finished second in the league. I nearly always played up front at that time, and it was the same in Gaelic football where I occupied one or other of the forward positions and liked nothing better than to score goals or points.

When I left primary school, I first attended St Paul's junior high school, for boys aged from eleven to fourteen, and here again football was my main preoccupation. I was just eleven and in my first year when I was selected to play for the school Under-13 side. We were a very good side under the charge of teacher Mr Kevin O'Neill, and I remember we beat our great rivals Killicomaine School to win the local school league and cup double. Again, I scored a hat-trick in the cup final, and we got our team picture with both trophies in the *Lurgan Mail* – always a sure sign of success.

As well as playing for St Paul's I was by then enjoying myself with Lurgan Celtic. Our Under-13 team went through the entire season unbeaten and won the Michael Casey Memorial Cup into the bargain. I also had my first taste of 'foreign' football when I went over to Scotland and played against Greenock Shamrocks and Greenock Boys Club. Shamrock at that time had one of the best young teams around and had strong links to Celtic. We beat them 3–2 and

I remember the trip well as it was my first visit to Glasgow and I got to meet some of my relatives on my father's side who lived in Scotland.

I was still playing Gaelic football for St Paul's and the Clan Na Gael club at this time, winning the Armagh Under-13 championship with the school.

I soon took and passed the exams which meant I could continue on to senior high school, in my case St Michael's Grammar School in Lurgan. One of the great things about St Michael's was that it was co-educational. Since it was a Catholic school run by a strict nun, any sort of contact between boys and girls was frowned upon, but that didn't stop your hormones rampaging. Like every other teenage boy, I was awkward around the opposite sex and it would take me ages to pluck up the courage to talk to a girl or ask her for a dance at the occasional 'hops' held at the school or the local social club. I'll confess now to having had a big crush on a very pretty girl of Italian extraction, Anita Cafolla. I must have carried a torch for her for a year or two when I was fourteen or fifteen, but nothing ever came of it and we went our separate ways with me moving to Motherwell and later Manchester.

Like everyone, I had my favourite teachers at school and one of the teachers who had considerable influence on me was Seamus Heffron, who taught me French at St Michael's. More importantly, he was in charge of the school Gaelic football team. He was the kind of teacher you need in any school, the sort who encouraged young people to do their best at work and play, and who put in many unpaid hours looking after the team. Seamus has subsequently followed my football career closely, coming over to see me play at Leicester and Celtic, and he is in regular touch with my family and myself.

When I first attended St Michael's, it became clear that I faced something of a problem, one that almost got me expelled from the school and nearly ended my career in soccer almost before it started. St Michael's was a highly traditional school and preferred the Gaelic version of football, which of course I loved, but not as much as soccer. Schoolmatches were played on a Saturday morning which sadly was also the same time that Lurgan United, the boys club for which I then played, held their games.

At that point in my life I came up against a person who was very determined to get her own way. Sister Mary St Anne was the nun in charge of St Michael's, and she was determined to uphold the school's traditions.

One of those traditions was the cane. Anyone above a certain age will remember that corporal punishment was once routine in schools, the teacher's weapon of choice being the tawse or the cane. Sister St Anne was one of those strict no-nonsense nuns who did not mind dishing out sentences but would send for a male teacher to administer the actual punishment.

I was a typical schoolboy, I suppose, and got in my fair share of scrapes and pranks, such as playing truant or 'bunking' as we called it, so in my time at St Michael's I was caned perhaps two or three times.

The occasion I remember most was a beautiful sunny day when the attractions of a double period of biology could not compare with the farm which adjoined the school. After lunch, three or four of us decided to scale the wall and make our escape from school. I'll name no names – for reading this will be the first time my own mother will know what I did, and I wouldn't like to get anyone else into the trouble I'm going to get!

We had climbed a tree and were sunning ourselves when

one of the teachers spotted us and came running over. We jumped down from the tree and unfortunately for one of the lads, he landed in a giant cowpat. Even worse for us was the fact that our escape route was sealed off by three other teachers. We were all hauled off to be caned, with the smell of cow dung accompanying us everywhere we went until my poor unfortunate classmate was sent home.

The caning ceremony was bizarre. You would go into Sister's room, and there would be no sign of the cane at first. The weird thing was that she kept the cane hidden in a box behind a picture in her room. The box would be produced with great ceremony and the assistant headmaster or other teacher would take out the cane. On each occasion the sentence was the same – three strokes of the cane on each hand, which you placed one on top of the other to receive the stroke. I suppose the cane was supposed to be an encouragement of sorts, but if so, then it did not achieve its purpose as your hands were so traumatized that you couldn't lift a pen or do any serious work for the rest of the day.

Tradition meant everything to Sister St Anne. As far as she was concerned, it was to be Gaelic football or no football at all. I, on the other hand, just could not envisage life without soccer. I was about fourteen, I was already in the school Gaelic football team, and was also playing for the local Clan Na Gael club. But I was doing so well with Lurgan United soccer club that my name was already in the books of several scouts from senior clubs across the water in Scotland and England. So I knew by then that I had a chance of playing football for a living and, more and more, that was what I wanted to do. But Sister St Anne decreed that I would play for the school Gaelic football team and that meant giving up Saturday morning soccer. Or so she thought.

The penalty for disobeying the order was simple – I would

be expelled from St Michael's. I was in tears at the thought – I had worked hard to pass the exams to get into St Michael's and now I faced expulsion for playing football.

The annoying thing was that all these orders were relayed in public at school assembly. My sister Orla was in the sixth year and she confronted Sister about this before telling my parents.

My father was very angry when he and mother went to the school office. He pointed out that I had made a commitment to the soccer club and somehow he worked out a compromise with Sister. At that time it was close to the end of the soccer season, so I was able to carry on playing but had to switch to Gaelic as soon as the season ended, and in the meantime I played only in the important school matches.

I would not have liked to have left St Michael's under a cloud. I loved my time there, and the standard of education was very high and academic achievement was not just demanded but expected. I was no swot, but there were some subjects which I did enjoy, mainly languages such as English literature and English language, Spanish, French and Irish Gaelic – I got 'O' levels in all of those. I passed seven 'O' levels in all, the others being religious studies and chemistry. I could have done better, but by then my mind was on other things, namely where I would start my football career.

The only other profession I considered was that of veterinary surgeon because I always loved animals. I still do, and have shares in several racehorses.

We always had cats or dogs in our house, and we also had a canary for years – one who never stopped singing! He was called Sweep, and the cat was not too impressed with his constant noise.

Perhaps if I had passed my biology 'O' level I might have carried on to study veterinary science, but I failed and that was the end of any thoughts of becoming a vet. To be honest, by that time I was already set on a career in football.

By the time I was fourteen I was on the fringes of the Northern Ireland schoolboy team. It was a very exciting period for me which also saw me widen my horizons a little.

For some reason of which I'm not aware, Lurgan Celtic had dropped their boys' team but the people who ran it went off and formed Lurgan United which I joined, because it was really Lurgan Celtic by another name. At that time we had a rare crop of players and we were frequently watched by scouts from dozens of clubs in Britain, and also representatives of other more senior boys' clubs in the area.

One of the best boys' clubs in Armagh, indeed the whole of Northern Ireland, was Lisburn side Hillsborough. Its officials and players were all from the 'other side' of the divide, so when Gerry Taggart and I were asked to join them, I was a bit sceptical. I had plenty of friends who were Protestant and Unionist, but joining Hillsborough from Lurgan Celtic was something of a bridge crossing, as we would be the only two Catholics in the club. I need not have worried a jot. We were welcomed with open arms and in the five years I played for Hillsborough, nary a cross word was spoken about the religious and political problems in my town and country.

One of the players was Noel Baillie, and he and I went right through the ranks at Hillsborough together before he went on to play for Linfield, the Belfast club traditionally associated with the Protestant and Unionist sector of the city's population. Strange to think that the two of us, one who played more than 600 games for and also captained the 'Rangers' of Belfast and myself, who captains Glasgow Celtic, were once both wee boys in the same team.

Those were busy days for me, especially at weekends. I would play soccer twice a day on the Saturday, for Lurgan

United in the morning and Hillsborough in the afternoon, and then turn out for my Gaelic football club on the Sunday. I was at the age when you felt you could play all day, every day. No one had heard of the phrase 'teenage burnout' in those days. I would pay for the excessive football a few years later, as you will learn in a later chapter.

My Gaelic football career was going very well, too. I seemed to have the natural ball-playing skills needed for both versions of football, and my ability to hit a long shot came in handy in Gaelic in particular. Playing for St Michael's and Clan Na Gael, in total before I left school, I won Armagh county league championship medals at Under-13, Under-14 and Under -15 levels; two more Under-16 league medals and two minor league medals; plus an All-Ireland Community Games medal and a winner's medal in the prestigious Herald Cup tournament.

The pinnacle of my school Gaelic football career came in an All-Ireland final. St Michael's won through to the Under-16½ Colleges B Championship which was played at mighty Croke Park in Dublin, the home of Gaelic football. It was a huge day for everyone at the school, but we were not fancied to beat the big strong team from Clane Community School in Kildare.

We were much more skilful, however, and I thoroughly enjoyed the game if not the match report in the local Lurgan paper – it mentioned something about me being 'exciting to watch' but spoiled things by adding 'the red-haired youngster . . . spoils his performances occasionally with his fiery temper'. The anti-ginger brigade in the media had it in for me from the start, it seems . . .

We won a close match by a goal and three points (1–3) to four points (0–4), and instantly became heroes to the rest of the school. In that year I also played for Clan Na Gael's

Under-16 team which won the North Armagh championship, as our club performed the remarkable feat of winning the league at every age level.

Despite my Gaelic football success, soccer was more and more the main focus of my life. As I approached my final year in school, I was already set on a path to try to become a professional footballer, and senior clubs from Scotland and England were taking a great interest in me, including one rather surprising club indeed.

CHAPTER THREE

First Steps on the Ladder

As I progressed through the ranks of school football and played for both Lurgan United and Hillsborough Boys Club, several senior teams in Scotland and England had begun to take a look at me with an eye to securing my signature in the future.

One club in Glasgow in particular seemed to begin taking a genuine interest. That club was not Celtic, but Rangers.

That is correct. Your eyes do not deceive you. I am relating the story here not to make any great fuss, but because it really did happen and in fact was reported in the local Lurgan paper at the time, though not with any great prominence. The first sign of interest from Rangers came after I played for the Northern Ireland Under-14 select against the Scottish Schools team in Stranraer. We won the match quite convincingly and I played particularly well that day. It was after that match that I came into contact with Harry Dunn, the well-known scout who would eventually help me to get a start in professional football.

He told me that Motherwell FC might be interested in giving me a trial, but a couple of weeks later he called the house to say that Rangers were also interested and would like to invite me to visit Ibrox Park for the day.

My dad was stupefied. But shortly afterwards we received a letter from Jock Wallace, the then manager of Rangers, confirming their interest in my future. You can read that letter and see the picture of me at Ibrox in the illustration section – proof positive that Rangers were following my progress as a fledgling footballer.

It was one of the few times in my life that I saw my father look absolutely stunned as he read the message on that Ibrox-headed notepaper. He just could not believe it at first, but when he realized it was serious he expressed his grave reservations about me ever signing for Rangers, not least because it could place my personal safety, and that of the rest of the family, at risk from the actions of extremists – given what happened to me when I was chosen to captain Northern Ireland, his fears were sadly justified.

Despite my father's concerns I also consulted Dessie Meginnis and it was decided all round that I should go over to Glasgow to see what Rangers had to offer.

The visit took place after an international youth tournament at Ayr where I was lucky enough to be named best player in the Under-14 section. The *Lurgan Mail* reported that 'Neill (sic) Lennon has attracted the interest of Birmingham City, Glasgow Celtic and Rangers.' Later on it was reported that '13-year-old Neil Lennon accepted an invitation from a top Scottish Premier League side to view their set-up. Neil, who was accompanied by his father, enjoyed the experience and may well be invited back at a later date for a trial. The club asked that their name should not be disclosed at this stage.'

That is probably a reference to the fact that the whole situation of Rangers taking an interest in a Catholic schoolboy was very delicate, to say the least. At that time, because of their culture as the club of the Protestant and Unionist tradition, Rangers did not sign Catholics. The club had stated several years earlier that it would sign a Catholic if he was good enough, but funnily enough by the early 1980s, Rangers still hadn't signed anyone of my religion. The first boy to sign for them who was reported to be a Catholic was John Spencer later in that decade.

It was obviously going to be problematic for me to sign for them and perhaps that's why everything was kept pretty hush-hush, but I have never doubted that their interest in me was genuine, not least because Jock Wallace told my father face to face – and as people who knew him will recall, Jock didn't do whispers . . . he could be heard out on the pitch!

With my father along to watch over me – and make sure I didn't sign anything – I enjoyed my trip to Ibrox, in company with three other boys from the Northern Ireland Under-14 side. We were accompanying the Under-15 side which went to Glasgow to play a Rangers' youth side, and after the game we four were given our own guided tour of Ibrox, including the dressing rooms and the trophy room, which was empty as usual – only kidding!

Ibrox was very impressive, particularly the marble halls, and Jimmy Nicholl, the Northern Ireland international who then played for Rangers, looked after us well. My dad had a conversation with Jock Wallace in which the Rangers manager said that he had known about me for some time. The subject of my religion was mentioned and my dad recalls that Wallace knew it would be a problem. Even so I was only thirteen and the time for deciding my future was a long way away, though even by then I was pretty certain that I wanted to be a professional footballer.

Over the next few months, Harry Dunn also assured me that Rangers were keeping an eye on me. The interest from Rangers was intriguing, but never came to anything. I reckon

I would have been about fifteen or so when Graeme Souness took over and started the revolution which brought Rangers their first high-profile Catholic signing of the modern era, Maurice Johnston, and Catholics have played a considerable part in their subsequent success. Could I have been the one to break the mould before John Spencer and Mo Johnston? I don't know, because the question never arose. Still, it's certainly something to ponder.

With nothing concrete coming from Rangers or any other club, I began to wonder if anyone would sign me up, but I need not have worried. The occasion which really brought me to the attention of scouts was the Milk Cup in Coleraine in 1985. Although I had only just turned fourteen, Dessie Meginnis asked me to captain a 'Craigavon United' select side which contained several older players.

The Milk Cup was a huge tournament for youngsters, and the best teams from all over Northern Ireland as well as visitors from as far away as Italy and San Francisco participated in a week-long competition with the final being watched by 10,000 people.

We played as Craigavon United but in reality it was the Lurgan Celtic team of two years earlier. Given our loyalty to the club in the east end of Glasgow it was somewhat pleasing that our best performance came against Rangers in the final. We had done well to get that far, but Rangers were hot favourites. Ironically, their side was managed by none other than Harry Dunn. His boys had wiped the floor with everyone, scoring fifty-five goals and losing none in romping to the final, and had the likes of John Spencer and Gary McSwegan playing for them. They were a very good side, but we gave them a huge fright, only losing to them on penalties after drawing 1–1 at full-time. At the end of the tournament, players were selected to contest a Northern Ireland versus the

Rest of the World match. With Dessie Meginnis as manager, I was chosen as captain of our side which won 1–0.

There was high praise at home for this bunch of youngsters from Lurgan who were representing Craigavon. When I got back to my house it seemed as though the telephone did not stop ringing. Scouts from Manchester City, Oxford and Motherwell all called my dad, but the interest which excited me most was that of John Kelman, chief scout for Celtic, who knew Dessie Meginnis. Kelman told my father that Celtic would like me to come over for a trial at some point in the future. I was ecstatic that I was even being thought of in connection with Celtic. When I was first told, I bounced about the house like some crazy fool, jumping up and down and doing somersaults.

I was now on the fringe of the Northern Ireland schoolboy team, so it was a very exciting time for me. Football was almost taking over my life, but then I suffered my first major setback. I had been selected in the initial squad of eighteen players of ages fourteen and fifteen who would train together to prepare for schoolboy internationals. That training period lasted about six or seven months, at the end of which the squad was reduced to sixteen. I was one of the players cut at that point, and I felt as if the roof had fallen in on me. I had put a lot of effort into my training for the national squad, and I was gutted to be left out. I kept thinking of the other players going off to feature in matches at big stadiums in Scotland and England while I was stuck back in Lurgan. I seriously began to doubt whether I would make it into the ranks of professional football.

Looking back on that period, I was probably carrying a bit too much puppy fat – like any teenager, I was quite conscious of it. I decided that I needed to get fitter and then perhaps my turn would come. Motherwell and Manchester City were still interested in signing me, after all, though I had heard nothing more from Celtic and a trial for Oxford United had produced nothing solid.

Everyone at Hillsborough Boys Club was really good to me at that time, encouraging me to carry on. I went back to play a full season for them, which proved to be highly successful. In 1986, when I was fifteen, Craigavon United returned to the Milk Cup but I was too old to play for the junior side which won the tournament that year.

As I studied for my 'O' levels, Harry Dunn assured me that there was still very strong interest in me from Motherwell. Indeed there was – one of the directors of the club, Malky McNeill, came over to see my parents and me, and he took us for dinner to a very nice restaurant at the Chimney Corner, an upmarket hotel on the outskirts of Belfast. I will never forget that meal, because not only did it lead to me starting my professional career with Motherwell, it was also the first time I had seen someone cracking open a bottle of champagne. Malky stuck a silver coin into the cork and handed it to me saying 'you keep that for luck'. I remember that the bill came to £48, which was an absolute fortune to my parents in those days.

After that dinner, I was made a formal written offer by Motherwell of a two-year apprenticeship plus a year's professional contract.

At around the same time, Manchester City's scout Peter Neill, who had seen me play in the Milk Cup in his home town of Coleraine, invited myself and Gerry Taggart to take part in trials for the Maine Road club. The trials went very well and City let me know through Peter that they wanted me to sign for them.

So I now had two offers on the table. After much discussion with Dessie, Harry and my parents, it was decided that

I would sign for Motherwell. The main reason I signed for Motherwell in preference to Manchester City was that we thought I would have a better chance of progressing more quickly at a smaller club where I might get more opportunities to break into the first team.

I was hugely excited at the prospect of playing full-time professional football, even as an apprentice, and couldn't wait to finish school and get over to Scotland.

But joining the Steelmen, as Motherwell were nicknamed because of the forges around the town, turned out to be the wrong choice for me. In fact, I would go as far as to say that my move to Scotland and Motherwell was a complete disaster.

Motherwell were then in the Scottish Premier League, and the previous year the club had celebrated its centenary. They played at Fir Park, so called because it was once the corner of Lord Dalziel's country estate in which fir trees grew.

In the 1987/88 season the manager was Tommy McLean, the former Rangers and Scotland player, and his assistant was Tom Forsyth, also a former Rangers player. That season the club had a staff of thirty-three full-time footballers, and they had a lot of players who were either already well known in Scottish football or who would become so, such as former Celtic player Tom McAdam, ex-Rangers man Robert Russell and a certain Tom Boyd whose name will reappear later in this book.

In July 1987, having just turned sixteen, I packed my bags and left home for a new life as an apprentice footballer with Motherwell. It was the first extended period I would spend away from my family, and I have to say that I did not enjoy it one bit.

It was certainly a huge shock to me to have to move into digs. My very first lodgings were with the grandmother of one of the Motherwell players, Chris McCart. Some thirteen years later when I signed for Celtic, one of the first people to greet me was the selfsame Chris, who by then was on Celtic's staff as a youth coach. Football can be a small world at times.

It can also be tough and uncompromising, especially for young apprentices. Among the boys who joined at the same time as me was Scott Leitch, who later captained Motherwell and is now the manager of Ross County. Scott was slightly older than me – in fact, every signed player at the club was older than me.

Our day consisted of an early rise in order to take the public transport I needed to get to Fir Park. We had to be there before the senior players as we apprentices had to clean their boots and make sure the kit was laid out and the place was tidy before training began. We were nominally under the supervision of chief scout and youth development officer Bobby Jenks, but from the start we were coached and trained by Tommy McLean and his coaching staff.

I was surprised to be thrown in at the deep end by being made to train with the first-team players and the rest of the senior squad. I was still a raw boy, and not physically up to the task of training like a full-time professional footballer. We would be taken to Strathclyde Park near Hamilton and made to run up steep slopes, then there would be all sorts of running and exercises that really were more suited to adults than a teenager. I was constantly getting it in the neck for my lack of fitness and I had to admit that I was struggling as I was overweight and had never experienced anything like the intensity of this training. After the senior players went off for the afternoon we apprentices would have to go back to Fir Park and do more cleaning and tidying of the stadium in preparation for the forthcoming season. Was it any wonder that I went back to my digs exhausted most nights?

I loved playing most of all and when I finally got the chance to play in a few warm-up games, I thought that I performed quite well. I definitely held my own among my age group, and went with Motherwell's Under-16 side to play in the Milk Cup at Coleraine where I had happy memories. We did well in our first game, beating Newcastle United's boys 5–2, before losing to Liverpool in the semi-final, the Reds eventually going on to win the tournament. Once again I was selected to play in the closing match, this time for the Rest of the World which beat a Northern Ireland select eleven 2–1. I must have set some sort of Milk Cup record having played for the Northern Irish select at Under-14 level and then for the Rest of the World at a higher age group – and I was on the winning side both times.

Back at Fir Park, there was just a chance that I might have made it into the reserves. The training was murder, however, and though I was determined to stick it out, I picked up a thigh injury and that set me back several weeks.

I was also suffering badly from homesickness. It did not help matters that for various reasons, I was shunted about from landlady to landlady, and I was in three different digs in three months.

The fact that I was the only Irish apprentice brought me some unwelcome attention. Not to put too fine a point on it, I was picked on and singled out to be the butt of a few jokes, usually involving 'Irishness', a subject beloved of the politically incorrect comedians of the time. I remember that my being a Catholic from Northern Ireland was also the subject of some remarks. On one occasion a senior player grabbed the broom I was using and showed me how to sweep up. 'There,' he said, 'that's bit more Protestant-like.' I had never heard that phrase before and though I now know it's a common expression in the west of Scotland to describe things being neat and tidy, back then at the age of sixteen, I didn't know how to deal with this kind of banter.

I was very unhappy and couldn't see me getting anywhere fast, and on a pittance for a wage I couldn't exactly live the high life. Like quite a few clubs, Motherwell had taken advantage of the Government's funding of youth training and my wage was set at the Youth Training Scheme allowance of £28.50, although the club, to be fair, paid for my lodgings.

The last straw came when I was moved into my third digs with an old lady who was perfectly civil but bordering on the stone deaf. We had nothing in common and conversation was minimal. My life consisted of cleaning boots, training, more cleaning, then going home to eat my dinner, watch some telly and go to bed. I was fed up and miserable, and something had to give.

Part of the contract I had signed entitled me to a couple of holidays during the season and by the beginning of September I decided to use up one of my breaks to go home to Lurgan. I had a long chat with my dad, during which I told him how nightmarish things had become. I told him that my brief flirtation with professional football, Scottish style, was over and that I wanted to come home and start my studies again.

My dad then had a long telephone conversation with Tommy McLean during which he told the manager in no uncertain terms that he was not happy with the way I was being treated. Tommy made it clear that he very much wanted me to stay and that things would improve, but my mind was made up and that was the end of my time with Motherwell. I don't blame anyone for what happened and I've never held it against the club that I had a poor start to my career. It was just one of those things that happens in football, and at least I had shown enough potential for Tommy McLean to want to keep me on.

I returned a wiser lad to Lurgan and home, and also to St Michael's School. I had only missed a few weeks of term, and I was sure I could catch up and eventually sit my 'A' levels. Despite my harsh experience at Motherwell, I also wanted to continue playing football.

Nothing better illustrates the topsy-turvy nature of football than what happened to me next. Within days of my arrival home I was invited to train with Glenavon, the local side who played in the Irish League. Their manager Terry Nicholson had heard of my return and moved quickly to sign me on professional terms, albeit for only a few quid a week. There were the usual complications over the cancellation of my registration with Motherwell, but the Scottish Football Association finally cleared me to play.

Glenavon played at Mourneview Park in Lurgan and it was there that I trained and played with the reserves. As part-timers, we trained on Tuesday and Thursday nights and the park was close enough to my home for me to jog there and back. I played a couple of reserve matches and scored twice, but as a sixteen-year-old schoolboy it looked as though I might stay in the reserves for a while. Glenavon's first team had made a dreadful start to the season, however, so Terry Nicholson decided to give me a chance in the senior side.

I made my debut as a senior professional footballer for Glenavon on Saturday 26 September 1987, in an Irish League match against Cliftonville at Mourneview Park.

I played in midfield and did particularly well in the first half, hitting the bar with a long-range effort after seventeen minutes. I was enjoying myself being back at home and playing football, and the training at Motherwell had certainly made me fitter. In the seventy-seventh minute I went forward, picked up a pass from substitute Billy Drake, beat one defender and sent goalkeeper Bobby Carlisle the wrong way as I shot home with my left foot. Cue a great roar from the home fans and a jig of delight from me.

It proved to be the only goal of the game. I had scored on my debut and into the bargain I had ended an eight-game losing streak for Glenavon. I think I was a bit of a hero in Lurgan that night . . . and all the miseries of Motherwell had vanished.

The *Lurgan Mail* duly reported: 'A debut goal is something worth celebrating and Neil certainly savoured the euphoria of it all. It was a score which may go down in history, marking the birth of a star.' Just shows you, the press can get things right at times!

I was amazed at the reaction to my debut. I was congratulated by people I had never met, I had my picture taken in my school uniform by the local paper, and because it was an Irish League match, the national newspapers covered the game. I was even given a special mention in Ireland's *Sunday World* column about football in the north.

I couldn't wait to play again and the following weekend I did it again, scoring the first goal in Glenavon's 3–1 win over Bangor in the TNT Gold Cup. I might have played a third game, but of all things I went down with 'flu.

By then, however, I had received the call which would put my soccer career back on track. I had turned down Manchester City for Motherwell, but they were a forgiving lot at Maine Road and within weeks of my arriving home the club contacted my dad through Peter Neill and said they would still like to take me. I needed no second invitation. In late October 1987, I put pen to paper and signed for City.

My friend Gerry Taggart had been signed as an apprentice that summer and was already over in Manchester, so this time, at least, I would not be the only Irish boy in the squad. I had to say goodbye to Glenavon but I would never forget the start they gave me as a senior player, and probably because of that experience and my feelings that things couldn't go as badly as they had done at Motherwell, I packed my bags with a lighter heart.

City's scout Peter Neill accompanied me on the trip to Manchester, which included ten hours on a ferry from Belfast to Liverpool – not fun, I can tell you – followed by a bus journey to Manchester. We arrived at my digs where the landlady warned me I had an early rise as I was wanted at Maine Road at 8.30 a.m. the following morning.

The guest house was just fifteen minutes' walk away from the stadium in Rusholme. As I set out for the ground my first thought was that I had somehow woken up in the wrong country. I had seen maybe only a few brown- or black-skinned people in my life, and here was I now in the Asian quarter of Manchester. I think I probably stared goggle-eyed at women in saris and men in turbans with big long beards – sights I had only seen on television before. As I walked along the road to Moss Side, which is the Afro-Caribbean area of the city, I really did begin to wonder where the white people had gone. It shows you how naïve I was when I arrived in Manchester, and it was to be the first of many culture shocks that I would experience over the next few weeks and months. It was a whole new world to me, yet I never found it intimidating. On the contrary, it was exciting to find new cultures on my doorstep, and I thoroughly enjoyed exploring Manchester.

I was back on the apprenticeship treadmill, having signed a two-year contract. Once again I was on the government's Youth Training Scheme stipend of £28.50 per week, but City did pay us an extra £10 for travel expenses. I was also determined not to repeat the Motherwell debacle, and the main difference in my environment this time around was that within a few days of arriving at Maine Road, I was put into digs with an incredible, wonderful family called the Ducketts.

They lived in a rambling three-storey Victorian house in

Stockport. Len and Jackie Duckett were the mother and father in charge of the household which included their two grown-up married daughters, a younger son and a grandson. Everyone in that house brought their own distinctive personality to a warm and supportive environment in which I was immediately made to feel at home. They were all hard-grafting people who contributed to the household income, and while you had to toe the line and respect their house rules, there was always plenty of humour and laughter around.

Len Duckett became almost like a second father to me, looking after me and making sure I knew my way about Manchester. I still talk to him to this day, and indeed I regret not keeping in touch more regularly because the Ducketts really were very good to me over a number of years. At City and later at Crewe Alexandra I would sometimes move into a flat with other players, for instance, but the Ducketts would always take me back if I needed somewhere to stay.

What makes their kindness and support of me even more astonishing is that Len was a season-ticket holder at Manchester UNITED. But he would often come to watch this City boy play, even travelling to Ireland when I started playing for Northern Ireland's youth side. They are still a warm and caring family, and I will always be grateful to the Ducketts for the start they gave me in England.

In my first year with them I had the whole of the top floor to myself, but after that they provided lodgings for three more players, namely Michael Hughes from Larne, later a Northern Ireland international who is still playing, Mike Sheron who went on to become a prolific scorer at several clubs, and John Wills. We four had a great time together, and all played in the FA Youth Cup Final of 1989. Regular as clockwork, we would catch the bus to Maine Road each morning, and, unlike Motherwell, training was something I looked forward to.

Billy McNeill had left the manager's job to return to Celtic in September 1986, and that had triggered something of a slide at City. During the summer before I arrived at Maine Road, Mel Machin had taken over after Scottish manager Jimmy Frizzell had taken over briefly and presided over the club's relegation to Division Two. Jimmy was kicked upstairs to become general manager, while Mel's job was simple – to get City back to the top flight as soon as possible.

It helped him that the club had a brilliant youth set-up producing some talented players, as evidenced by the fact that City had won the FA Youth Cup in the 1985/86 season. We apprentices were looked after by coaches Tony Book and Glyn Pardoe, and it is these two men that I credit for giving me the basis of my professional career.

Tony had captained the side in a vintage era for City in the late 1960s and early 1970s when the likes of Colin Bell, Mike Summerbee and Francis Lee were at their peak. He had also later managed the club. Glyn was an outstanding full-back who had been forced to retire prematurely. He had suffered some appalling injuries including a horrific broken leg in a tackle by George Best, but it was a knee injury that finally forced him to stop playing.

What these two City men did not know about football was not worth knowing. The quality of their coaching was superb. They concentrated always on teaching us the correct things to do on the pitch, such as passing the ball accurately time after time. As all good coaches should do, they tried to get us to develop good habits both on and off the pitch.

Our routine as apprentices consisted of making sure that the kit for the senior professionals was properly prepared for them. Each of us looked after two players, and at first mine were striker Trevor Morley and the big goalkeeper Eric Nixon. Trevor went on to play for several clubs and is now a scout, while Eric later became something of a living legend at Tranmere Rovers. He was a huge fellow, six feet four inches tall, who would happily give you a thump on the shoulder if his boots weren't prepared exactly as he wanted them.

It was the sort of apprenticeship where, if you got sent for a pot of tea, then you went without argument and fetched it. Another of my jobs was to clean out the toilets and the baths. It may sound as if it was slave labour, but I didn't mind as I knew I was getting a good grounding.

The coaching by Tony and Glyn more than made up for the more tedious aspects of the job. They always tried to keep things varied and interesting, though we concentrated a lot on retaining possession, playing hundreds of hours of the game called 'keep ball'. We would also play small-sided games, while Tony would give me special coaching in the afternoon sometimes, working on my ability to trap and pass the ball. I think it's fair to say that the sort of player I became was established under the tutelage of Tony and Glyn. Later, Dario Gradi and Martin O'Neill would add to my game but my basic grounding was at City.

There was one unexpected development for me right at the start of my time at Maine Road. I had spent most of my youth playing in the forward line or at half-back, but as soon as I got to City, they tried to turn me into a right-back. Is it any wonder that I struggled a bit at first in that position? The move came about because I was put in at right-back in one of the early trials that I played for City. I didn't do too badly, and then the club became short of cover at right- and left-back so that was me stuck in defence for the next three years. Though I mostly played on the right, they also tried me at left-back and even centre-half. It wasn't until I moved to Crewe Alexandra that I got back to playing in my favoured midfield position again.

Mel Machin took a real shine to me when I first started at City. Almost from the start of my time there, I was able to do what I loved best which was playing. Mel put me into the youth team but as the 1987/88 season wore on, I began to play a lot of matches in the reserves.

It was terrific experience for a youngster, as we would often be playing against top professionals. I recall one particular match against Liverpool reserves when their team featured the likes of Jan Molby, Kevin McDonald and Craig Johnston. I was credited with having kept Johnston quiet during the game, which we won 2–0.

The club was suffering an injury crisis in February and March 1988 and I found myself becoming a regular in the reserve team. We were due to play Hull City when Mel Machin told me that I was on standby to play for the first team. I was covering for Paul Lake but in the event he passed a late fitness test and my debut had to be postponed. There were some pundits who queried putting a teenager in the squad, but Mel said at the time that 'if they are good enough, they are old enough', and it was only a few weeks before I did indeed make the starting eleven.

On 30 April, we were going to St Andrews to play Birmingham City, and I was delighted to be told I was travelling with the first team. I just thought I was going along to make up the squad numbers, but then, half an hour before the game, Mel read out the team to start the match and I was named at right-back. I was completely taken by surprise, just amazed that only six months after leaving school, I was going to make my first-team debut for one of England's best-known clubs. I also knew that I had been given a great chance by the manager to stake a claim for a place in the first-team squad for the next season as it was well known that veteran defender John Gidman would be leaving the club at the end of the season.

I did not find out until much later that I was the second-youngest player to be picked by Manchester City for a first-team debut in modern days, the youngest ever having been Glyn Pardoe.

Before the kick-off I was a nervous wreck, and shortly after the referee blew the whistle to start the match I was nearly a wreck of a different sort.

I remember running about the pitch and savouring the atmosphere. I was determined to enjoy myself, but Birmingham's Scottish player Andy Kennedy had other ideas. About a minute into the game I took a pass and was moving down the right wing when Andy absolutely flattened me, taking my legs away and thumping me right over the touchline. It was late and dangerous and he was yellow-carded.

Our physio Roy Bailey and Mel Machin both came to attend to me and it took me a minute or two to get to my feet. Having been given a first-team opportunity, I was determined to carry on, even though I was still sore, and at least I showed I wasn't going to be intimidated.

At that stage of the season we already knew City were not going to make the promotion play-offs, but Birmingham were deep in relegation trouble and perhaps that is why they tried to kick us off the field. I thought I had played reasonably well and was comfortable with the pace of the game, but five minutes into the second half, Ian Handysides came through and hit me just as hard as Andy Kennedy. He caught my ankle and it was very painful, I can tell you.

Handysides, too, was booked, which provoked the Birmingham fans into booing me. They appeared to think that the victim was guilty of getting their players booked, but then who says a football crowd is a thinking creature?

By now the physical punishment was taking its toll on me so Mel Machin brought me off the field after about sixty-four minutes. We went on to win 3–0, with two goals from Ian Brightwell and the third from Imre Varadi.

In the dressing room afterwards my ankle was swollen like a balloon, and indeed the injury prevented me from playing in any of the remaining matches of the season.

Despite the 'treatment', I had thoroughly enjoyed a great experience, and I remember calling home to Lurgan that evening where my dad couldn't believe that he had missed my debut.

He never did get the chance to see me play for Manchester City's first team, because that match at Birmingham turned out to be the one and only appearance that I made for the club at the top level.

Of course I had no idea that things would turn out the way they did, in fact I reasoned that having made my debut at the age of sixteen, I could look forward to an exciting time.

The sky was my limit, or so it seemed, because I was also back in the international frame. During that first season with Manchester City I was called up to play for the Northern Ireland youth side against the Republic of Ireland in Dublin, a match which ended in a no-scoring draw. It was further proof of how far I had come in a short time as it was only three years since I had been cut from the schoolboy squad. And there was more good news on that international front during the summer of 1988, when Billy Bingham, the manager of Northern Ireland, invited me to join the Under-23 squad and attend the Irish FA's four-day coaching seminar at Stranmillis near Belfast.

Gerry Taggart was there, and he had also made his first-team debut for City, so it seemed that life was going to be pretty good for the two boys from Lurgan. It was certainly a quiet life – on YTS wages we were not exactly Jack the lads at that time, and indeed we rarely had a night out in my first two seasons at Maine Road, as we simply couldn't afford it. The funny thing was that all my mates back home thought that Gerry and I must be loaded because we were playing for such a big team. If only they knew that we were dependent on the government for our YTS wages, and the occasional rock concert was a big event for us.

My second season at City turned out to be less than satisfactory, however. Mel Machin had added players to the squad, and I found myself further down the pecking order as the team made a strong bid for promotion to the First Division. Perhaps I tried too hard, but things just did not seem to work out for me, and I was stuck playing in the reserves and youth team. Looking back, I should have been less frustrated than I was, but I had had a taste of first-team action and I wanted more. When you're seventeen and eighteen, you want to do everything in a hurry and rightly or wrongly, I felt that I was not making the progress I should have.

Playing for Manchester City at any level was no great hardship that season. The senior squad did indeed win promotion as we youngsters won the Lancashire Youth Cup and embarked on a tremendous run in the FA Youth Cup, winning at Mansfield, Bradford, Tottenham and Newcastle before facing Watford in the two-legged final.

With future England goalkeeper David James in goal, they restricted us to a 1–0 lead at Maine Road, and we eventually lost after extra-time in the return leg at Vicarage Road. It was a heartbreaker, especially as we had been so well supported by the City fans, 8,000 of whom had turned out to watch the first leg.

The end of the season did bring some good news, however. I had concluded my YTS apprenticeship and the club now exercised the option of giving me a one-year professional contract, which at least earned me a bit more money. Mel

Machin had confidence in half a dozen of the Youth Cup finalists and gave us all professional contracts.

We also went on a wonderful summer trip to Italy, playing four games for City in a prestigious youth tournament in Bologna, in which we lost the final to Juventus. We then moved to Venice where Gerry Taggart, Michael Hughes and I played in the Northern Ireland Under-18 youth team which won a tournament that involved sides from Russia, Holland and Italy, who we beat in the final on penalties.

I celebrated my eighteenth birthday back home in Lurgan where I decided that I would make a special effort to stay fit by playing Gaelic football. And in my 'other' footballing life, things could not have gone much better for me. My old teacher Seamus Heffron had been appointed coach of the Armagh county junior side, and he invited me along to train with them. As always, I enjoyed my 'Gaelic' and thanks to Seamus, this Manchester City player got to play for his county side.

But all too soon it was time to return to City for my third season with the club and my first as a fully-fledged senior professional footballer. It would prove to be a season I would not forget, but not for the reasons I had hoped.

CHAPTER FOUR

Joining Dario's Crewe

It was not all work and no fun for me at that time. In a bar in Manchester I had met a lovely girl called Claire Whiteoak and I plucked up the courage to ask her out. A stunning blonde, she was slightly older than me and worked as a hairdresser. Soon we were 'going steady', as the phrase was in those days, and I met her folks and got on well with them. She was my first love and we were very serious about each other. All of a sudden I was a very happy young man with a terrific girlfriend and good prospects even if I wasn't earning fantastic money. I was on about £100 per week, but out of that I had to pay digs as these were no longer provided by the club. After tax and outlays, I had about £20–£30 per week to live on – it certainly wasn't the high life at that time.

Manchester City were back in the top flight, however, and good earnings would surely come my way if I could break into the first-team reckoning and City could stay in Division One. From the youngest apprentice to the manager and chairman Peter Swales, there was huge anticipation for the season ahead. You couldn't help but get caught up in it, especially as City had bounced straight back after relegation. Personally I felt that, at eighteen, this could be my time to seal my place in the first team.

Yet from the start of the 1989/90 season, things did not go according to plan. There were times when the first team played very good football, but in retrospect there were not enough quality players to sustain the effort over a whole season – you need strength in depth simply to survive in a top league, especially when you make a bad start to the season, as City did in 1989.

There were some very good days, however. We had won only one of our first seven matches before we faced our great Mancunian rivals at Maine Road on 23 September 1989 – a date emblazoned on every City fan's memory. United had paid millions for Gary Pallister and Paul Ince to strengthen a squad which already had the likes of Steve Bruce and Brian McClair, but they were not going well either and the pressure was growing on manager Alex Ferguson. The atmosphere was electric at Maine Road that day, and by the end it was the City support which was celebrating, a record victory over their deadliest rivals, a feat which I know lives on in the memory of City fans to this day.

I was not playing that afternoon but was in the stand to watch an unforgettable match as we ran riot, blitzing United with terrific attacking football. Two goals from David Oldfield and one each from Trevor Morley, Ian Bishop and Andy Hinchcliffe earned us a final result of 5–1. You had to feel sorry for Mark Hughes as he scored United's only goal and it was one of the best I've ever seen, a hitch-kick into the top corner performed about five feet off the ground.

We all thought that such a sensational victory would spark a mini-revival but it was not to be. By December we were deep in relegation trouble and had lost heavily on occasions, Derby County beating us 6–0 away, Nottingham Forest winning 3–0 at Maine Road and Liverpool also hammering us at our place, 4–1.

Mel Machin then paid the price for the poor run when Peter Swales sacked him. Joe Royle, then manager of Oldham Athletic, was appointed in his place but changed his mind before Howard Kendall, who had managed Blackburn Rovers, Everton and Athletic Bilbao, took the job. Howard had but one aim, to keep City in the First Division, and that was going to be a tough task given our lowly position at the time.

Not surprisingly, he sent for some of his Everton 'Old Boys' to help out, including Peter Reid, Alan Harper and Mark Ward. Every manager needs people around him he knows and trusts, but new signings also mean that younger players get pushed to the back of the queue while other players are sold or swapped to make way for the newcomers. My mate from Lurgan, Gerry Taggart, for instance, had made ten starts for the first team but in January was sold to Barnsley for £75,000. It was a very good move for my friend as he made such an impact at Barnsley that within a few weeks he was called up to make his full international debut.

I knew I was going to miss Taggs and I also wondered what fate lay in store for me. For in truth, the reserves were not Howard's priority, though I could soon see that he was a great coach, a very good man manager who knew how to build a team.

He didn't seem to notice me so all I could do was keep plugging away in the reserves where I hardly missed a game. However, I was soon spending more time on the treatment table than I would have liked, due mostly to a succession of niggles which affected my groin area in particular. Still, I played every reserve match and thought I was doing well, and I was quite confident of having my contract extended at the end-of-season talks with players which every manager held in those days before Bosman pre-contracts and transfer windows.

Sometimes in the reserve matches you would find yourself playing against big-name players who were either coming back from injury or had been dropped to the reserves for some reason. I remember having a rare old tussle with Nigel Clough, for instance, and Viv Anderson was another famous player I faced on the pitch.

Playing Manchester United was always a bit special no matter what level it was. Reserve matches were played more often at Maine Road than Old Trafford, which was probably just as well for my landlord and friend Len Duckett. He would come along to support his City lodgers, such as Michael Hughes and myself, and when we played United he would use his season ticket and find himself shouting for us while sitting among his fellow United fans. They would tap him on the shoulder and ask him, 'Why are you sitting here with us and shouting for them?'

Undaunted, Len would reply, 'I'm a season-ticket holder but that's my boys out there.' That's the type of character Len is – loyal to a fault.

We went out of the League Cup at the quarter-final stage, beaten 1–0 by Coventry City, and lost in the FA Cup to Millwall after three games. First Division survival was all that mattered and the club spent £1m on Niall Quinn to see if he could provide the goals that would save us from the drop.

He scored on his debut to earn a 1–1 draw with Chelsea and then we beat league leaders Aston Villa away which sparked a run of victories. Howard Kendall had managed to turn things around and by Easter Monday of 1990, City were safe from relegation. All that remained was for me to make it into the first team and get my contract extended.

I thought I might get a run out in the first team in the end-of-season games but that did not happen. All the contracts were sorted out on one day shortly after City had ensured

First Division survival. I remember being in the dressing room waiting to be called up. Another young player, Ian Thomson, and myself were the first to be called out. I thought it was not a good sign that only two of us were given the call, and I was slightly apprehensive when I was the first to be summoned to the manager's room, though I still did not feel too worried at that point. Although I had only played for the reserves, I had done consistently well so I did not think there would be a problem.

Howard had Peter Reid with him, as he was his assistant at the time. The manager got straight to the point. 'This is the time of year when it is good news or bad news for players,' he said. 'I'm afraid that in your case it is bad news.'

He proceeded to talk to me for at least another five minutes, but I'm afraid I can barely remember a single word he said. My mind just could not take in the enormity of the fact that I was being sacked, though football calls it by the supposedly nicer name of 'free transfer'.

There have been thousands of boys like me in that same position. I doubt if any one of us could really explain how it feels when you hear the dreaded verdict that someone thinks you are not good enough to make a career as a professional with his club. You really do feel as if it is the end of your world, and in a sense, it is. If you're with a top-flight club as I was, then the only way to go is down, or even completely out of the game.

Maybe Howard Kendall and Peter Reid advised me to look for another club down the leagues. At least that's what I assume they said, but I was so deeply in shock that I really cannot recall much of what they said. I do remember Howard finishing by saying that he would put my name on the flyer containing the names of players who would be out of contract that went round every club. He added that he did think I had a future in the game but it just wasn't going to be with Manchester City at that point.

What really hurt was that the two members of the coaching staff who had worked most closely with me, Tony Book and Glyn Pardoe, thought otherwise, believing that I could have a future with City.

I was angry and bitter for some time afterwards. I felt I had done enough to justify being kept on, but I learned as I progressed in football that such oustings are often not the fault of the player and that managers can get it wrong, about youngsters in particular. I myself have often said that I am a late developer, so I want to make it clear that I do not hold any grudges against Howard or Manchester City in any way whatsoever. He had a decision to make and he took it with a view to what was best for the club at the time. He just concluded that either I was not going to make the grade at Maine Road or that I would not be suitable for the kind of team he was trying to create. I don't blame him for that – even though he was wrong!

The worst thing was that I then had to go back to the dressing room and relay the verdict to my colleagues and peers. I just could not face them. I went into the toilet beside the manager's office and immediately burst into copious tears. It must have taken me about five minutes to compose myself. Eventually I made my way into the dressing room but as soon as I had told them, I started crying again anyway.

My first thought was for Claire. Things were going so well between us, but here was I with no job, no prospects and probably no money in a few weeks' time. It already looked to me as if I would have to go home to Lurgan and start all over again, so I just could not see a way ahead for us. It appeared that I would lose my career and my girlfriend in one go.

All the lads in that dressing room were sympathetic and

gave me plenty of advice, most of which was not to panic and try to find another club as soon as possible. I think I have shown over the years that I'm a pretty resilient character, but back then as an eighteen year old it was difficult to bounce back. Eventually I told myself that I would show Howard Kendall that he had made a mistake and that I could make it as a professional.

Luckily for me, there were seven or eight reserve games left so I could put myself in the shop window. My contract did not expire until the end of June so I had about two months to find another club, and I soon became pretty determined to do so as I wanted to stay in England and hopefully play for a team near Manchester and Claire.

I also had another method of showing the football world that I was worth signing. At the beginning of April 1990, I had been picked for Northern Ireland's Under-21 squad to play against Israel at Coleraine – the place where I had enjoyed such good times in the Milk Cup. Perhaps that was a good omen for me, because manager Billy Bingham put me straight into the team to play Israel.

This was a memorable game for me as it marked my debut at that level, but I'm sure the other players who took part and the small number of spectators who attended will remember it for other reasons, as there was a blizzard in the second half. The match had to be abandoned two minutes from time as the floodlights failed – the second time that had happened in matches between the two countries, the first time being in Tel Aviv in a World Cup qualifier.

I have to say I was never totally impressed with Billy Bingham, not least because he had the annoying habit of calling me Noel, and my dad was amazed and angry that the manager of the national football team couldn't even get my name right. He did it so often that even the football writers picked up the habit and one of the reports of that match against Israel refers to me as Noel Lennon. It was not as if they could confuse me with Noel Bailie, who was also in the team that night, as we look nothing like each other.

It was Noel who set up the move for our opening goal, scored by Iain Dowie of Luton Town. Banini should have scored for Israel after thirty-eight minutes but he dallied and I just managed to nick the ball off his toes. Israel did equalize after eighty-five minutes but Paul Gray of Luton, who had come on as a substitute, scored three minutes later. We were still celebrating when the floodlights failed, and since the game was a friendly the score stood in the record books.

I knew I had done well and a few weeks later I was delighted to be picked for a rather more prestigious game, this time at Under-23 level. Although the players of both sides often play alongside each other in England, games between Northern Ireland and the Republic of Ireland are always keenly contested and the match at Shamrock Park, Portadown, on 15 May was no exception.

By that time, I was feeling rather better about life as I was doing very well in the City reserves and had already received a couple of calls from scouts and one manager. The first person to take an active interest and come along to see me play was Des Bennett, a scout acting on behalf of Crewe Alexandra of the Third Division.

Des watched me play a couple of times and persuaded Crewe's manager Dario Gradi to come along and see me. After he had watched me a couple of times, Dario called to say 'We would like to take you aboard at the end of the season.' No details were discussed but at least I had an offer.

Obviously I was still hoping for an offer from a bigger club, and the Under-23 game gave me an ideal opportunity to show what I could do. A couple of newspapers highlighted the fact that I was in the shop window and I told them that I felt I had been badly treated but was still 'determined to make the grade'.

Gerry Taggart captained the side that night, having already made his debut at senior level, and my City colleague Michael Hughes also played. There were several managers from big clubs in the stadium that night, such as Chris Nicholl of Southampton, and I wasn't the only one out to impress them.

In the first half in particular I played out of my skin, as did several others in our team, and we went in at half-time 2–0 up. The Republic fought back and equalized when John Sheridan tripped over me in the penalty box and the referee pointed to the spot – the match reports say I brought down John but of course we full-backs, as I was then, never see it like that. David Kelly of Leicester scored from the spot and also hit the winner ten minutes from time.

To lose 2–3 after being 2–0 up against our old rivals was hugely disappointing to put it mildly, but at least I had performed well overall. Back in Manchester, there was better news for me as John Rudge, the manager of Port Vale who were then in Division Two, called to say he was interested in signing me. He explained that he still had to sort out who was going and who was staying but he would get back to me once that process was completed.

Dario Gradi, meanwhile, had invited me down to Gresty Road, home of Crewe Alexandra. I did not know much about the town or the club, so I was in for something of a surprise. I knew the Alex, as locals called them, were nicknamed the Railwaymen because of the town's huge train station and links with the rail industry, and I knew of Gradi's growing reputation, but that was about the extent of my knowledge.

It was a complete culture shock when I arrived at the club. Maine Road was not the biggest and best stadium in the First

Division, but it was a light year ahead of Gresty Road. I suppose it was very traditional in an old-fashioned Spartan way, but the facilities left a lot to be desired. The gym, for instance, was nothing more than a sweatbox with some weights – I was to get to know it all too well though, as you will discover.

Dario was impressive as he communicated his plans for the club, but when we began to talk money I was a bit disappointed. As a reserve player at City, I had earned £100 per week, so as a first-team player – even in the Third Division – I was expecting to earn double that. But Dario outlined the club's budget and financial problems, and offered me a two-year deal worth £110 per week, plus bonuses.

I had been hoping for a bigger club and more money, but Dario proved very convincing and he did have a reputation for his work with young players. In particular, he was good at improving players freed from other clubs and selling them on, as he had done with David Platt, who he got for nothing from Manchester United and sold to Aston Villa for £200,000. Also, when I had played for City's youth team against Crewe Alexandra, they had always impressed me as a team who were trying to play good football.

I had to make my mind up quickly as my contract was running out, so though I was bitterly disappointed at having to join a club two divisions lower, I only had one concrete offer on the table and it was a two-year deal, so I decided to sign. I suppose I could have waited to see whether an offer materialized from Port Vale or some other club, but Dario had done such a good job selling Crewe Alexandra to me that I plumped for them. At the time it seemed a disastrous backward step, but in hindsight it was the best thing that could have happened to me. I have long since learned in life that sometimes you have to take a step backwards to go forwards.

Dario did indeed live up to his reputation as a fantastic coach, particularly of youngsters like myself. At times he could be very straightforward, even curt, but at other times he would be funny and he was always very encouraging. He kept telling us to go out and play football and enjoy the game, and try to express ourselves on the pitch.

He was very 'hands on' or should that be 'feet on'. I particularly remember that when we were practising set-pieces, if we did not get it correct and hit the wrong spot with the ball, he would march up and get hold of the ball, then deliver the free-kick perfectly to the exact place he wanted it.

He taught us a whole range of things which were new to the game in England. He had been very influenced by Ajax of Amsterdam and their training methods, and in a way it was he who brought the continental philosophy into the game in England, following their approach a few years before the big influx of players and managers from abroad in the 1990s. He emphasized movement on and off the ball and told us to try to copy the good European teams.

Goodness knows how he managed it, but he persuaded Red Star Belgrade to play Crewe in a friendly, and even though we lost 0–4, it was a really pleasurable experience to take part in a game with such skilful players. They scored four, but it could have been fourteen, and afterwards Dario told us that he would love us to play like them – we ended up getting relegated and Red Star won the European Cup that season, so that plan didn't exactly work out.

Although much of the attention focused on Dario's youthful brigade, the Crewe squad at the time were not just a bunch of raw youngsters. Kenny Swain was the assistant manager and he had won the European Cup with Aston Villa in 1982. He was still playing even though he was coming up for forty and was fantastically fit. Apart from being a really nice guy, he taught us a lot and for all his achievements in the game he was a modest man.

Steve Walters was another fine player. He had been Crewe's youngest-ever first-team player and had captained the England youth team. He was a very talented boy but he didn't make the impact expected of him later in his career.

One of the players who joined us for a season later in my time there was someone I knew quite a bit about. Jim Harvey hailed from Lurgan, and like myself he had started out with Glenavon FC, though he had played rather more than my two matches with our home-town side. He had gone on to have a long stint with Tranmere Rovers before moving to Crewe. He was in the later stages of his career, and went on to become assistant to Sammy McIlroy when he was manager of Northern Ireland, where I encountered him several years after I had left Crewe. Jim was manager of Morecambe of the Nationwide Conference League for a dozen years and twice took them to the brink of Football League qualification, but he was sacked in May 2006, to be replaced by none other than Sammy McIlroy.

Other players at the time included Rob Jones who went on to sign for Liverpool for £300,000 and then played for England, while Craig Hignett was a Scouser who was transferred to Middlesborough for £500,000. I recognized one player as soon as I walked in the door – Andy Gunn had played against me in the Manchester City v Watford Youth Cup Final.

It was a happy dressing room at the start of my time at Crewe and would generally stay that way for the rest of my time there. It took me a while to get to grips with the demands of playing for the first team even at that level, but Dario had confidence in me and picked me from the start of the season, which sadly began disastrously as we took just one point from our first six league games.

The first really big games I played for Crewe were against a club who were legends of world football. After knocking out Grimsby Town, we were drawn against Liverpool in the League Cup. We actually took the lead against them at Anfield, but that probably only served to annoy them and they came back to overwhelm us 5–1. The return leg was an all-ticket affair at Gresty Road, which at least showed that the stadium when full could generate plenty of atmosphere, but we were on the wrong end of a 1–4 drubbing. In fairness to us, that was the Liverpool team who were league champions and even to be on the same pitch as the likes of Ray Houghton, John Barnes and Ian Rush was a big thrill for all of us, especially since I was still only nineteen.

I had decided to stay in Stockport, and even though I wasn't being charged the earth for my digs, money was very tight. Those were the days when a tenner could buy you five or six pints, which was just as well as that was usually how much I had left for a night out.

My favourite local pub was the Elizabethan in Heaton Moor Road, Stockport, and it was there that I met and drank with two friends, Chris Mooney and Scott Woodhall, who are still mates of mine to this day. There were a lot of talented people who drank in the Elizabethan at that time and formed a loose grouping of friends. There were actors such as Craig Cash who was in *The Royle Family*. He and a guy called Phil Mealey wrote a television sit-com called *Early Doors* which was based loosely on The Elizabethan where they both drank. Sally Lindsay, who played Shelley Unwin on *Coronation Street,* was another regular, and it was a place where a lot of musicians gathered, including two brothers called Gallagher. I was just getting seriously into music at that time so you will not be surprised to learn that I was a big fan of Mancunian music at the time of 'Madchester', when bands like the Stone Roses and Happy Mondays burst onto the scene.

Noel and Liam Gallagher were a class apart from the start. They were just putting their band together and it was great to watch them develop and became bigger than all of the other Manchester bands. I'm still a huge fan of Oasis today. From the first time that I went to see them I was blown away by their live performances, and I saw them quite a few times before and after they were famous.

One of their best-ever gigs was at Maine Road in Manchester in 1996. Everybody wanted to be at that concert and it was generally reckoned to have been a high point in the Manchester scene of the 1990s, but I don't have the fondest memories of that day.

I had just signed for Leicester City and Steve Lomas, a great friend of mine who was captain of Manchester City, managed to get us backstage passes for the day. It would be fair to say that we had enjoyed a drink or five before the gig even started. I remember there was a long corridor backstage and as we went along it I spotted Liam and Noel and Liam's wife Patsy Kensit, plus Stan Collymore and a few of the Liverpool players. As we went outside to stand beside the executive boxes, for some reason Steve Lomas and I started to have an argy-bargy. I cannot even remember who started it or why, but we were soon rolling about on the floor in front of all the VIPs, trying to punch each other but failing miserably because we were under the influence. The bouncers took a dim view of our scrapping, but for some reason it was me who got thrown out and not Steve. A few years later Oasis played a gig in Glasgow and we managed to get backstage to meet the band, the Gallaghers being great Celtic fans as well as Manchester City diehards. The first thing that Noel said when he saw me was 'Right, you, no fighting tonight.'

Back in the early 1990s I was happy to be on the edge of what was a hard-drinking, drug-using scene, but I was a little like a spectator looking in. As I played football for a living, I could never get involved in that sort of heavy stuff, but I did enjoy the craic and the music.

The early 1990s were exciting times to be in the Manchester area and I was reluctant to leave when Crewe was only thirty-five miles down the road, but transport was a problem. Even though I had learned to drive and had a licence, I was so badly off that I couldn't afford a car and at first I had to hitch lifts off other players to make the journey back and forth to Stockport. My young person's bus pass came in very handy at that time.

Eventually I managed to scrimp and save enough to get myself some wheels. My first car will strike a chord with those who remember British Leyland and some of its more 'charming' products. The second-hand – or maybe about tenth-hand – Austin Montego that I bought during my first season at Crewe was at least an improvement on the bus.

One day Dario asked me to pop up to the train station in my car and pick up the scout who had spotted me in City's reserves, Des Bennett. I parked my car at the top of the hill outside Crewe station, and went looking for Des. I couldn't find him and when I went back to where I had parked it, my car was gone. My first thought was 'who would nick an Austin Montego' but as I looked around I spotted my car rolling down the hill. There were a lot of cars parked by the station that day, and my Montego hit four of them on the way down. I did the honest thing and left notes with my details on the windscreens, and the insurance company picked up the tab, but the Montego didn't last long after that.

As I totted up the appearances for Crewe I knew I was doing well, and I was flattered to read in the newspapers that the great Brian Clough, legendary manager of Nottingham Forest, was apparently having me watched. But as would happen so often in my career, reports and rumours proved to be just that.

In late November, we were deep in the relegation zone and things were looking very glum when we went away to play Cambridge United who were then chasing promotion. I remember that game well because it marked my first goal for Crewe.

Kenny Swain was making his 100th appearance for Crewe that night, becoming only the second player after Peter Shilton to reach that mark with five separate clubs.

Dion Dublin, who would come to Celtic late in his long career and end up scoring in the Scottish League Cup Final, notched the opener for Cambridge after two minutes, but we equalized before Steve Claridge, later to be a colleague at Leicester, put United ahead on the stroke of half-time.

About a minute into the second half I got the ball and went on a run past three of their defenders before poking the ball past John Vaughan in the Cambridge goal. I was ecstatic and remember running over to the Crewe fans and jumping onto the barrier in my excitement. I would score three goals that season, which proves I could actually hit the net with somewhat more regularity than I have done with Celtic.

Our league form was dismal from then on, frankly, but we went on a fair old run in the FA Cup, beating Lincoln City, Atherstone United, Bristol Rovers and Rotherham before drawing West Ham in the fifth round. There were television cameras at the ground and I had told all the people in the Elizabethan to watch out for our game – it was slightly embarrassing when only thirty seconds of the match was shown.

I wish they had shown more because we played really well

in that match. Dario had told us to go out and have a go at the First Division side, and we certainly did. United had my old Manchester City colleague Trevor Morley playing that day while Frank McAvennie was back with them and proving dangerous. But we not only held out, we attacked them and could have scored when Craig Hignett missed a relatively easy chance. It looked as if we would earn a money-spinning replay but with about twelve minutes left, Jimmy Quinn scored for them and we were out of the cup. I recall their fans as well as ours giving us an ovation as we trudged off Upton Park. We just could not replicate that form in the league, however, and despite a late surge when we won four out of our last five matches, the terrible start cost us dear and relegation became inevitable when Chester City beat us 3–1.

I enjoyed a bittersweet end to the season. Relegation was heartbreaking, though Dario had us all feeling pretty confident that we would get straight back up again. My own form had held up, Dario had made me captain for a few of the later matches, and there were reports that Nottingham Forest and Oxford United were watching me, but of course these came to nothing.

What really boosted me was that I was voted Player of the Year not once but three times. I was the Players' Player, the Junior Player and the Supporters' Player. I particularly relished the latter award because from the start the fans seemed to have taken to me, and I certainly appreciated their encouragement.

For good measure the club's Vice Presidents' Association also voted me as their Player of the Year which is how I got to meet the one and only Denis Law. He presented me with the trophy at a black-tie dinner just twenty-four hours after watching United beat Barcelona in the European Cup Winners' Cup Final.

As we prepared for the summer break, Dario told the lads to take a good rest but be ready for hard work in pre-season training. We would bounce back to Division Three, Dario was certain, and I personally had already come a long way since that dreadful day when Howard Kendall showed me the door at Maine Road.

I was club captain at nineteen, I had enjoyed a terrific season and was player of the year three times over. I should have been happy, but I had lived under a secret cloud for many months. No one outside of my family and friends and a few people at Crewe knew just how serious the 'niggling injuries' I had suffered in recent years had become. They had never stopped me playing and didn't really affect me too much during games, but I had become aware of the deep-seated reason for them. So as my first full season in the first team ended, I knew that in the months ahead lurked the greatest test of my life, one where my future, quite literally, would be in someone else's hands.

CHAPTER FIVE

Out of the Depths

I know what the word nadir means. I've been there. Indeed, I was there for more than a year.

People tend to remember where they spent special birthdays like their eighteenth or twenty-first, but the birthday I remember most is my twentieth. The reason why is that I spent it in hospital in Belfast, facing an operation on my spine that would determine whether or not I would ever play football or even walk properly again. Here was I, a professional footballer with dreams of a long career ahead of me, stuck in a living nightmare in which I could only look ahead with fear and dread.

The worst crisis of my life had begun when I started playing regularly for Manchester City in the youth team and the reserves. During training but especially after matches, I began to notice some niggles – no more than twinges – in my lower back and then inexplicably I picked up some injuries to my groin and hamstrings.

I began to think that I had better get something done about these injuries as they were affecting my progress at Maine Road. The medical staff at City were concerned and I was sent for an X-ray as a precaution. When nothing showed up, I was told it was just 'growing pains' and they would probably heal themselves in time. So I just had to carry on playing. Though the pain was irregular, I was always aware of the niggling feelings in my lower back. Yet I had to continue training and playing as normally as possible because I was so anxious to complete my apprenticeship and get a long-term contract at Maine Road.

I dealt with my exit from Manchester City in the last chapter, and to be honest I do not know what would have happened had I stayed there. Less than six months into my stay at Crewe, the strains and niggles started to occur again, making me feel that there was something more serious underlying the various problems. At that time at Crewe, there were a couple of part-time physiotherapists and we also had access to a physio called Craig Simmons who worked at the FA's training centre at Lilleshall.

Craig examined me thoroughly and said 'Neil, I think you may have a serious problem with your back. The niggles that you are having with your groin and hamstrings are stemming from the back problem. You need to go into hospital to get it checked.'

At this point I was going well in the first team so this was really the last news I needed to hear. But when the specialist at Leighton Hospital, Dai Rees, examined me, the verdict was the worst possible.

My back was X-rayed again and this time the specialist said, 'You have a real problem here as you have quite a serious injury in your lower spine. You will need an operation to correct it.'

As I was only nineteen at the time I immediately thought it was just something that I could shrug off in six or seven weeks and be straight back to playing, but the specialist said 'I don't think you realize the seriousness of what I'm saying. The fact is that you have a stress fracture of the fifth bone in the lumbar section of your spine, and if you do not get this operation you will be finished playing football at twenty-two or twenty-three.'

Now he had my full attention. I could not take in what he was saying at first as the room seemed to swirl and my mind went blank for a few seconds. When I recovered I realized that, in effect, he was saying that I had been playing football with a broken back.

My mind began to race and I asked him a load of questions: what was the likely outcome for me as a footballer? How long would I be out for? What sort of work would I need to do to get back to playing? That was my whole focus – to get back to football.

The real shock came when he told me that I would be out of football for at least a year and that I would require extensive physiotherapy for many months. The alternative was that I would almost certainly have to give up playing football completely within three years. I was utterly dismayed – the thought that I might have to stop playing had never even crossed my mind.

The consultant made it clear that there was no absolute guarantee that the surgery would be successful. Not only might I never get back to playing professionally, there was even the remote possibility that I might never walk properly again, though he stressed that this was highly unlikely. However, there was no doubt in the specialist's mind that if I did not get the operation then I certainly would have a very short career in professional football.

All of this was a lot to take in for someone who was, after all, still a teenager. When I was given a free transfer from Manchester City it seemed as though my whole world had collapsed around me. Now here was I at just nineteen being told that my career might be over before it could even really start. It just seemed so unfair that I had put the disappointment of City behind me, done so well at Crewe that I had been made captain and won the Player of the Year award, only for this injury to surface and threaten my whole future.

I was only earning £110 per week at that point, of which £50 went for digs and food, so it was not as if I was going to lose a fortune if I had to give up. However, that wasn't the point. I just desperately wanted to carry on playing, because I was sure I could have a future at a higher level in the game.

I suppose I could have gone without the operation and let nature run its healing course, but that would have meant stopping playing football there and then for anything up to three years, or perhaps permanently. I was now forced to consider retirement, but that thought lasted only a few seconds. I wanted to play football more than anything else in the world, but I was being presented with the dilemma from hell – take a year out and risk my career, or know for certain that I'd be finished in two or three seasons' time.

I cannot speak highly enough of Crewe Alexandra for what they did for me in the wake of this dreadful news. Dario told me not to worry, that the club would look after me, and they were as good as their word, paying for me to go to Belfast to see another specialist who confirmed the diagnosis. Ian Adair was one of Europe's leading orthopaedic surgeons in the field of spinal treatment, practising at Musgrave Park Hospital in the city where the British Army sent its soldiers for treatment throughout the Troubles. You can imagine the horrors he had to work on over the years.

Mr Adair explained that, as its name suggests, a stress fracture comes about because of undue pressure on a particular bone. It particularly affects growing bones and physiotherapists are now much more aware of the problem in teenage footballers because of the experience of players like me. The surgeon said that I had simply played far too much football for too long, but the fact is that when you are a kid you want to play every game you can. I had been playing football at every opportunity, whether it was soccer or Gaelic and my body had to pay the price at the age of nineteen. In other footballers it shows up much later on in life when joints get crippled by arthritis which is often caused by twisting and turning too much – you would be surprised just how many former footballers get hip and knee replacements some time after they retire.

Here was I showing signs of long-term damage while still a teenager and there was no way to replace a bone in my spine. There was, however, a surgical procedure which could strengthen the damaged bone considerably and leave me nearly as good as new.

He said that the operation itself would involve a long and complex procedure that would include the removal of a piece of bone from my hip which would then be fused to the fractured bone and secured with wires. Mr Adair added that the operation should cure the problem, but success was not guaranteed and I might have some residual stiffness. I was also to prepare for a long haul back to fitness.

At that time Crewe were deep in relegation trouble so it was decided that I would play out the rest of the season before undergoing the operation which would make or break my footballing career.

The hardest part was having to tell my parents the extent of my injury problems. Understandably, they were very upset to hear the news. There were a fair number of phone calls between my dad and myself in particular, me virtually in despair and him trying to raise my spirits. Indeed, all my family and friends rallied round to try to boost my morale, though I think they had a hard task.

At least I was still able to play and could lose myself in training and playing. I could get by in games without taking painkillers but I did avail myself of the latest fashion accessory in football at that time. Cycling shorts had just appeared on the scene and several players with a history of groin injuries swore by them, so I think I was one of the first people in the Third Division to wear them. They were not the smooth Lycra shorts which are ubiquitous nowadays. These shorts were bulky rubber efforts designed to keep the groin area warm and whenever you took them off there was so much sweat in them it looked as though you had lost two pounds off your backside.

Still, they seemed to do the trick and I was able to play out the season. I told people the shorts were to protect against groin strains, but I did not let on that my injuries were much more serious. Indeed I tried to play them down, not least because I was anxious to retain my place in Northern Ireland's Under-21 squad.

After the final league match, against Mansfield Town on 11 May 1991, we were relegated to the Fourth Division and now I faced a major operation. Happy days, or what?

After collecting my various Player-of-the-Year awards and having a short break, I went home to Lurgan to prepare myself for the ordeal ahead, though in truth it was largely a question of waiting. In the middle of June I went in to Musgrave Park Hospital, the first time I had been in hospital for anything serious in my life.

I was in a ward full of people with back problems and I was by far the youngest. I was there for four days before the operation and ten days after it. My twentieth birthday fell on 25 June 1991 and I celebrated it, if celebrated is the word, in hospital. Now hospital food isn't always the best, so for my birthday my mum brought me a special present – a Chinese takeaway. I was starving and it tasted wonderful, I can tell you.

After the operation, Mr Adair assured me that the procedure, which took several hours, was very much as it had been outlined to me though it had been complex and taken longer than expected.

The sliver of bone from my hip was now fused to the fracture and tied up with wire in the butterfly knot which can be seen in X-rays to this day. This wire also led to several newspaper headlines about the 'bionic footballer' after I returned to Crewe.

Mr Adair is a truly brilliant surgeon and within days it was clear that the operation was a total success. It was only much later on that I found out that the problem of spinal stress fractures was not uncommon in young footballers and that similar operations had been carried out on a number of players. I know of only two of us who have had the operation and enjoyed long-term careers in football, which just shows how risky the operation actually was.

At the start of my recuperation, I had to remain immobile as much as possible. I spent the first three months of the rehabilitation period in something which resembled an armoured jacket. It was really a glorified plaster cast, a plastic shield that went round my body with Velcro straps at the side. I could take it off only at night so that I could sleep on my side. It was extremely uncomfortable to wear at first, though the nurses were great in trying to help me get used to it. When I think back on what those nurses have had to deal with over the decades, I realize that my problems – massive though they were for me – were probably minor compared to bomb and shooting victims. I have nothing but grateful thanks for the work they did for me and countless others at Musgrave Park. They are not called angels for nothing.

For ten days after the operation I was on drips and had various tubes running in and out of my body and was examined every few hours. Normal sleep was nearly impossible, but at least I could rest all day – I didn't have any choice.

The worst part was not being able to go to the toilet in the usual manner. I was lying motionless on my back and being fed and given juices so, not surprisingly, I developed constipation. The nurses measured the liquid I had drunk and the amount I had produced at the other end, so to speak, and concluded that I was very constipated indeed.

They sent for Matron who was a lovely lady but had a slightly distressing resemblance to Hattie Jacques, the actress who always played a matron in the *Carry On* films. She even had the same no-nonsense manner. Matron loudly asked 'Who's constipated around here?' before looking at the notes beside the bed and saying 'So it's you that's constipated . . . well, we'll soon fix that.'

If I could have moved I would have run for the hills to escape that big woman, but the next thing I knew was that the curtains were round the bed, my backside was exposed, and I had an enema suppository inserted in a very private place. The inevitable results appeared with indecent haste, and afterwards I was acutely embarrassed to realize from the smiles on my fellow patients' faces that everyone else in the ward had heard everything that had happened. Still, you had to laugh . . .

The first time that I took off my body protector I just about collapsed, but with shock rather than pain. After about a week of lying virtually motionless, the doctors said I could get up and go for a shower. It took what seemed like an hour to get out of bed and go to the shower room.

In there I got undressed and couldn't help looking in the

mirror. Immediately I wished that I had not done so. I looked as if I had been attacked by an axe-wielding assassin, like Jack Nicholson in *The Shining*. The skin of my lower back was being held together by sixteen metal staples and there was still a trickle of blood oozing from the scar which was about a foot long and followed the line of my lower spine. There was bruising everywhere and another scar on my hip where the piece of bone had been extracted. It looked completely horrific and I wondered how I was ever going to play football again. I don't mind admitting that there and then in that shower room, I cried my eyes out at the sight of my stapled back.

I took my shower and put my body protector back on, wishing that I hadn't taken it off, and apart from nighttime it stayed there for three months. I washed in it, ate in it, went to the toilet in it and sometimes slept in it. At times the pain in my back was quite unbearable, but I could not take off that damned thing. It was also incredibly itchy on my skin – believe me that sort of itch can drive you demented and it really did nearly send me over the top.

Immediately after the operation my main concern was finding out whether or not I would actually be able to play again, but after Mr Adair's reassurances that things had gone well, all I could think about was how long it would take me to get fit. I should just have been happy that the operation had been successful, but my mind was preoccupied with my future and in many ways I felt as if I had been handed a prison sentence. I had always known that a football career was going to be short, and here was I looking at a year out, or perhaps even longer. It was soul destroying to contemplate such a future – when you're twenty, a year seems to stretch ahead of you like an eternity, and though I was obviously thankful that at least I had the chance of playing again, I was nevertheless full of frustration that the resumption of my career was so far away.

It was also further away than I anticipated. The extent of the work done by the surgeon was such that I think I became a bit of a textbook case, but just as the operation itself went on longer than expected, so too did my recovery.

The physiotherapy experts were wonderful, but the actual work itself was mind numbing in its tedium. Every day I would have to spend four or five hours in the gym. At first I was only allowed to sit on an exercise bike and pedal away for hours on end or lift a few weights. Gradually I moved on to being allowed to do some stretching and moving the trunk area of my body. I could not bend my back at first so the exercises were concentrated on strengthening my waist and abdominal muscles.

As ever, my family were supportive and once I got home to Lurgan, I began to feel a bit more positive about things and soon got into the discipline of doing my exercises. All I could think about was getting back to playing for Crewe, but had I known how long and tortuous my recuperation was going to be, I might well have quit. Indeed many times in the months ahead I seriously contemplated giving it all up.

There were some really bad days when I thought my career was over. I really did wonder if it was all worth it. I was almost in despair, but somewhere within myself I found the strength to carry on, even after various setbacks meant that my recovery period kept being prolonged.

They had told me it might take a year to get back to playing. But several times during my rehabilitation I suffered slight setbacks and at those times I began to wonder how many seasons I was going to miss, never mind matches. It was at times like that, when the future seemed so bleak, that I realized I had reached the end of my tether, that I was at my personal nadir. I wanted to call a halt and get myself out of the gym or wherever, and just walk away from it all. But then my inner voice would kick in and remind me that what I was working for was worth the agony.

At one point, I was told to stop all exercises completely as Mr Adair felt I was not giving the bone in my back enough time and rest to knit together properly. That was a devastating day, and once again there was the frustration of having to sit motionless for hours, but that period of enforced rest did the job and I was soon back in the gym grinding out the hours.

The biggest problem I faced was the sheer boredom of the physiotherapy and the hundreds of hours I spent in the gym building up the muscles around the site of the operation. As any athlete or bodybuilder will tell you, there is nothing more mind-numbingly wearisome than staring at a wall while you pump iron, counting the repetitions as you sweat it out. Yet there is no alternative to sheer bloody hard work, though you do think you are going slightly bonkers at times.

The very thought that you have to be patient makes you madly impatient. I remember wondering how prisoners managed to do their time, because I was slightly 'stir crazy' myself.

All the time I was worrying whether that little tweak I had just felt in my lower back was the one that signified that all the surgeon's work and my own efforts had been undone and I would have to start all over again. Or worse . . .

Eventually I went back to Gresty Road where there was a small room set aside for gym work. It was tiny enough with one person in it, but sometimes there would be other players trying to recover from injuries and it became rather crowded. Mostly I did repetitive work with weights and circuit training, all aimed at strengthening the muscles supporting my back.

Though Dario, Jim Harvey and all the lads at Crewe would

always drop in to encourage me, for a great deal of the time I was alone. Often I would be locked up in my own mind wondering what the hell I was doing and just dreaming of the day when I would be able to kick a ball. Still, at least there was one beneficial side effect of all that hard work – I lost about a stone in weight and looked very trim.

Each week I would be measured on my progress and the physios would tell me if I had achieved some improvement and could move on to the next stage. As I got stronger, I was able to go cycling and swimming and that broke the monotony.

As the rest of the squad began the 1991/92 season, I was just getting into the swing of things with my various exercise programmes, but I knew I was behind schedule with my recuperation. I did not realize, however, just how far behind I would fall.

One year on from the operation I had still not recovered to the point where I could play any kind of football. It was only in the first week of January 1992 that Mr Adair finally decreed that I would definitely play again, and I was packed off to Lilleshall for two weeks of serious rehabilitation work. Before I went there, the doctors' estimated that I would be back playing after two months and therefore I would not miss the whole season. But at the FA centre the experts found that I had a much longer way to go to regain full fitness, and they told me it would be many months before I could play again. It was yet another setback in a series of them, and once again I was really downcast by the news. However, I had no choice but to soldier on and work my way through the schedule of exercises, many of which were designed to restore mobility to my lower body.

As it happens, I never did get back the full range of movements that I had before the operation. Some people who do not know my medical history like to make fun of my admittedly unusual running style. Perhaps they do not know that my upright stance is a legacy of that back operation. There are times when I look at myself on the television and say 'would you look at the state of that?' because I see myself running with such a straight back and a tense gait that looks awkward. You don't notice it over the first five or six yards, but in a longer sprint it's quite discernible. Of course, the great Olympic sprinter and world-record holder Michael Johnson runs in the same upright way and it hasn't done him any harm – I just wish I could run as fast as him!

The first time I began to believe that I would make a comeback to professional football was about eight months after the op, on the day I was allowed out for my first running session. Really it was just a gentle jog round the pitch but it felt wonderful to be out of the gym at last and into the fresh air. I hadn't finished with the weights and circuit training, not by a long chalk, but at least it was a start and I felt as if I had got out of prison.

I got one day off a week, but from Monday to Saturday I would either be in the gym or out on the pitch running, or cycling around Stockport. I also joined a gym near my home and would go along there in the evening for more sessions or a swim. Although it was great to be in their company, it was a bit uncomfortable when I went with the squad to matches, because all the time I would be watching them and wondering when my time would come to join them on the pitch.

Slowly but surely I built up my running until finally the time came to kick a ball. By that point I had missed an entire season and to be honest, my patience had long since worn thin.

As the season wore on I was able to take part in training games and eventually moved into reserve matches. When I emerged from the gym I was, if anything, a bit too muscular and it was not until I got back to playing that I regained the condition that I wanted.

Eventually, after nearly eighteen months out of senior football, Dario reckoned I was ready to play. I certainly felt fit enough and couldn't wait. My return to first-team action came against Bury on 24 October 1992, at Gresty Road. From the start it was a rough old game but I was just so pleased to be back playing that I got stuck in as if I had never been away.

After half an hour, I got forward and sent in a cross which Dave McKearney side-footed into the Bury net. We should have hammered them as we missed a load of chances, but it didn't look good when Bury equalized through Peter Valentine after sixty-eight minutes. Fortunately, my mate Craig Hignett made it a very happy comeback for me when he scored the winner with seven minutes remaining on the clock.

I was interviewed by the press after the match and told the truth about the problems I had faced, telling them: 'I'd be lying if I said I never thought my playing days would be over. An operation like that knocks the stuffing out of you – sometimes you ask yourself if it's worth all the pain and worry.'

The first test had been passed, but for a while afterwards I suppose there was a nagging doubt at the back of my mind that my damaged vertebra would fracture again, or that the knitted bones and wire would 'pop' at the first really heavy tackle. Although I was not bothered at having to make my own tackles, I wondered how I would react to being hit in the back or smacked to the ground.

That close encounter was not long in coming. We were playing Rochdale a couple of weeks later when I was almost cut in two by a tackle from Shaun Reid, brother of former England player Peter and one of the game's tougher customers.

His tackle was so hard it took away my legs completely and

dumped me awkwardly on my back. I'll confess that I was in a total panic as I lay there for two or three seconds. With some deliberation I slowly got to my feet. I was shaking like a leaf and feared the worst but then I realized there was absolutely nothing wrong with me. I had taken the worst that football could throw at me and there was absolutely no problem. The relief and euphoria flooded through me and, after that, I never gave my back another thought during a match as my fitness levels just got better and better. I think it took me about six months to regain match fitness fully and display the form I had shown before the operation. On reflection, there had been a two-year hiatus in my career but I was back playing and I was still only twenty-one – I had time on my side.

The injury did affect me in another way. I know that over the next couple of seasons, plenty of scouts and managers from clubs higher up the league looked at me as possible transfer material but wrote me off because they knew that I had been out for so long with a serious injury. Well, more fool them.

Crewe Alexandra and Dario Gradi had no such qualms and I like to think I justified their faith in me with my performances over the years. I'm also very glad that the club was repaid in the long term with a seven-figure sum going into the bank account from my next two transfer fees. They invested in me and my recovery and reaped the rewards.

The whole experience taught me a lot, especially about myself. I knew from then on that I had the mental strength to achieve what I wanted out of the game, but I also came to realize that everything you have worked for can be taken away from you in an instant. You can be flying high in sport and then you snap a cruciate ligament or get some other injury and that is you finished or at least out of the game for a very long time. Football can be a very cruel game and the trauma I suffered during my own eighteen-month struggle has made me very sympathetic to those players who get long-term injuries and indeed to long-term sick people and the disabled in general.

To come back from that operation and get back to playing football is one of the greatest achievements of my life. I have had fifteen years in professional football since that twentieth birthday, and I can honestly say that I have had no real problems with my back since returning to play. Obviously I do not have the fluid movement I had before the operation, but that has been a small price to pay for being able to run and compete again. Even though I have to exercise some care in what I do physically, by and large I have played on without pain or hindrance.

For that I have to thank Dario and everyone at Crewe, the people at Leighton Hospital and especially Mr Adair and all the wonderful staff at Musgrave Park Hospital. I have thanked them before, but I want to put on record my appreciation for what they did for me. I would never have enjoyed the career I have had without their professionalism and expertise. And for that I am truly, truly grateful.

Writing this book has made me think back on many periods of my life when things went wrong, and though there have been a few bleak times, nothing, but nothing, compares to those dark days when I thought I would never play again. I enjoy the fruits of my success and the wealth that football has brought me, but that enjoyment is greatly enhanced by the knowledge that I gained it after a period of sustained adversity, that I could have had nothing, but fought long and hard to win the toughest trial of my life.

In that hospital bed in Belfast and in that tiny gym at Crewe and on the roads around Stockport, I did the work that laid the foundations for my success. All those thousands of hours of solitary labour made me become a stronger, better person. From then on I would always know how wonderful it is to win and would fully appreciate what winning means, because I came so very close to losing it all.

While that was my worst injury by far, there have been other times when I have been seriously ill. Since I have just told you of the greatest health crisis of my life, I should also tell you of another, more long-term problem.

I have thought long and hard about what I am going to reveal here, and have discussed the matter only with close family and friends and medical experts. I am not 'going public' for sympathy – let's be honest, I am never likely to get that from opposition fans – but because I believe that by telling the truth, people will perhaps have a better understanding of me and things that have happened. There may also be some good come of it, in that people will hopefully discuss sensibly and with sensitivity a subject which sadly is still taboo in our supposedly modern society.

I have a recurring illness, one which I have kept secret largely because I generally keep my private life out of the media. I know that sounds incongruous from a person writing a published autobiography, but it is nevertheless true as I have kept many things out of the public domain until now. Indeed, were I not telling my story in this book, and doing so as truthfully and as comprehensively as possible, I would probably not mention this at all.

The nature of this illness is such that it is not the sort of thing you willingly talk about – the unfortunate fact is that there is still a considerable stigma attached to even the least serious disease of the mind.

The truth is that for a large part of my adult life I have suffered from bouts of depression. In the last six years I have had five serious episodes. Fortunately, my condition has been clinically diagnosed, and since the early bewildering occurrences I have had the fullest support of Doctor Roddy McDonald and the other medically trained staff at Celtic.

With their guidance, I have been taking medication for what I consider to be a disease as real and as damaging as any physical illness. Indeed, my form of depression often displays itself physically as I am unable to sleep properly, I sweat profusely, feel nauseous, lose weight and actually look ill – many's the time someone has said to me 'Are you okay? You don't look good,' and I have just mumbled and avoided telling them the truth.

Depression can hit you any time, and in my case I do not know what causes it. It may be genetic, because other members of my family have also suffered. I also know all the theories about it being brought on by chemical imbalances in the brain – all I can say is that sounds more than plausible to me as my medication is designed to affect those chemicals and by and large it works. I can also honestly say that it has not ever been triggered by any particular event on or off the pitch, not by death threats or assaults, or by losing leagues in the final minutes of the season – that was maddening, but not depressing! You see, I can even laugh about it now, though I could not do so for a long time as my condition was seriously debilitating for me.

Sir Winston Churchill suffered from depression and called it his 'black dog' as a way of personifying some oppressive entity you would love to shout at. I know how he felt – there have been times when I felt like screaming. When it first happened I was wandering like a lost climber in a dense fog, unaware of what was going on around me and within me, and frankly scared at the intensity of the mental anguish I was suffering.

A depressive state just comes upon me like a curtain closing and shutting out the light in a previously bright room. I feel darkened inside and it blights my whole life for weeks at a time. People who suffer from depression will know the symptoms. Everything becomes a toil, and you lose your desire to eat, talk and even get out of bed. When you do surface, it feels like you are carrying a dead weight on your shoulders and everyone and everything seems to be so much trouble. You feel as though you are being swamped by waves of queasy discomfort, but you cannot put your finger on what is causing the overwhelming feeling of listlessness that makes you want to curl up and hide.

You can't stand company because you know, you just know, that other people cannot possibly have any understanding of what you are suffering. And all the while you feel worse because you are maintaining a façade whilst inside you are dying.

How does someone like me who earns his living in public deal with the fact that you cannot opt out? You cannot lock yourself away, or else people start to ask questions and eventually the truth comes out.

Carrying on in the face of such internal turmoil used to frustrate me, which only added to my depressive state. I now recognize the onset of the symptoms and take my medication quickly, but when it first struck me, I frankly didn't know or perhaps refused to believe that I could be suffering from depression. It was a mental illness that happened to other people, not me.

I was also concerned that my condition might become public. I know only too well that football supporters can be cruel, and great players such as Andy Goram of Rangers suffered taunts after they were even suspected of being ill. Maybe that will happen to me now, but I'm nearing the end of my career and have had every insult under the sun directed at me, so a few more won't make a difference.

Possibly the worst episode happened around the time of our Champions League qualifier against FC Basel back in August 2002. I was lying in my hotel room hours before the match simply unable to move and in a cold, clammy sweat about the very thought of even putting my feet outside the door, never mind heading out to a football stadium full of exhilarated supporters.

I called Dr McDonald and he gave me sufficient medication to get me through the ordeal, but I did not play my best that night and being honest, I have played other matches where I let myself down because of this illness.

And it is an illness – as much a disease as influenza or whooping cough. Yet society does not see it like that. Depression is viewed as a taboo subject to be talked about in whispers. Some employers no doubt see it as a worker finding a convenient way to get an extra holiday, not realizing that the person who works on through depression will almost certainly underperform – I know, because that is what I did.

What about the great many people who go undiagnosed and whose lives could be so much better if they knew they could get treatment?

Perhaps the vast majority of ordinary decent people who follow football will realize what I am trying to do here and think about their attitudes towards mental health – after all, I would be very, very surprised if there is anyone reading this who does not know someone who has suffered from depression or worse. God alone knows how people deal with Alzheimer's or dementia, or how families cope with a loved one stricken by serious mental illness. As a society we are dealing with racism and sectarianism, so can we not also look at this other form of discrimination which affects vulnerable people?

Until we do there will be many people who will continue to

suffer in silence or perhaps even damage themselves in some way simply because they do not know anything about depression or are too scared to consult a doctor for fear that they will be stigmatized.

I have managed to cope with my illness, but it has not been easy. I always wonder how much more difficult must it be for people who are less fortunate than me and do not have the support I have received, support for which I am truly grateful.

At times things have been pretty tough for me, mentally and physically, but at least my sense of humour has seen me through plenty of the bad days. There you have it – I'm held together by bits of wire and suffer from depression. If only I was a hypochondriac, I'd have plenty to moan about . . .

CHAPTER SIX

Moving Up, Moving On

The period when I was recovering from my operation was a very emotional time for me. Claire and I had grown very close and, in 1992, our daughter Alisha was born. It was a bit difficult to adjust to being a father at twenty-one, especially since the injury was still blighting my footballing career, but from the start I adored Alisha. I still do and always will.

Claire and I were probably too young at the time and we later split up, but we are still friends and she has been the most wonderful mother to our daughter. I still get on well with her parents, Alisha's grandmother Pat and grandfather George. Claire later got married and has two other children and I know they could not ask for a better mum. As for Alisha, I have tried to be as good a father as possible, and though she lives with her mother in England, I speak to her all the time and we visit each other regularly. She knows that I am always in the public eye, but the best times are when we can get away from it all and go on holiday.

What had happened to Crewe Alexandra while I was away from playing? Quite a lot, actually. I was determined to stay part of the squad so whenever I could I attended the matches, though any professional will tell you there is nothing worse than having to sit in the stand and watch when you know you can't do anything to affect the result. The previous season I had started thirty-four times for the club, so to go from that to playing none at all was heartbreaking.

It was frustrating to be at Gresty Road and also at the away games, watching my colleagues enjoy a season that was so very nearly wonderful. They had started the 1991/92 season by scoring seven in a terrific game at Barnet, the final score being 7–4. We then beat Doncaster home and away to earn a League Cup tie against Newcastle United of the First Division. The boys gave them a real fright at home before losing 3–4, and we held the mighty Magpies to a 0–1 scoreline at St James's Park. We also enjoyed a good run in the FA Cup, putting out Carlisle and Chester before coming up against Liverpool in a cup competition for the second successive season, losing 0–4 this time.

The team stuck to Dario's plan to try to play good skilful stuff, and sometimes it didn't work out against sides who played in typical robust Fourth Division style. But we all had confidence in the manager's plan, and I found it fascinating to study his methods.

He had one main strength, which is what has made him such an excellent coach in the twenty-three years that he has been at Crewe at the time of writing. He was always intent on communicating things well to his players and making sure he had got his point across.

In my first season, I noticed that the training sessions would go on and on, seemingly forever. There might be nettles in the stand and we all had to do our own laundry, but in terms of preparation for playing we were second to none.

Dario always told me that at the lower levels you have to work harder with players. In the Third and Fourth Division, you have to improve your players individually, as well as try to make some kind of team out of them. That was Dario's forte – he was always concerned about the individual and if he thought you needed to work on something, he would stay with you after team training and make sure you practised until you got it right.

One thing that Dario did not like was a player who went out to kick people. He is a footballing purist and really believes passionately in the ethics of the beautiful game. I know he got big offers to go elsewhere but he had a strategy in place to take Crewe as far as possible and he was prepared to see it through.

He was also so dedicated and enthusiastic. Dario would often be at Gresty Road from before nine in the morning until late in the evening, as he would insist on coaching the youngsters when they came along after school. He would drive the kids to and from the coaching sessions in a minibus – on many occasions he would even drive the first-team bus. As I say, he was a total hands-on enthusiast, from whom I learned so much.

All the while I just had to keep on with my recuperation, but it was particularly annoying to be missing as we made a tremendous surge in the last few weeks of the season, losing just one of our last eight games to qualify for the play-offs in Division Four.

In a two-legged affair against Scunthorpe we drew 2–2 in the first game but they beat us 2–0 in the second leg. We had come so close to promotion in my season off. I vowed that, when I returned, I would redouble my efforts to help Crewe to get out of English football's basement where we did not belong.

But we would not have to play Fourth Division football the following season, because at the start of the 1992/93 season, English football changed forever with the creation of the FA Premiership as the new top flight. The Football League was reorganized and we went automatically into the new Third Division. It was the Fourth Division by another name, of course, but somehow it sounded better saying you played for a team in Division Three.

I was still sidelined at the start of the season, of course, but I was gradually getting fitter and returned to training as the boys went on something of a roll in the autumn. It was agony for me to miss out on thrilling League Cup performances, such as when we drew 0–0 with West Ham at Upton Park and then beat them 2–0 on a super night at Gresty Road.

That was shortly before I made my comeback against Bury. After a few weeks in which I got back to full match fitness, I was once again in the team and enjoying myself.

We were going well in the league and FA Cup, having trounced both Wrexham and Accrington Stanley 6–1, but we suffered a loss of form around Christmas before we came up against Blackburn Rovers in the Cup. We were given a lesson in the difference between top flight and bottom division as they beat us 3–0. But that encounter only heightened my appetite to play in a higher league.

Just when it seemed as though I was back to normal and playing well in midfield, we hosted Scunthorpe in a midweek match at Gresty Road. We had advanced up the league and were now challenging for a play-off spot, and Dario had been kind enough to say how consistent I had been in our good run. I've often said that football has a habit of kicking you in the teeth, but in that match it wasn't a boot but an elbow that did the damage.

About seventy minutes into the match, I was in a tussle with their midfielder David Hill when he lashed his arm back into my face. He said later it was an accident, but my view is that even so it was certainly nothing less than reckless. I felt an agonizing jolt of pain on the point of my jaw and the blood started to flow from my mouth instantly. I knew it was serious right away, but to be honest, I was so angry the pain became secondary to wanting to stay on the pitch and win the game to prove that such tactics should not win matches. In any case, Dario was not for letting me come off!

I would have gritted my teeth, but they were so loose I didn't dare risk it. Even though the pain hit me in waves I was determined to stay on, not least because our captain Darren Carr had been red-carded for a handball offence. The luck did not seem to be with us as Scunthorpe were awarded a penalty, but our young goalkeeper Mark Smith dived the right way and saved from Mark Elliott. We held on for a 1–0 victory which was vital to our play-off chances.

It was only when the doctor examined me afterwards that he detected that I might have a fracture in my jaw and the X-rays at the hospital confirmed his diagnosis. I also had to undergo dental surgery on my battered gnashers – indeed, my jaw and teeth had to be manhandled back into place by the surgeon – and the initial thoughts of the medics were that my season was over. That really made me very angry indeed, because I was one of several Crewe players to be injured in dubious incidents around that time – Darren Carr was concussed after an 'accidental' clash, Steve Macaulay was stamped on by a Gillingham player and Dean Greygoose had his leg broken in an unsavoury incident with a Wrexham striker.

The conclusion was unavoidable – some teams had decided that the only way to stop Crewe was to kick us off the park.

It all made me wonder if I should take some sort of action against David Hill, but in the end I decided it would only distract attention from our push for a play-off place which was gathering pace. I concentrated on getting well quickly, though Dario was convinced I wouldn't return until the following season.

A week after the match in which I suffered my injury, our striker Tony Naylor scored a club record five goals in a 7–1 win over Colchester United. In the next match a 2–1 victory over our nearest rivals Bury clinched a play-off spot for us. At that stage of the 1992/93 season we had scored more than 100 goals in all competitions and believed we could score against anybody.

Our opponents in the play-off semi-final over two legs were Walsall, who had beaten us twice in the space of ten days in April. Walsall had a wily manager in Kenny Hibbitt, whose tactics were to restrict the number of chances we got and hit us on the counter. Fortunately for us, Dario worked out a plan to counter that strategy.

My jaw had been broken on 20 April and the first leg against Walsall was due on Sunday 16 May. The fracture came together nicely as I was a quick healer in those days. There were still problems with my teeth but my dentist had made me a protective gumshield and three weeks after the injury I was able to resume training. Dario was amazed and delighted with my progress and in the days leading up to the match it became clear I had a chance of playing. It would be a gamble, but it was one both Dario and I thought was worth taking.

The gamble paid off as I played my part in a comprehensive thrashing of Walsall at Gresty Road. Tony Naylor was on fire at the time and notched a double as we hammered them 5–1. Tony went one better in the return leg, scoring a hat-trick as we romped home 4–2 for a 9–3 aggregate.

We had made the play-off final and that meant a trip to Wembley – the first time I had played at the famous stadium.

Our opponents that day were York City who were managed by Brian Little's brother Alan. They had reached the play-off final by beating Bury 1–0 at home after a goalless draw away.

They would be tough opponents, but we had matched them evenly in the league, beating them 3–1 at Gresty Road after losing 1–3 away.

It was an incredible feeling to know that we were going to Wembley and were just ninety minutes away from the new Division Two, with all that would mean for us in terms of increased prestige and better opponents, not to mention a boost to the pay packet. The build-up got to us all, and we were pretty high for days beforehand. When we got to Wembley and saw the famous twin towers and were then shown into the large and immaculate dressing room, we knew we had arrived on the big stage.

It seemed to me that most of Crewe's population had made the journey south and though Wembley wasn't full by a long chalk, with only 23,000 fans in the stadium, both sets of supporters made enough noise to make you think it was the FA Cup Final itself.

I was just so wrapped up in the clamour and glamour of the day that I don't think I did myself justice on the pitch and that remark applied to a few of us. York had the better of things in the first half but we came back strongly in the second and Tony Naylor had the ball in the net only to be ruled offside. Both sides missed chances, with Mark Smith in our goal pulling off a couple of fine saves, and there was no score at the end of ninety minutes.

Extra-time was all about the survival of the fittest. For a while it looked as though we would prevail, but in the first fifteen minutes York went ahead through Gary Swann. We were shattered, but somehow we dug deep and found a little more energy. We threw everything at them, but as the clock ticked by, it looked as though we would have to settle for Fourth Division football again. In the last minute we pressed again and won a corner. Dave McKearney swung it in and quite incredibly, York substitute Steve Tutill clearly handled the ball – penalty! I could hardly bare to watch as Dave strode forward to take the kick, which he put past Dean Kiely.

The final whistle blew seconds later and the play-off was decided on penalties. Our whole season had come down to this last ten throws of the dice. Dario gathered us all together and told us to keep our heads. There was nothing we could do but pray.

Jon McCarthy went first for City and scored, but Dave McKearney equalized. Paul Barnes made it 2–1 to City but Shaun Smith again put us level. Tony Canham's penalty for York went just inside the right-hand upright. Gareth Whalley was next for us and he opted to blast the ball down the middle, only to see the kick well saved by Kiely. Our hearts sank, and went even lower when City increased their advantage to 4-2 through Nigel Pepper. Ashley Ward pulled it back to 4–3, but we all knew the equation – City only had to score the next one to win and Wayne Hall made no mistake.

We were all devastated but Gareth was inconsolable. He was another of Dario's youth players who had joined the club straight from school and was still only twenty. Such a miss might have destroyed his career, but he fought back to enjoy a long spell with the Alex, his finest moment coming in another play-off final four years later, when Crewe beat Brentford 1–0 to enter the First Division, known now as the Championship.

We did win a trophy that season however, one that showed we were trying to play football correctly. The Bobby Moore Fair Play Award was given to us for having the best disciplinary record over the season, and it was a trophy Crewe would retain for the next three years.

A lot of people do not like the play-off system, but having played in them, I can only say they are always exciting and really do give a second chance to clubs who, like Crewe, occasionally make a bad start to the season but finish well. Crewe's loss to York was definitely anti-climactic – win a play-off final and you have weeks of ecstasy to follow, lose and you spend the summer in the doldrums.

There was no anti-climax about the following season, during which I signed a new two-year contract to stay at Gresty Road. We started poorly though, taking just four points from our first five matches, making me wonder if a bad beginning to the season would cost us dear at the end of it, as had happened before.

However, from the end of August we went on a nine-game unbeaten run and quickly rose up the league table. We really began to show our mettle at that time. We were still the same skilful side as always, but we also began to show a willingness to battle to the end.

Against Torquay United at Plainmoor, for instance, we lost two defenders through injury and I had to go back to a sort of centre-half position to help out. I can only say my unfamiliarity with the role was the cause of my howler of an own goal, lobbing my back-pass over Mark Smith. We were 2–3 down and under the cosh from a team which was at that time unbeaten in the league, but with seconds remaining we broke upfield and big Ashley Ward scored to give us a 3–3 draw.

Another game I recall was against Wycombe Wanderers, managed by a certain Martin O'Neill. Martin had taken them from the Conference League into Division Three and they were going well, but we were in second position when we went to Adams Park in late November 1993. They played good football and our attempts to defend against their free-flowing attacks were pretty suicidal. It was a happy Martin that evening as his side deservedly won 3–1.

The next time we met, Martin would not be so happy . . .

REGISTERED No. 4276 SCOTLAND

FOUNDED 1873

TELEPHONE:
041-427 0159
041-427 2346

R. C. OGILVIE
SECRETARY

TELEX:
778377

J. M. B. WALLACE,
MANAGER

THE RANGERS FOOTBALL CLUB plc

REGISTERED OFFICE
IBROX STADIUM · GLASGOW · G51 2XD

9th December, 1983

Mr. N. Lennon,
20 Richmond Gardens,
LURGAN,
N. Ireland.

Dear Neil,

I confirm herewith that Rangers Football Club are very interested in your future football career and we would certainly like to have you over at Ibrox some time in the future for some training and coaching..

Yours sincerely,

J Wallace

Manager.

ABOVE: The letter to me from Rangers FC signed by then manager Jock Wallace. How different life might have been…

RIGHT: Inside Ibrox with young fellow prospects and Jimmy Nicholl, now assistant manager at Aberdeen, and then a Rangers player.

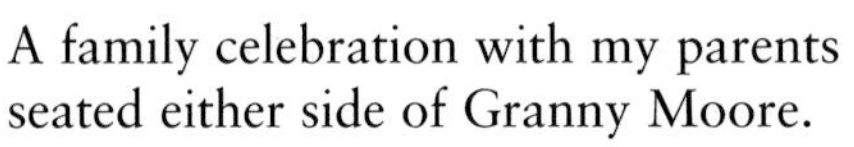

A family celebration with my parents seated either side of Granny Moore.

The class swot. Studying for my seven 'O' levels.

Playing Gaelic football for my county Armagh during a break in my time at Manchester City.

ABOVE: Showing off after Manchester City win the Lancashire FA Youth Cup at Blackburn 1988–9.

BELOW: Celebrating a rare goal for Crewe against Macclesfield Town in the FA Cup.

ABOVE: Denis Law presents me with the Crewe Alexandra Vice-Presidents' Association Player of the Year Trophy at Old Trafford in 1991.

BELOW: Dario Gradi's school for excellence: the Crewe squad that won promotion to the Second Division in 1993–94.

ABOVE: Let the champagne flow: Leicester City are heading for the Premiership after beating Crystal Palace in the 1995–96 First Division (now Championship) play-offs.

RIGHT: Head to head with Fabrizio Ravanelli in the replay of the 1997 Coca-Cola Cup Final at Hillsborough Stadium, Sheffield, 16 April 1997.

LEFT: Celebrating Steve Claridge's match-winning goal with Emile Heskey.

BELOW LEFT: The 1997 Coca-Cola League Cup belongs to Leicester City.

BOTTOM: *That* tackle. Alan Shearer's left boot is on the way to my head. Note the right boot's location.

RIGHT: Proudly wearing my Northern Ireland shirt as I head the ball away from Thomas Hassler in the 1996 World Cup qualifier against Germany.

THE Coca-Cola CUP
199 WINNERS

10

ABOVE: Tackling Patrick Vieira in our friendly against France at Windsor Park in 1999.

BELOW: My father's complimentary ticket for the Northern Ireland v. Cyprus match. It was, of course, never used.

Before then, however, was a match which I believe brought me to the attention of many managers up and down the country. After putting out Darlington and Macclesfield, we were drawn against Leeds United at Elland Road in the third round of the FA Cup. We were sitting top of the Third Division by then, but Leeds were still Premiership contenders and their side at that time included one of my all-time heroes, Gary McAllister. I had followed his career since my days at his former club Motherwell where people still spoke of him with something approaching reverence, even though he had left two years previously after the Fir Park side had won the First Division title.

With Leicester and Leeds he had become the epitome of the intelligent passing midfielder, and he would show with Scotland what a wonderful player he was at international level. Of course, he then went on to enjoy a spectacular Indian summer in his career at Liverpool in 2001, a year in which he won five medals and an MBE for services to football. I said at the time of our match at Elland Road that it was a privilege to be on the same pitch as him and I meant it. But of course, that didn't stop me trying to play him off the park.

I had one of my best-ever matches for the Alex that January afternoon. Leeds attacked us from the start, taking the lead through Brian Deane after sixteen minutes, but by the half-hour mark we were right in the game. I spotted Tony Naylor in a good position and he made no mistake from my pass. Jamie Forrester, who was just nineteen at the time, put them ahead with about an hour gone, and the same player made sure there would be no fourth round for us with a fine curling shot seven minutes from time. It was the sixth year running that we had been eliminated from the FA Cup by a big-name top-flight club. I played against someone who would later become my manager in that match. Gordon Strachan and

I had a bit of a battle in midfield, and I wouldn't like to say who won, though it was his mistake that gave me the ball to set up our goal.

My dad had come over to watch the big game and we were sitting in the players' lounge after the match talking about the tussles between Gordon and myself. My dad turned to the woman who was sitting next to him as she was obviously paying attention to the conversation.

'That Gordon Strachan,' said my dad, 'he's got a bit of a temper.'

The woman nodded: 'I couldn't agree more,' she said. It was only when Gordon came over and gave her a kiss that Dad discovered he had been talking to Mrs Lesley Strachan!

The FA Cup exit seemed to affect us as we were inconsistent after that and dropped off the top of the table soon afterwards. It didn't help when our goalkeeper Mark Smith set an unwanted record – he received the quickest sending-off in League history, red-carded after just nineteen seconds for a professional foul against Darlington.

We lost that match 1–0 and struggled a bit thereafter, but a 0–0 draw with eventual champions Shrewsbury Town and a 4–1 win over Wigan Athletic meant that victory over Martin O'Neill's Wycombe would mean that the season would go down to the last match. If the visitors won, they would be promoted and we would have to be content with a play-off place.

Ashley Ward put us ahead early on, but Wycombe got a bizarre equalizer when Darren Rowbotham mishit a clearance and the ball ended up in his own net though Tony Hemmings claimed the goal as all good strikers should. It was looking like a draw until Ashley popped up with a late winner. Martin O'Neill's face was a picture at the end, but no words were exchanged between us.

That left a simple equation. In the last game of the season, if we beat Chester, who had already gained their place in the Second Division, it didn't matter what Wycombe did at Preston North End – we would be in the third promotion spot and would go up automatically.

Once again it was Ashley Ward who did the trick for us with a late winner. He had been the club's record signing at £80,000 from Leicester City but had paid back every penny with those late goals against Wycombe and Chester. Ashley was a good striker who would be transferred to Norwich City the following year and would play for numerous clubs in the Premiership and elsewhere before his retirement.

Wycombe could only draw with Preston but that didn't matter – we had won promotion to the Second Division and were no longer basement boys. As it happened, Wycombe Wanderers got through the play-offs and joined us in the higher league anyway.

Winning promotion put our wages up – to £300 per week in my case. The following season I would get a welcome £20,000 signing-on fee and a rise to £500 a week. As you can see, we were not millionaires at Crewe.

I was enjoying life with Claire and Alisha at the time, and the 1994/95 season almost brought more promotion success for my club. Far from being intimidated by playing in a higher league, we prospered and after five games we sat top of the division with maximum points. But we all knew that promotion was not going to be easy to achieve as the composition of the leagues was going to be changed at the end of the season with only two places available for promotion. The division champions were guaranteed to go up with the next four teams taking part in the play-offs for the second place.

We remained committed to Dario's philosophy of playing good football with the belief that no matter if the opposition scored, we would score more, and we had plenty of players capable of getting the goals – I even managed six myself that season, my best-ever annual total, at least since my days as a teenage scoring sensation back home in Lurgan.

One of our most entertaining games was when we defeated Hartlepool 8–0 in the first round of the Auto Windscreens Shield. Amazingly, all eight goals were scored by different players.

Just look at a couple of names from the list of goalscorers that night – Danny Murphy and Robbie Savage both went on to be great players. That was no accident, because Dario always gave us the belief that we could all make the grade, and the style of football we were playing at that time was a cut above the rest of the division. Interviewed by Andrew Longmore of *The Times* during that period, Dario explained his annoyance at the coaching system which he felt was damaging the game: 'We are trying to produce footballers who can play at a higher level, partly because we need to sell them, partly because we want to win. We've been quite successful but, on the whole, the system is not working hard enough at producing footballers. It is easier to produce kick-and-rush players.'

Such a philosophy was anathema to Dario and to those of us he had nurtured. We played football to win, sure, but we wanted to win by playing skilful football.

We featured in a few more high-scoring encounters that season, including a 5–1 thrashing of Peterborough and a 7–1 hammering of Gresley Rovers in the FA Cup. Unfortunately, that latter scoreline was recorded *against* us by Hull City, and Birmingham put five past us with no reply only two days later.

We were displaying a baffling inconsistency, but from early April onwards we began to play some solid stuff and went on a run of eight wins from our last ten matches to finish third in the division – enough to gain automatic promotion in most years but only enough for that season's play-offs, in which we would meet Bristol Rovers.

Again it was a two-legged affair and we gave absolutely nothing away at Twerton Park. The defence had to be re-organized after Shaun Smith went off with a facial injury after eighteen minutes, and both substitutes Gus Wilson and Danny Murphy had to clear off the line, but we came away with a 0–0 draw and felt pretty confident about the return leg.

The second leg in front of a capacity crowd at Gresty Road was a mirror image of the first as we attacked them incessantly but just could not score.

Darren Rowbotham eventually put us ahead in extra-time and in sight of another trip to Wembley, but Paul Miller hit a late equalizer to give them victory on the away-goals-count-double rule.

Our whole season had gone in a few minutes. We were all totally gutted, in agony that we had yet again missed out on promotion in the play-offs. It is difficult to describe the feelings of a side caught in that experience, but it makes you realize the bittersweet nature of the words 'so near and yet so far'. I could only hope that my next play-off experience would be happier.

In the summer before the 1995/96 season, I was wondering what I had to do to get a move up the leagues. I was beginning to get itchy feet at Crewe. I had celebrated my twenty-fourth birthday in June and I reckoned that I should have had a move by then. I had played three solid seasons since my return from my year-and-a-bit out and any manager who still had doubts about my fitness following my back operation should surely have been reassured by then.

One club did want me – Reading of the First Division. In October they approached Crewe and asked to speak to me.

Jimmy Quinn, who had played for Northern Ireland, was the manager at the time and I knew they were a good footballing side. As is often the case, news of their interest was leaked and the transfer fee mentioned was £350,000. Dario told me he did not think they were good enough for me, saying that I had the chance of playing in the Premiership. I was very keen to join Reading, however, and I was pretty miffed at the club's attitude. Let's just say that Dario and I exchanged words on the matter.

Events were to prove him correct, of course, and again he had seen the whole picture better than me. He had been looking after my future and had my best interests at heart, thank goodness.

After Reading were turned away, there was nothing else for me to do but try my best and hope that some other, bigger club would finally come in for me. In the first half of the season we were always in the top three or 'bubbling under' the promotion places. We went on another FA Cup run and confirmed our status as the lower league team nobody wanted to draw when we beat West Bromwich Albion 4–3 in the third round after putting out Altrincham and Mansfield Town. We charged into a 4–1 lead but West Brom battled back and came close to grabbing a replay. That was one of my best games for Crewe and might have been the match that sparked renewed interest in me.

At that time we were topping the Second Division and that display showed that we would be able to handle ourselves in a higher division. I certainly felt my performance indicated that I was ready for a move up.

For the fourth round we were drawn away to Southampton. We put up a typical Crewe cup performance and took the lead, but Matt Le Tissier scored a goal of sheer class to gain the Saints a 1–1 draw which meant a replay the following week at Gresty Road. Matt was in the midst of his well-publicized difficulties with football in general at the time and frankly looked a bit fed up – what would he be like if fully enthusiastic, I wondered.

The replay was another thriller, which we lost by the odd goal in five. In both matches against Southampton, I had again played well against a team from a higher division, and things began to happen quickly after that. Dario pulled me aside later that night and gave me the news that I had been waiting for – a Premiership club would like to speak to me. At the time, Ron Atkinson was the manager of Coventry City and Dario confirmed that the board of Crewe had given him permission to approach me. Dario emphasized that Coventry were very interested in signing me. He asked if I would be interested in going there, and of course I said yes. True to his word, Dario never stood in the way of someone getting what he thought was the right move for them.

So I went to see Big Ron the following day. It was Valentine's Day 1996, and it wouldn't have surprised me if Ron Atkinson had turned up with a bunch of roses – like everyone in football I knew of his reputation as a larger-than-life, jovial individual who also happened to have been a very successful manager. We met at the Haydock Thistle Hotel which is just beside the racecourse. At the time, Jim Melrose, who I had known since my days at Manchester City, was representing me, but Jim did not hold a FIFA agent's licence which meant that he could not finalize any deals on my behalf. We called in another agent named Phil Morrison who did hold the appropriate licence and before the meeting he told me what he thought I would get. Almost word for word, Ron Atkinson offered me exactly what Phil Morrison had predicted.

To be honest, I wondered if a deal had been done before I

even entered the room. Ron then proceeded to ask me a series of questions, which I have to say I found just a little patronizing, and his manner was a bit aloof. He was asking me things like if I could play at right-back and what my heading of the ball was like. That led me to ask whether Ron had actually watched me or not. He admitted he had not actually seen me play himself, but had sent scouts to see me several times.

I wanted a clause in the contract which would reward me with a bonus after I had played a certain number of games for Northern Ireland, on the basis that becoming an established international would also boost my value as a Coventry player. Ron pooh-poohed that, saying that it was a certainty that I would become a regular international and that if I could not get into the Northern Ireland team as a Coventry player, then I would never play for them. His confidence was remarkable for a man whose club were then in the relegation zone, though funnily enough, the prospect of joining a club under pressure did not concern me.

Ron offered me tickets for the FA Cup replay match which Coventry were playing that night at Maine Road against my old club Manchester City. It was handy for me as I was staying in Stockport at the time, so I said I would be happy to go along.

Ron then said they would need to hold a medical examination the following day, which I knew was routine. We shook hands but I specifically asked for time to think about things.

I went to the Cup game which frankly wasn't up to much as Coventry were beaten 1–2. Nor did I much admire the way Coventry had played.

Fully intending to sleep on the matter, I went back to the end-of-terrace flat in Stockport that I was sharing with Chris Mooney at the time. Now two bachelors sharing a flat is always a recipe for untidiness, but we took it to extremes.

Our pad made the flat in *The Young Ones* sitcom look like Buckingham Palace. There were no rats or mice – they had left in disgust.

We were sitting having a couple of beers when the phone rang. It was Jim Melrose, who said that he was in the car with Martin O'Neill and John Robertson, now manager and assistant manager of Leicester City. They had been to see the Port Vale v Everton match together, and were on their way to see me to discuss my signing for Leicester. I suppose it was probably a technical breach of the rules about talking to other clubs, but I presumed that since Crewe had given me permission to talk to Ron Atkinson then it was going to be okay to speak to another club. Anyway, I wasn't prepared to hang about and check the small print so I told Jim to come on up.

They were not far away and arrived within minutes. I suppose it must have seemed slightly surreal to our neighbours to see this big black Mercedes pull up outside our flat at the end of a cobblestoned terrace in Stockport. It just looked so out of place parked there.

Jim came in first and told me they were desperate to sign me. He asked me what Big Ron Atkinson had offered earlier in the day. I told him they had offered £100,000 as a signing on fee plus £1,000 per week, and he immediately said 'Tell them £1,500 a week.'

Into the flat came this whirlwind called Martin O'Neill, with John Robertson behind him. I had met Martin several years before in Lurgan but it had only been a brief meeting and we hadn't actually spoken since then. The pair of them had to step gingerly over empty pizza boxes and old clothes, while in the kitchen there were piles of dishes waiting until they fell into the sink of their own accord. Martin would later describe our bijou apartment as 'a hovel' – he should have seen it on a bad day.

Chris went upstairs and told me later that he listened in on everything. I had always admired Martin and John as players, and as a fellow Northern Ireland international, I felt I had a lot in common with Martin. We had both played Gaelic football, for instance, and both of us had won medals at the sport before switching codes to become professionals, moving to England after spells with Irish league sides, in his case Distillery FC.

His playing career spoke for itself, most of it under Brian Clough at Nottingham Forest, with whom he won the European Cup. He had also captained Norwich City, Manchester City and Northern Ireland, for whom he played sixty-four times. As a manager, he had already enjoyed success. I had played against his Wycombe Wanderers side and liked their football and he had been going well at Norwich until a dispute with the club chairman over budgets led him to leave on a point of principle. There had been much talk of him going to Nottingham Forest as manager but instead he had taken over at Leicester at the end of 1995 and was now building the team he wanted.

I liked Martin from the start. He was a charismatic figure, talking persuasively and with humour, and he was very clever with his words. He had trained to be a lawyer at Queen's University in Belfast before going off to play football, and you could easily see him winning any argument in court.

Leicester were then sitting seventh or eighth in the First Division and a play-off place was not out of their reach. No matter if his side did not make the Premiership that season, Martin said it was their ambition to make it into the top flight as soon as possible and perhaps even by the next season. Martin absolutely convinced me that they would be there shortly, and in no time at all he had sold me the virtues of joining him at Leicester City.

He told me he really wanted me to sign and that they had watched me many times. He and John were convinced that I would do a good job for them. His manner was also something of a contrast to Ron Atkinson's.

Then he asked me how much Coventry had offered me as a signing-on fee and in wages. I did as Jim suggested and said '£150,000 and £1,500 per week.' Martin immediately offered £200,000 and £1,800 per week. I was flabbergasted – I was only on £500 a week tops at Crewe and it all seemed like an absolute fortune to me.

Martin then wrote out the terms of my contract on the back of a pizza box which he had rescued off the floor. I didn't quite sign for Leicester City on the back of a take-away box, but I certainly got my written offer on one.

I asked for a minute to talk to Jim, so the pair of us went outside and walked around the block. I told Jim that I had a much better feeling about Martin and Leicester than I had about Ron and Coventry, and in return he said that Martin was a good young manager who had done remarkably well at Wycombe Wanderers and was surely destined for greater things. He was convinced that Martin was desperate to sign me, and after all, the money was much better than Coventry's offer. I had not signed any deal with Ron Atkinson so I was free to negotiate elsewhere.

We then called my dad in Lurgan and Martin spoke to him as well. Dad said that if I was not entirely happy about going to Coventry then I should leave it, and he certainly seemed to be taken with Martin.

In the end it was my decision, however, and not much later that night I decided to sign for Leicester. I rang Coventry in the morning and told them of my decision and Ron was not best pleased. However, I was not too chuffed either when he later told the press 'I thought we had agreed and shaken hands on the deal,' as that was not my recollection of the way we had left things.

The ironic thing is that had I gone to Coventry, within a short space of time I would have been playing under the managership of Gordon Strachan. He was then aged forty and playing in his last season, was already on the coaching staff and took over as manager in November 1996, when Ron Atkinson became the club's director of football.

I told Dario and the board of Crewe of my decision not to join Coventry and asked them for permission to speak to Leicester City as I was aware of their interest in me. Of course, I neglected to say just how interested they had become.

Dario was amazed and not a little miffed that I had turned down Coventry of the Premiership and was now looking for a move to First Division Leicester City. I told him it was just a gut instinct, a feeling that Martin was going to take his club places. He still shook his head, but I knew that he had admired what Martin had done at Wycombe, so maybe in time he would come round to my point of view.

The formalities of contract, fee offer, medical and signing took a few days. Coventry had offered Crewe £750,000 for my signature and Martin had agreed to match that, so for the club it was not a question of having to sell to the highest bidder. The ball was very much in my court and I had made up my mind, for good or ill, to join Martin O'Neill's Leicester City.

As when I joined Crewe, I did not know much about Leicester, either the city itself or the club. I knew that they had never won the English League or FA Cup, but I also knew that Gary Lineker had played for them and also the great England goalkeeper Gordon Banks, but that was about it. Once again it was going to be a bit of an adventure to be joining a new club, only this time I would have to move away from

Stockport and all my friends in Manchester, though I did promise to keep in touch.

Even though he was disappointed that I had not gone to a Premiership club, Dario said he accepted my reasons for moving to Leicester. He gave me a few last words of advice and we parted with some emotion. I left with his best wishes and a legacy of footballing nous that will last me for ever.

The £750,000 Crewe received for me was then a club record, but it would last only to the following year when Danny Murphy went to Liverpool for double that sum. The signing also came with a condition that if Leicester sold me within a certain number of years, Crewe would be entitled to a cut of the fee. I knew little about that clause at the time, and it was a condition which would cause me some grief later in my career.

I played my last game for Crewe in February 1996, and sadly it was not to be a happy ending as Stockport County beat us 1–0. I had been with the Railwaymen for the best part of six years, and so much had happened to me in that time – the birth of my daughter, the back injury which had nearly finished me as a player, relegation and promotion and my becoming a fully-fledged professional.

It was genuinely a wrench to leave Gresty Road and I was extremely touched by the good wishes of so many individual fans who wrote to me or shook my hand at the stadium and in the street. Dario was kind enough to tell the newspapers that Leicester had signed the new David Platt – his highest compliment.

Like so many people who have played for the Alex, I had developed a real affection for the club and I still follow their fortunes to this day. If you go to Crewe now it is a totally transformed club, with a fine all-seater stadium, holding more than 10,000, with excellent facilities to match.

Back in September 2003, Crewe played Leicester City at the Walkers Stadium. It was the first time that I had a free week in the season and was able to go to watch a match between my two old clubs and thus catch up with a lot of old friends. I was specifically looking forward to seeing Dario, but that was the very day on which he was taken into hospital for heart surgery, from which he has fully recovered. Not even Sir Alex Ferguson can match his longevity as a manager, and personally I think he will be manager of Crewe until they carry him out in a box.

For everything that they did for me, I will always be grateful to everyone at Crewe Alexandra, to Dario and all the staff and especially the fans. But the call of Leicester and Martin O'Neill had proven irresistible. Very soon I would be what I had always wanted to be – a player in the very top flight of English football.

CHAPTER SEVEN

The Flying Foxes

My career with Leicester did not exactly get off to a flying start. I watched the team come from behind to beat Wolves 3–2 at Molineux on the Wednesday night in what was Martin's first victory in charge of the team. Perhaps I am his lucky charm, because when I joined Celtic I also did so at the start of a very good period for a side managed by Martin.

I joined the squad for training on the Thursday morning and I have to say there was a mixed reaction to my arrival as most people at the club did not know me. Leicester at that time had some great players such as Emile Heskey, who was only seventeen or eighteen but was already a key player and you knew that he was going to become a major star. He certainly had an unforgettable middle name – Ivanhoe.

If you had met his father Tyrone you would know where Emile gets his athletic build from. Tyrone worked as a bouncer in the city and he must have been in his late forties or early fifties when one day a would-be robber tried to hold up one of the clubs where he worked. Tyrone chased him down the street, got hold of him and pinned him down, even though the guy was carrying a gun.

Right away I was impressed by the methods that Martin

had introduced, though I was also slightly taken aback by the fact that some of the players and staff still harked back to Mark McGhee's time in charge. Mark had left to join Wolverhampton Wanderers in a manner which did not please the Leicester board or the fans, but there were plenty of people around Filbert Street who looked back on his management days as a halcyon period.

Martin was still in the early days of his time at City and people didn't yet know what to make of him. He had not been helped by the fact that Leicester had suffered a real drubbing in the FA Cup at the hands of Manchester City, losing 5–0 at Maine Road after a goalless draw at Filbert Street.

I was delighted to learn that I would be joining the squad for the league match against Reading on the Saturday – the very same Reading that I had been prevented from joining the previous autumn.

I wish I could say that my debut went very well, but it was a bit of a mixed bag. I went on at half-time, made the opening goal for Neil Lewis by hitting the by-line and cutting the ball back to him, but then gave away a penalty for a challenge on Lee Nogan. Steve Lovell scored from the spot. It was a day of conflicting emotions for me because I felt I had played well, but I had been penalized and given away the goal which cost us two points. That's football for you – nothing ever goes completely right.

I made my home debut the following weekend against Derby County. It wasn't much of a match and ended in a goalless draw, but over the next two weeks our position in the league fluctuated, with victory over Grimsby but two losses to Ipswich. I have to say I was not overly happy and my form was inconsistent as I made the adjustment to playing in a higher league.

Against Oldham, I committed the cardinal error of getting

myself sent off for two bookable offences. The first yellow card was a bit harsh and the second was for retaliation after being stamped on, but I should have known better and afterwards Martin tore strips off me – believe me, you do not want to be on the receiving end of an O'Neill lecture. It was the first time in my career that I had been sent off and it could not have come at a worse time, for me personally and for the team. I had been so desperate to make a good impression at the start of my career with Leicester and the team needed everybody to be available for the challenge ahead. I felt I was really beginning to get a grip of things in midfield and was coping with the transition from Second to First Division more than adequately, but then I went and let the side down. I did not feel very clever that day.

I did my best to redeem myself in our victory over Millwall, for which I won my first man-of-the-match award as a Leicester player. The sending-off meant I was suspended for the game against Sheffield United however, a match which I believe was a turning point in the career of Martin O'Neill.

He had decided to introduce some new blood, including Steve Claridge. Steve was one of the game's characters, a real enigma. He would turn up for training at the last minute already wearing his kit, having been down at the bookies – he was quite open about his gambling habit. He was never much of a trainer but what a fabulous player he turned out to be. I will never forget him because he was responsible for scoring two of the most important goals in my career.

Like John Hartson at Celtic, Steve was often at his most dangerous with his back to the goal. But he could do nothing for us that day against Sheffield United. We were beaten 0–2 and the crowd were extremely unhappy as it now looked as if we were going to blow our chance of promotion to the Premiership. There was a demonstration by some fans, some of whom were calling for Martin's head, but not for the first or last time, Martin dealt with such outpourings of anger very sensibly.

He called the players in on the Monday and I remember the brilliant way he handled things when many other managers would have collapsed in the face of such a crisis. The following night we were due to play Charlton Athletic who at that time were lying third in the league. It looked a difficult task for us to come away with any kind of result, but Martin told us we would win. He went on to say that he would take the flak from then on and we were just to relax and go about our business on the park. He ended by telling us that we would get it together as a side and would go on to the play-offs and win promotion. 'And having taken the flak,' he added, 'I'll take all the glory when it comes!' Humour coupled with inspirational words are the key things in Martin's talks to his teams. There is no such thing as a typical O'Neill talk as he varies them to suit every occasion, but he never does anything less than encourage you to play to your best, and he does it with a bit of wit.

Martin was as good as his word and we beat Charlton 1–0 to get back on track for the play-offs. Though we were beaten by West Brom, we then won three home matches in a row. In the last of these games, against Birmingham City, I broke my duck for Leicester by scoring one of our three goals. As you can guess, my celebrations went on all night.

The victory ensured that in the last game of the season, against Watford, we only needed to win to secure a place in the play-offs. I say 'only' – if we took all three points, Watford would be relegated to the Second Division, so we knew that we faced a tough battle, and it turned out to be exactly that.

Mustapha 'Muzzy' Izzet was on loan from Chelsea at the time and he popped up to score the only goal of the game on the hour mark. We had finished sixth in the First Division, enough to put us into the play-offs.

Success in the play-offs was something the older players really craved as they had been through thick and thin at City. Steve Walsh, for instance, was a legend at the club. He was one of those tough-as-teak centre-halves that you had to respect. His disciplinary record – he got sent off about a dozen times – showed that he was no saint, but he was such a great leader of the team. He played through the pain barrier so many times it was ridiculous, as he often had to take medication for the various injuries to his knee and back.

Mike Whitlow was a solid defender who had been over the course, having won the championship with Leeds in 1992. He was very fit for his age and a real example to the younger guys like myself.

Backstage we had John Robertson and Steve Walford. I'll have much more to say about these two major influences on my life later, but from the outset I could see what an effective team they formed with Martin, how much he relied on them and vice-versa.

What I remember most of that time is the way we all gelled so quickly and that stemmed from the manager. He appeared to have a knack of picking and developing a squad that worked well together.

In the first round of play-offs, again effectively a semi-final, we played Stoke City. The first leg at Filbert Street was not a good game and ended in a goalless draw, handing a huge advantage to Stoke. However, before the second leg at the Victoria Ground, Martin hammered it home to us that we were not done for and we could get the result we needed, even though Stoke had beaten us twice in the league.

We knew the prize was the chance to play one more match to gain entry to the Premiership and the riches that would bestow on Leicester. With so much pressure on both sides it was no classic, but we took the fight to Lou Macari's side and dominated most of the first half. At the start of the second half, Emile Heskey went charging down the right wing and sent in a cross which was met on the volley by Garry Parker. Garry had been the captain of Leicester but had been deprived of the armband after a row with Martin, but he popped up at just the right moment to send us to Wembley, as there was no further score.

That play-off final against Crystal Palace is one of the best memories of my entire career. There were around 100,000 people crammed in Wembley on 27 May 1996 and I doubt if a single one of them will have forgotten that amazing match.

Even though we were the form team and had beaten Palace the previous month, they were considered the favourites. Around 40,000 fans made the journey down from Leicester to Wembley on that Bank Holiday Monday. The build-up to the match had been incredible in the city and the prospect of playing the likes of Arsenal and Manchester United had our supporters in a fever pitch. We were all determined not to let them down.

We basically dominated the game from start to finish, but it was Palace who took the lead in the fourteenth minute when Andy Roberts hit a twenty-yarder past an unsighted Kevin Poole. Steve Claridge almost got an equalizer right away and he might have scored just before half-time, but things were not running for us.

Scottie Taylor was one of the best players on that day at Wembley. He was a real box-to-box player but during his career he sadly suffered several injuries. He had promised that if we got to Wembley he would bleach his hair and he duly surprised us all by turning up with peroxide locks – it certainly made him stand out and I made a mental note of that haircut.

Palace made a strong start to the second half and captain Walshy was lucky to escape with just a booking when they broke away and he halted the play in his own fashion. But we turned things around and once again began to dominate. In the seventy-fifth minute, just as I was beginning to worry that we'd never get back into the game, Walshy sent Muzzy Izzet away down the left wing and, as he made his way into the penalty box, he was brought down by Marc Edworthy. Referee David Allison had no hesitation in pointing to the spot. It was only the second penalty that City had gained in the league that season. Garry Parker made no mistake with the kick and we could have scored twice in the final minutes of normal time as Steve Walsh had headers cleared off the line.

In extra-time we continued to dominate but couldn't get that winner. In the first half of extra-time I even had a go myself from twenty yards and their keeper Nigel Martyn spilled the ball, though none of our strikers was close enough to net the rebound. Just when it looked as if we were going to have to go to penalties, Martin O'Neill did something that showed how much he thought about the game. In the final minute, Emile Heskey was brought down by Kenny Brown, and as referee Allison showed Brown the yellow card, Martin took off Kevin Poole and sent on Zeljko Kalac. The latter was a giant Australian, about six feet seven inches tall, who went on to become the reserve goalkeeper for AC Milan. He was one of the many people who lost an argument with Martin over the years. We were on the way back from a game and were playing cards when he made the mistake of saying to Martin 'What have you ever done in the playing side of the game?', which allowed the manager to go on at length for at least five minutes about the championships he won, the League Cups, and of course the European Cup. 'And I captained my country and won 62 caps – just tell me when you want me to stop . . .'

Sending Zeljko on against Palace was a clever psychological ploy by Martin, because it distracted the opposition. Anybody due to take a penalty against such a giant would wonder how they could score against a man able to spread himself so wide. But in the end we did not need anyone to save penalties.

We were now in injury-time at the end of extra-time. After 120 minutes and thirty seconds of the final, as Zeljko took his place in goal, Mike Whitlow hit a free-kick long and diagonally towards the Palace box. The ball was nodded down and then sat up nicely for Steve Claridge to shoot home from eighteen yards. He did not catch the shot cleanly but it hit the back of the net anyway. I could barely believe what had happened. It was one of those moments when you hesitate for an instant before realizing what has actually happened. Here was I at Wembley in the biggest game of my career to date, and we had won the match in the dying seconds of extra-time. I remember dropping to my knees almost with relief at the thought 'we're there' while Martin and all the other coaching staff went crazy. Later, there was a photograph in one of the papers showing Martin a clear four feet off the ground as he leapt for joy.

There was barely enough time for the restart before David Allison blew the final whistle. The Leicester City end of the ground erupted in bedlam and, as Steve Walsh lifted the play-off cup, I felt the sheer joy of knowing that at last I was going to be a Premiership footballer.

It was the start of celebrations which went on for several days. The bus ride back up the M1 was memorable – there were crates of beer flying about and everyone was soon merry. We returned to our pre-final base, the Sketchley Grange at Hinckley, for an all-night party which was the perfect end to a perfect day. My family were there to join in the celebrations and, having chewed their fingernails down to the bone because we left it so late, all our relatives and friends could now enjoy themselves. Just like Freddie Flintoff and the English cricketers in London after winning the Ashes, I was still half-cut when we got back to Leicester the following evening and boarded a blue and yellow open-topped double-decker bus for a triumphal tour of the city. There were thousands of people lining every street and they were ten and twenty deep in places with people leaning out of windows and others trying to gain the best vantage point they could.

I remember one young fan who climbed a lamp-post to be at exactly the same height as the top deck of our bus. He clung on with one arm and reached out with the other and I was able to shake his hand as we went by slowly. The next day the picture of us shaking hands appeared in the *Leicester Mercury*.

All this was new to me. I had never experienced anything approaching this and I had only ever seen anything like it on television. To be in the middle of it was overwhelming and just a bit surreal for all of us.

The scenes of joy as we paraded around the town had to be seen to be believed. We then had a civic reception hosted by the Lord Mayor of Leicester, Councillor Culdipp Batty, but to be honest we couldn't wait to get back out and start partying again.

There was one irritation in the aftermath. I had been picked for the Northern Ireland squad to play Germany in the friendly on the Wednesday, but due to a mix-up I thought I was going to be allowed to travel over on the Wednesday morning and meet up with the rest of the lads then. I was not tired despite the long final, was keen to play and had even booked the flight to Belfast, but Bryan Hamilton sent a message to say not to bother travelling. Maybe he had heard about the parties!

Yet nothing could spoil that wonderful feeling of at last having made the big time as a player.

The entire city of Leicester seemed to be on a roll at the time. Leicester was a one-team football town, but in the mid-1990s the Leicester Tigers rugby union side and Leicestershire County Cricket Club were also doing spectacularly well.

Leicestershire were county cricket champions, Leicester Tigers had won their title the previous season and now we had won promotion. Steve Walsh was interviewed on television along with Dean Richards of the Tigers and James Whitaker, the captain of the cricket club. The interview was going very well until Walshy forgot that he was on live television and let slip one of those words the television people usually bleep out. At that point, the camera diverted onto the faces of Richards and Whitaker who were seen to be laughing uncontrollably.

Not surprisingly, we all enjoyed a great summer break but all too soon we were back in pre-season training, which included a week in Dawlish, undergoing some pretty intensive physical work at a nearby naval establishment. Two or three days before the start of the season, Martin signed Kasey Keller and Spencer Prior from Millwall and Norwich respectively. That was part of the manager's psychology – he would sign a player and throw him right into the team so that he didn't have time to think about things and just got on with the job.

In training we had been practising a 4–4–2 or 4–5–1 formation, but on the opening day Martin switched to a 3–5–2 system – he liked to keep us guessing. This was to become

Martin's favourite system, with three big centre backs who could defend set-pieces, a mobile midfield and two strikers who could hold the ball up and nick goals.

Before the season, most experts predicted that we would go straight back down. Although we got off to a good start with a draw at Sunderland and a win over Southampton, we took only one point from our next four league matches, losing at home to Arsenal and Liverpool, the latter beating us 3–0 in a match in which Patrick Berger was outstanding. We had started well against Liverpool, but they eventually played us off the park. It was a sign that we had to raise our game substantially.

After that match, and with just five points gained, Martin called all the players in on the Sunday and spoke to us about how we had given Liverpool too much respect and how we needed to start believing in ourselves. It did the trick as we promptly went to White Hart Lane and beat Spurs 2–1. I always enjoyed visiting White Hart Lane which became one of my favourite stadiums as I liked the way Spurs played football and I can't recall ever being in a poor game there.

The man who came off the bench and scored the winner that day was Ian Marshall, who was one of the great characters at Leicester. Marshy was a big Liverpudlian with a dodgy mullet, a face that would have won any gurning contest and a Scouse wit that was terrific to have around the dressing room. Marshy could score, too, and I used to love the look on his face as he wheeled away after bagging a goal.

By the time we beat Leeds United, we had already disposed of Scarborough in the Coca-Cola League Cup, a trip I remember chiefly for the massive card school on the bus to Yorkshire. Those Leicester card games could be fierce, but they did help to while away the hours of travelling which are the bane of every footballer's life.

In the second round of the Coca-Cola Cup we were drawn away to York, where I scored my first goal of the season as we beat them 2–0. For the next round we were drawn against Manchester United at Filbert Street.

After the York match we visited Newcastle United which brought me my first brush with the 'beaks', the disciplinary panel of the FA. Towards the end of the game, I was booked for a tackle on Robert Lee. We were winning 2–0 at the time, and obviously upset at the prospect of losing, the United fans reacted as if I had shot him. Not thinking about what I was doing, I gave them a half-hearted V for Victory sign. It all depends on your point of view when you see these things – it's either a Churchillian gesture or a Harvey Smith sign, and I suppose the Geordies chose to interpret it the latter way. I couldn't believe it when the police wanted to talk to me after the match. Apparently some Newcastle fans had made a formal complaint about my action. The police superintendent then spoke to the press about the need for players to behave. What with all the publicity, the FA got involved and I found myself on a misconduct charge. The hearing didn't take place until the following February where I was given the chance to explain that I had acted out of frustration at being booked. The Professional Footballers' Association's assistant chief executive Mick McGuire represented me at the hearing. He told the panel that I had a good disciplinary record, adding that he had known me since my days as an apprentice with Manchester City and the offence was out of character. Mick did a good job as the panel took a lenient view of my offence, but I was still fined £500.

I came up against the indomitable Roy Keane for the first time when we played Manchester United in the League Cup at Filbert Street. This was the period when United were not supposed to be taking the League Cup too seriously and resting key players, but any team with Roy Keane in it is going to be trying to win. In any event United's so-called second rankers were internationals wanting to stake their claim for a more permanent place in the first team.

The programme for that match contained one of its regular features, a sort of *Through the Keyhole* item. It was my turn to be profiled, and I was looking pretty pleased with myself as I had moved with Claire and Alisha into a new five-bedroomed house in Leicester just ten minutes from Filbert Street. I also had a new sponsored club car. There was barely any furniture in the house at the time and the photographer did well to make it look habitable, and I have to say I was quite pleased with the way the feature turned out. Personally, I thought my house looked big and amazing.

Midway through the match, Roy and I got involved in a tussle and as we got up, he turned to me and said 'I saw your house in the programme.' 'Did you like it?' I asked. 'Huh,' he replied. 'My double garage is bigger than your whole house.'

What a put down – a real classic piece of quick-witted Irish insult. It annoyed me at the time as it was supposed to, but it was just banter on the pitch, sledging as the Australians call it, and we have had a good laugh about it many times since. I definitely got the last laugh that night as we won 2–0 and advanced into the quarter-finals.

In the second part of a double header, United beat us 3–1 at Old Trafford three days later, but we played really well and at least I got on the scoresheet – beating Peter Schmeichel late in the match with a twenty-yarder was a real thrill.

Another terrific game was a 1–1 draw at Anfield, the start of a long run of fine performances by Leicester against Liverpool. In fact, after that initial 0–3 defeat we never lost to the men in red in Martin O'Neill's time at Filbert Street. I remember that game for another reason – I broke the fourth toe on my right foot. It never did set properly and you can see the damage to this day. But it was only a wee toe so I soldiered on, though for the next few months after it happened I had to get injections of anaesthetic into the base of the toe before I could play.

Martin was always looking to strengthen the squad and he soon bought Matty Elliott for £1.6 m from Oxford. It was one of his best signings, as Matt was a colossus for us, a big ball-playing centre-half who was very nimble on his feet. The 3–5–2 formation suited his game exactly and he slotted into the middle of the defence immediately. He also scored a few vital goals for City over the seasons.

The Coca-Cola League Cup was now taking up more of our attention and the draw looked to be kind as it had paired us with Ipswich Town of the First Division. We exacted a bit of revenge for two defeats the previous season, however, by beating them 1–0 at Portman Road. We played well that night, showing how much we had progressed.

In the very next game, the FA Cup fourth-round match against Norwich, I was made captain for the day as Steve Walsh and Simon Grayson were both out. Perhaps it was the extra responsibility that made me try so hard – too hard in fact. In the thirty-third minute I was chasing the ball when Mattie Jackson let it run through his legs and barged into me. I pushed him back but there was nothing in it, just one of those clashes that happen ten times a match. Referee Alan Wilkie was normally very good and I had a rapport with him, but he didn't see things my way that day and, after some discussion, he sent us both off. In no way did the incident warrant a sending-off. It was just heat-of-the-moment stuff, handbags at five paces if you like. I departed feeling very aggrieved and angry.

As I came off the field, Martin let rip at me and chased me

up the tunnel. I can reveal, as they say in the papers, that our famous relationship might well have ended in that tunnel right there and then as we very nearly came to blows. Indeed, Steve Walford had to intervene and keep us apart as two Irish tempers flared. I dread to think what might have happened had we actually begun fighting, but Steve's actions kept us apart.

I was so angry that I stormed off home straight away after getting changed. I would have been no use to anyone at the time because I was so frustrated and enraged. I knew I had to get away from the ground to let off steam, or else I would have kicked every door in the stadium.

I sat in the house and listened to the rest of the game on the radio. Only after the final whistle when I'd finally calmed down a little did I go back to Filbert Street. Martin gave me a second bollocking, although he understood that I had only reacted to a situation and not caused it. I suppose it was part of the learning process of a Premiership player, but it was very hard to take.

My broken toe was still bothering me. Before the match against Newcastle at the beginning of February, the doctor was injecting me with painkiller when the needle broke. He had to go off and find another one, so there was I sitting in the dressing room minutes before a big match with half a hypodermic needle sticking out of my toe. Luckily he found one in time and the game itself was a cracker. We took a 3–1 lead only for Alan Shearer to catch fire and score a hat-trick in fifteen minutes or so, making the final score 3–4.

After that match most of the players went to a boxing dinner, which turned into a whale of an evening after a few refreshments were taken. When Garry Parker went up into the ring he managed to trip over the bottom rope and smash one of the prizes. The comedian who had been hired for the evening was a lot less funny than Garry's fall and we thought we were hilarious as we kept shouting 'When's the comedian coming on?' He was heckled off after five minutes. We thought it was all good fun but some complaints were made and it hit the newspapers – Martin was not best pleased.

My three-match ban for the sending-off meant I missed the first leg of the Coca-Cola Cup semi-final against Wimbledon at Filbert Street. It was a drab 0–0 draw, in which Robert Ullathorne, who had been bought from Osasuna for £600,000 to replace the injured Mike Whitlow, broke an ankle just eleven minutes into his debut. Sadly for Robert, he was ruled out for the rest of the season

I also remember that match well because Sky television invited me to be part of the commentary team along with Lawrie Sanchez. I was much more nervous doing that than I ever was playing in front of huge crowds.

I also missed the FA Cup fifth round when we came up against Chelsea and gained a 2–2 draw at Filbert Street which earned us a replay at Stamford Bridge. It was the Ruud Gullit management era, when Chelsea had world-famous stars like Gianfranco Zola and Gianluca Vialli, but we did not fear them one bit. We should have been afraid of the replay's referee, however, as in my opinion, Mike Reed had an absolute shocker, booking ten players including myself in a game that in my view was not dirty at all. Kasey Keller was outstanding, making four magnificent saves. At the other end, we almost won the game through Matty Elliott's last-minute header but Frank Leboeuf cleared off the line. As extra-time progressed we sensed we could win, but with two minutes to go Erland Johnsen played a one-two with Vialli and as he raced into the box he brushed against Spencer Prior and went down. I couldn't believe it when Mike Reed blew for a penalty – neither did half the Chelsea side. There was a huge commotion before Leboeuf stepped up to score.

After the final whistle it was Martin who had to be restrained as he gave Reed his verbal verdict. Celtic fans who have seen his excitement in the technical area will not believe that he was once even more animated when demonstrating his passion for the game. We were all furious, because we were convinced that we were on a roll and could win both cups that season. As it was, Chelsea went on to win the FA Cup. To cap it all, during the match I broke the same toe again, so it was back to the injections before each match.

We were left with the Coca-Cola Cup and a hard second leg of the semi-final. Playing Wimbledon was always tough. They were a big physical side but had several good players and Robbie Earle was doing particularly well. But we had the players to match them in the physical department and we also had several skilful players of our own. One of the new additions was Steve Guppy, who had been bought from Port Vale for £650,000. Steve had played under Martin at Wycombe for four years who knew that he would give us valuable width on the left. He was a very fit player who could play as an out-and-out winger, in midfield or as a wing-back, ploughing up and down all day, and he was a deadly crosser of the ball.

With us having failed to score against them at Filbert Street, the second leg started with Wimbledon in the driving seat. Marcus Gayle put Wimbledon ahead, but then Simon Grayson went upfield to head home a magnificent equalizer. From then on it was a case of hanging on as the away goal meant we would win the tie.

Late in the match, Wimbledon sent on Mick Harford who was one of the toughest guys in football and whose job was to put himself about. Watching him and big Walshy going at each other was tremendous stuff, but I'm not daft and I kept out of the way of that battle. At the whistle, Leicester had made it into the final of a major trophy at Wembley for the first time in twenty-eight years.

Our opponents in that final were Middlesbrough. We knew just how dangerous they would be at Wembley because we had met them in the league three weeks prior to the final. Middlesbrough had a great team at that point with Fabrizio Ravanelli and Juninho their two biggest international stars.

At Filbert Street in the league, Juninho ran riot as they steamrollered us, winning comfortably 3–1. In terms of the forthcoming final however, their display was something of a mistake, because it allowed Martin to see certain things and make some changes to our approach before we went to Wembley.

There was an extraordinary atmosphere in the city before the Cup Final, but I didn't take much part in all the hype and hoopla because I was away with Northern Ireland, playing Portugal in Belfast and the Ukraine in Kiev.

The game was dubbed the millionaires against the paupers. For us it was just a great achievement even to be in a final considering that most people had predicted that we would go straight back down out of the Premiership. Not only would we survive but also we had reached the final of a domestic trophy which also brought with it the chance of qualifying for Europe, as the winner was automatically entered for the Uefa Cup. We were underdogs because of that defeat three weeks prior to the final, but that suited us.

Martin's masterstroke was to bring in Pontus Kaamark, who was normally in the reserves. The Swedish player spoke of the moral dilemma about his task of man-marking Juninho to stop him playing. He did the job superbly, however, and Juninho hardly got a touch of the ball. As sometimes happens with a final, the game did not live up to expectations, with chances few and far between. Kasey Keller made a brilliant early save from Ravanelli and then saved from Juninho late on. It was mostly Middlesbrough doing the attacking, but we held on and forced the match into extra-time.

Juninho managed to get space and pushed the ball through but I got across to clear it. As luck would have it the ball went straight to Ravanelli and his shot got between Kasey and the post. It looked as if we were done for, but we had a never-say-die attitude at that time. Martin decided to gamble and sent on Mark Robins for Mike Whitlow – an attacker for a defender. We kept battering away until three minutes from time when Mark sent in a lovely cross to the back post which Walshy nodded back to Emile. His header came off the bar, Steve Claridge got to the rebound first, but Gianluca Festa blocked his effort on the line. Emile's athleticism then told as he got to it first and forced the ball home. For the second year running, we had scored a late goal in extra-time at Wembley.

In one sense we were grateful to get a replay because we knew we had not done ourselves justice at Wembley. The replay on 16 April 1997, took place at Hillsborough, home of Sheffield Wednesday, which was the nearest large stadium to the midway point between the two cities. It proved a good choice as Hillsborough was packed to bursting point and the atmosphere was tremendous, though a lot of our fans got stuck in a jam on the M1 and some were late, even though the police delayed the kick-off by fifteen minutes – during which time we stayed in the dressing room and kept each other's spirits up.

This time we played much better. I remember putting Emile clean through after about forty minutes and he charged in on Ben Roberts in the Boro goal. Later, on the video replay, we saw how a camera had focused on Martin O'Neill as Emile made his sprint towards goal. The gaffer followed him all the way and he leapt in the air as Emile's shot flew by Roberts, only for the ball to cannon off the upright. Martin just about fell over with his head in his hands and it was only then that he realized he had gone all the way into Middlesbrough's technical area and had to make an embarrassing retreat.

Muzzy Izzet almost scored in the second half before Ravanelli put Juninho through but somehow the Brazilian shot over the bar. It was one of the few occasions that Kaamark let him free the whole night.

Althought it was a much more entertaining game, there were still no goals in normal time. In the first half of extra-time we were the dominant side and after nine minutes we won a free-kick which Garry Parker hit long into the box. As he had done so many times before, Steve Walsh rose above the defence and nodded the ball down to Steve Claridge who thumped it home.

We held on for the remaining minutes as Boro attacked incessantly. That final whistle was so good to hear, and sparked scenes that I will never forget involving the players, Martin, the staff and our fans. The euphoria was incredible, there was sheer elation in everyone's eyes and another party began. Later on, I reflected quietly that in the space of five years or so, I had gone from lying flat on my back, wondering whether I would ever play football again for a Fourth Division side, to landing a major domestic trophy with a Premiership side and qualifying for Europe. It had been some journey.

A few days after that final I was brought back down to earth when Claire told me she wanted to go back to Manchester. She was homesick, we had not been getting on and I had been absent a lot. That television series *Footballers' Wives* makes their lives out to be glamorous, but it can be difficult when your husband is away sometimes two or three nights a week during the season.

Alisha had not settled in school so we talked things over

and decided to split up and I got her a house near her parents in Manchester. I blame myself for a lot of what happened, but it was the right thing to do at the time and turned out for the best in the long run.

We had a bit of work to do after the final to consolidate our place in the Premiership. Chelsea and West Ham beat us, but when we drew 2–2 at Old Trafford – Peter Schmeichel foiling me with a terrific save – we were definitely safe and we went on to win our last two matches and leapt up the league table.

The season had finished and we had ended up tenth in the Premiership and won a cup. We had done so with a squad of players who were not the greatest in the land but who worked hard and who had been moulded into a team by Martin O'Neill. It was a magnificent achievement, but how would we better it?

Over the summer, reports appeared in the press that Ruud Gullit was interested in taking me to Stamford Bridge. I was flattered, but then Martin came waving a revised contract which gave me a substantial boost to my wages.

This would happen year after year at Leicester. I had never earned more than £800 a week at Crewe, but within a couple of years I was on ten times that amount at Leicester. It was the era when television-driven huge salaries arrived in the Premiership and all I can say is that I was not about to say no. Representing me in negotiations with the club at that time was Mel Stein, one of the most distinguished agents in sport. He and I enjoyed a great relationship over many years – all I can say is that he did so much for me that even though we parted later on, I will always be eternally grateful to him.

Thanks to the inflation in salaries and Mel's skills, I became a very wealthy young man indeed. My wages went up year on year at Leicester so that, with bonuses, eventually I was making £1 million a year and more. Some Premiership players, of course, are now making several times that sum. People might say those are obscene amounts of money, but if those same people were forced to live under the pressure which top players experience, they would demand the same cash. A footballer's career is also short and only a small percentage move into coaching and management, so you have to earn enough while playing to last you the rest of your life.

Probably as a result of having practically none of it for such a long time in my teens and early twenties, I am still pretty insecure about money. Cash isn't the driving force in my career nor the most important thing in my life – I would prove that later at Celtic.

I did make some particularly bad investments, including one which caught out a lot of top players who bought shares in a company whose share price was supposedly going to soar. In fact, it did the opposite and it cost me and plenty of others a packet.

My finances have improved considerably since my adviser Peter Kelsey took over. He looks after all my investments and I have also put money into property. Let's just say I'm comfortably off and should remain so.

Back then when Martin offered me a new and improved contract to stay at Filbert Street, I grabbed it gleefully. He had just signed a new three-year contract himself, so I could see that he was committed to the club. Being honest, I should have told him that I didn't ever want to leave as life at Leicester was just so good.

I did get into a few scrapes at the time though, mostly as a result of drinking and being in the wrong place at the wrong time. I was young, single and earning good money and I had plenty of female company when I wanted it. Martin was forever asking how I managed that, because he didn't consider me male model material – the cheek of it! I just used to say to him that when you have a bit of Irish gab, a glint in your eye, a devil-may-care attitude and you treat women properly, you'll go a long way. I certainly did . . .

There was also a great camaraderie among the players, never more so than at our weekly sessions at the snooker hall owned by former world champion Willie Thorne, who was a great fan of City. We'd play snooker or cards for hours and it all helped to bind us together as a squad.

It was always good when an old acquaintance arrived to join us, as happened a lot with Martin over the years. Robbie Savage was a colleague from Crewe Alexandra who had started his career as a centre-forward before becoming a midfielder. At Leicester, he began as a right wing-back before joining me in midfield. He went on to enjoy a great career and become one of the best-known players in England.

But as one mate joins, another leaves – that's the way of football. Simon Grayson left to go to Aston Villa for a fee of £1.35 m, not a move that was guaranteed to retain his popularity with the Leicester fans who took their Midlands rivalries very seriously. There was nothing really to match a good set-to with the likes of Villa or Derby County in the first season I was at Filbert Street.

As the 1997/98 season approached, life was pretty damn fine for me, though I found the transfer talk unsettling at the time. That sort of stuff can make your head spin and when it happens during the season it can become hard to concentrate on what you're doing. Being linked with other clubs has happened to me all my career and I usually found out where I was supposedly going when I heard it on the radio or read it in a newspaper. Eventually I learned to take it all with a spadeful of salt.

While I believe I am the same sort of person I was as a

young player at Crewe – a fierce competitor, ambitious, with the odd moments of temper that I have learned to control – I consider myself to be honest and loyal. I would have found it impossible to look Martin O'Neill in the eye and tell him I was walking away from Leicester in those days at Filbert Street. We knew something very special was happening, and under Martin's leadership we were committed to going as far as we could. The Foxes were flying, the only questions were how high would we fly, and how far could we go?

CHAPTER EIGHT

Life is a Rollercoaster

Over the summer break I did something which suddenly brought me a whole lot of attention – I had my hair dyed platinum blond. Gerry Taggart and I were over in Donegal and frankly, we were bored stiff one day when we were passing a hairdresser's shop. Gerry got his head almost shaved to the bone, while I went for the full peroxide monty. I really did it just for a change, because after all, I had been looking at my carrot top ever since the first time I glanced in a mirror.

I was amazed at the reaction my new hairstyle provoked, not all of it entirely positive. It did make me stick out a bit more on the field and was certainly a talking point at the club, but I did not know how much I had become associated with my peroxide looks until I came to Celtic and some entrepreneur produced a mask of me with white hair. I have to say it was a flattering likeness.

Martin was one of those people who never really liked my bleached blond looks. He was convinced that it made me a beacon for trouble from referees who did not like that sort of thing. Once, after yet another bout of trouble in a nightclub, which not surprisingly made its way into the newspapers, he called me in to his office. He had the cuttings spread out on his table. In the course of giving me an entirely deserved lecture, mentioning the fact that I was then thirty and should wise up, he suggested that it might help to avoid trouble if I reverted to my original hair colour. He asked me why I dyed my hair at all and I replied that I just liked to do something different now and again.

'You want to do something different? Well, how about scoring a hat-trick!' he replied. Talk about a tongue like a barber's razor! And it only took me five years to get those three goals . . .

We got Leicester's 1997/98 season under way with a cracking series of games. A local derby win over Aston Villa was followed by a superb performance at Anfield where we won 2–1 against a team featuring their recent signing Paul Ince – always 'fun' to play against – and a certain seventeen year old making his home debut. I remember thinking that the boy looked quite useful. It was Michael Owen.

A home draw against Manchester United set us up for a memorable match against Arsenal. I have played against some of the greatest players in the world such as Ronaldinho, Andriy Shevchenko and Michael Ballack, but Dennis Bergkamp's performance at Filbert Street that night was the finest I have ever seen on a football pitch. He was magnificent, completely dominating the game and scoring the best hat-trick I've ever seen.

His first was from a shot he curled inside the post and the second was all about his shooting power. Somehow we got back to 2–2 through goals from Emile Heskey and Matty Elliott, but in the final seconds of the match Dennis ran upfield and scored an astonishing goal which looked to be the winner from heaven.

David Platt hit a long diagonal ball which dropped over Dennis's shoulder. He controlled it instantly and flipped it over Matty Elliott all in one movement, then dinked it by

Kasey Keller. I remember standing open-mouthed in admiration at the genius of the goal, even though my heart was broken because it looked as though we had lost the match.

But our steel showed and we raced into the attack and forced a corner, from which Steve Walsh headed the equalizer for us three minutes into injury time – a fantastic end to a great game.

I also remember that night because it was my first encounter with Patrick Vieira. I couldn't believe the athleticism and skill of this big gangly 6 ft 2 in guy who was only twenty-three at the time. I got booked for hauling him down early in the match. I couldn't help it – he was away past me and I was lucky to catch him at all!

That was Arsene Wenger's double-winning side which contained the likes of David Seaman, Marc Overmars, Ray Parlour, David Platt, Emmanuel Petit and future Celtic player Ian Wright. They were all very impressive, but mostly I recall just how good Dennis Bergkamp was.

We were in good form as we prepared to take on Atletico Madrid in the Uefa Cup. Leicester had not been in Europe since 1961 and Atletico Madrid were one of the best teams in Spain at the time. They had signed Juninho from Middlesbrough and had also signed Christian Vieri, the Italian international striker. Atletico also had a number of Spanish internationals, so it was a team packed full of class players.

The first leg was in Madrid so we went over a couple of days early to see some of that beautiful city, which is not something that always happens when you're travelling in Europe with a team. We were outside Real Madrid's Bernabeu stadium when John Robertson said fondly, 'Tell you what, boys, that was heavy.' We were wondering what he was talking about until he pulled out a picture of himself lifting the European Cup. 'Aye,' he said. 'It was really heavy on the arms. Did I tell you

I scored the winner that night? Just across the road there . . .' he said, pointing to the Bernabeu.

In the Calderon Stadium of Atletico we surprised everyone, including ourselves, by taking the lead after only eleven minutes. I put Ian Marshall clean through but his effort was deflected over the bar. But with a well-worked and often-practised move from the corner, Steve Walsh headed down and Marshy thumped the ball home. It was one of the funniest things that I have ever seen – this big mullet on top of an open-mouthed grin running towards our fans in the corner who were going ballistic while everybody else in the stadium sat in stunned silence. The Atletico players were all looking at each other in total shock as if to say 'that wasn't in the script'.

Steve Claridge came on for Marshy and missed a good chance just before half-time, and we came to regret that as Atletico came out for the second half all charged up. The miss haunted Steve, as Martin O'Neill blamed him for it and he rarely started a game after that before he was loaned to Portsmouth and then transferred to Wolves – a man of many clubs, Steve is now best known as a very able broadcasting pundit.

We held out until the seventieth minute when Atletico scored two goals in two minutes through Juninho and Vieri, the latter from a penalty. But we had that vital away goal and we were pretty confident that we could score against them at Filbert Street.

Our stadium could be very intimidating at times for the opposition. It was quite an enclosed ground with the big stands and two sheds at either end, and the fans almost sitting on top of the pitch. On the night we played Atletico there was a very special atmosphere, which was not surprising given how long it had been since the Leicester fans had been able to watch their team play in Europe.

We played well that night but when you have £30 million worth of talent in your ranks, it is almost inevitable that class will tell, and Atletico eventually won 2–0. But it does help to have the referee cocking things up in your favour as well.

The performance of Frenchman Remi Harrel that night was *merde*. Just before the hour mark, with their player Juan Lopez already red-carded and with the score still at 0–0, Garry Parker took a quick free-kick. To our utter amazement, Harrel stopped the match, flashed the yellow card, and since that was his second of the match, Garry had to go off. The referee had not told Garry to wait or anything, he just seemed to lose the plot in the heat of the moment. In effect, Garry had been penalized for a piece of quick thinking. That decision turned the match, because Atletico were able to attack as the numbers were even once again. We were also denied three clear penalty chances and, obviously encouraged by our travails at the hands of Harrel, Atletico scored twice to put us out of the Uefa Cup. Afterwards, we all let rip at the referee. I chose my words carefully and said that I felt cheated, while Martin looked back to the 1979 European Cup Final when he had been left out of the Nottingham Forest side by Brian Clough. That had been his biggest disappointment in football, but the way that Leicester City lost to Atletico was worse. His criticisms of the referee were fierce, though he stopped short of directly comparing Harrel to the referee in the Notts Forest–Anderlecht Uefa Cup semi-final of 1984, where two bad decisions helped to oust Forest and the referee was later found to have been bribed by an official of the Belgian club – the row over that lasted for years.

'I thought it was a match we could not win,' said Martin. 'The referee must seriously look at his performance and analyse his game and ask "Was this OK?" I think his performance was shocking and I am absolutely, thoroughly disgusted.'

Those comments led to the usual inquiry by the beaks, but for once Uefa decided not to throw the book at the people who were making their criticisms but at the referee who had deserved them. After viewing the video off the match, Uefa's refereeing committee decided that M. Harrel would not be allowed to officiate at any more matches in the competition that season.

When Uefa were prepared to take him off the list it showed what a dreadful performance the referee had given. It still rankles with me to this day, as I am convinced we could have gone far in that competition, but for once at least, some action was taken by footballing chiefs against the real culprit.

We had a break early in November when we all took off to Ireland, basing ourselves near Dublin. A squad of us played golf at the Portmarnock golf and country club before going off to the Grove Hotel in Malahide, run by Alan Clancy, who has since become a good friend. We all had a bit too much to drink and, as we were waiting for taxis, I felt an urgent need to answer a call of nature. Rather than make my way into the crowded premises, I popped round the corner and was in the middle of my business when I felt a big hand around my shoulder. 'Okay, lad,' said the voice behind me. 'That's enough of that. Zip up.' Two officers of the Gardai Siochana, the republic's national police force, had appeared from nowhere. As they say on *Mastermind*, I had started so I finished. They then arrested me and, in time-honoured fashion, asked me to accompany them to the station.

I pleaded with them to let me go, but they were having none of it. They bundled me into the back of a police car and I'm afraid the red mist descended and I gave them a shower of abuse. Any chance I had of going free disappeared at that point.

They took me down to Malahide police station and left me

to cool my heels in the cells where I continued to protest. Garry Parker and a friend of mine, Adie James, came to the station and asked the gardai to let me go as I had not been causing any trouble and had just had a couple of drinks too many.

The officer apparently gestured along the corridor to where I was still giving it long and loud with the insults. 'We'll let him out when he has calmed down,' said the cop, so that was me stuck in the cells until six o'clock the following morning.

By that time, Martin O'Neill had got to hear of what had happened. Spookily, just as I lay on my uncomfortable bed wondering what sort of punishment he would inflict on me, a familiar shadow appeared at the cell door. It was the manager himself, dressed in his long coat.

'Right, you,' said Martin. 'Out!'

In the back of a taxi pulling away from the police station I sat with Eadie and I had to bite my knuckles because I had looked at him and he had looked at me and we both nearly had a fit of giggles. That would not have been a very clever thing to do with Martin sitting in the front seat – you could almost see the steam coming out of his ears.

We got back to the hotel and Martin ordered me to go to my room and get some sleep. 'I'll deal with you later,' he said, with more than a hint of menace.

It was an unpleasant experience trying to explain what had happened. It turned out that the gardai might have dropped the charges, but the arresting officer said I had been abusive so they threw the book at me. I was facing four charges under the Public Order Act, including being drunk, causing a breach of the peace and behaving violently in Malahide police station.

My court appearance had been set for the Tuesday, when the squad was due to fly back, so Martin ordered me to stay behind and face the music. Paul Franklin, the reserve-team coach, was deputed to stay behind and look after me and Martin told me I would have to pay for his fare and my own.

'Get yourself sorted out and I'll deal with you when you get back,' said Martin.

Paul and I got into a taxi at the hotel and the driver asked where we were going. When I said 'Swords District Court', the driver asked if I was in trouble. When I explained that I had been charged, he shook his head sadly and tut-tutted. 'Today being Tuesday, the judge will be Sean Delap, and that's a terrible shame for you. Sure, now, did he not go and fine a guy 1,000 punts for emptying his ashtray in a car park last week?'

With that sort of punishment being handed out for such a minor offence, by the time we got to the courthouse I was convinced that this particular 'hanging judge' would send me to prison.

In one way, it was interesting to see the inside of a courthouse for the first time. In the dock there were five or six young lads all handcuffed together, none of whom recognized me. My main concern was that the case should not reach the newspapers, so the good news was that there did not appear to be any photographers or reporters in the vicinity.

I was the third case up and when Judge Delap called my name I could see why he had such a fierce reputation – he just looked the part. The statement of the gardai officer, named as Padraig Grey, was that I had been 'roaring and shouting and urinating' in front of a crowd of 300 people, and I had been abusive at the police station.

I couldn't remember there being 300 people watching me have a wee-wee, but I wasn't exactly in a position to argue. I pleaded guilty all round and waited for Judge Delap to do his worst.

In fact he dealt with me quite reasonably and was even

funny. He asked me what I did for a living, so I said I was a professional footballer with Leicester City. 'How are you going this season?' he asked, and I replied that I thought we were about eighth in the Premiership.

He couldn't resist a dig, however. 'So you will be used to performing in public then?' Ouch.

He then asked me how much I earned, so I just said 'Enough'. I then had the good sense to apologize profusely and sincerely to all concerned.

He told me that he did not take kindly to people coming over to Ireland and disrespecting its laws and warned me not to do so again. To my surprise, he dismissed three of the charges, but fined me 250 punts on one count of breach of the peace.

I thought that I had got a terrific result, considering that ever since I had met the prophet-of-doom taxi driver, I was sure I was going to jail. There had also been no media people that I could see around the court, and although I still had another 'hanging judge' to face, i.e. Martin O'Neill, I had got off lightly so far.

I returned to Leicester and was delighted to see that there was nothing about me in the national or local press either. My dad called that night and asked if I had enjoyed a good weekend off. I decided to play the innocent and told him everything had gone well. The craic had been great but I hadn't got up to much, I foolishly insisted.

'That's not what it says in the *Belfast Telegraph*,' he replied acidly, and right away I knew my goose was cooked.

It turned out that there had been a reporter in the court-house after all and the details of my crime and punishment were soon all over the papers. Not only was I now in trouble with Martin, but my parents were on my case, too.

It was something of a wake-up call. I had to face the fact

that I had committed an offence and been hauled up in front of court, that I had humiliated myself, although not 'in front of 300 people' as had been claimed – it was more like a couple of million newspaper readers.

I realized that I had overdone things with the booze and that was what had got me into trouble. I resolved to be a bit more careful in future, but didn't actually realize at the time what the source of my problem had been.

Many months after the court case, indeed after the Worthington League Cup Final in which Spurs beat us 1–0, I went on a bender for a couple of days. Not surprisingly, I had the 'booze blues' for a few more days afterwards, and was still under the weather when I joined the Northern Ireland party to play a couple of internationals.

For some 'light reading', I bought Tony Adams autobiography *Addicted* and began to flick through it. Within a few pages I was hooked, if you'll pardon the expression.

The former captain of Arsenal and England had gone public over his battle with the bottle and, as I read the first chapter, I began to realize that I could relate to quite a lot of the early problems he had experienced. Footballers do have spare time and money, and the devil makes work etc., but I had never considered myself to have a drink problem. I had never got into fights as a result of drinking, but at the weekend after matches I would sometimes go out with the lads and not return home until the wee small hours. Occasionally I would find myself waking up in my armchair, still fully dressed.

However, reading Tony's brutally honest words convinced me that I had better get a grip as I was clearly at the top of a slippery slope. I had a good long think to myself. I was then twenty-eight years old, in my physical prime and finally earning excellent money. Yet with the court appearance still in my mind and suffering the hangover from hell, I could see that I was where Tony had been near the start of his ordeal. I resolved to cut out the heavy boozing stuff, and with a few exceptions – you will read about a couple of them later – I have stuck to that pledge. I do still enjoy socializing over a drink but a beer or two is my normal limit – anyway, I absolutely detest hangovers and do not miss them.

During the 1997/98 season, there was one match which would have driven any Leicester fan to drink. Grimsby Town from the division below us were our first opponents as we set out to defend the Worthington League Cup. But on a dreadful October night at Blundell Park, we just never got started and even though we had several players injured, that was no excuse as we should have dealt with them comfortably. To be fair, Grimsby played superbly and in the end we could not complain about their 3–1 victory. I had enjoyed several highs at Leicester, but that was by far the lowest point of my time at Filbert Street to that date.

Other clubs might have resorted to panic buying at that point but that was not Martin's way, though he did make a few astute signings in his time there. One was my big friend Gerry Taggart, signed from Bolton in the summer of 1998, while Leicester also took a chance on the 'forgotten' Tony Cottee. Steve Walford's connections came up trumps when he heard that Tony, who was then out in Malaysia, was wanting to come home. Martin duly signed him and Tony had a couple of very good seasons for us. While he was at Leicester he got his 200th league goal at Tottenham, which speaks volumes for what he achieved in his career. He was a very nice fellow into the bargain, a decent professional who had looked after himself and who the younger boys could look up to.

One import was Theo Zagorakis from Greece, who was a class player – he later captained his country to victory at the

European Championships in 2004 – but did not really adjust to the Premiership. Martin sometimes had trouble getting through to Theo, whose English was not fluent. Once Martin gave him a bit of a bawling out and the rest of us couldn't believe it as Theo just sat there nodding and smiling. It was only after Martin had left that Theo turned to me and asked: 'What he say?'

That season saw me involved in a couple of on-the-field incidents with two men who by a twist of fate captained Scotland and England. Having said how much I admired him and much enjoyed playing against him, I was pretty upset when I was involved in a collision which led to an injury to Gary McAllister. He was playing for Coventry City at the time and in a purely accidental clash in our match at Highfield Road in late November 1997, his studs caught in the turf just as I tackled him and the result was that he got a bit of damage to his cartilage. It was just one of those things and Gary did not blame me. On the contrary, he later said I had done him a favour as the knock showed up some underlying problem which might have prevented him from taking part in Scotland's World Cup campaign.

As the season wore on, it was clear that inconsistency was our main problem. For every brilliant performance such as our defeat of Manchester at Old Trafford, or our terrific 2–0 win over Chelsea which ended their unbeaten run, there was an equally depressing performance such as our baffling 3–0 defeat by Crystal Palace in the FA Cup.

My season almost came to a premature end at Bolton in March. Alan Thompson clattered me and I went down like a ton of bricks. With me lying on my back, Tommo and I exchanged pleasantries and the Bolton fans booed me thinking that I had taken a dive.

It just shows you how fans view a match through glasses

that only see one side of things. I went off to get strapped up and tried to struggle on but eventually had to be substituted. Tommo was on my personal hit list for a while after that, but the ironic thing, of course, is that we have since become very good friends since we both fetched up at Parkhead.

The initial diagnosis was that I had damaged ankle ligaments and would be out for the rest of the season, but a specialist was able to confirm that there was no damage. I returned to the team in time to play my part as we went unbeaten through the last nine matches of the season.

Part of me wishes that I could have missed out on one match though, against Newcastle at Filbert Street on 29 April 1998.

I remember the date and the match only too well. It was a really busy game, full of incident with no quarter asked or given. Newcastle were struggling in the league at that time and were sixth from bottom. They needed every point they could get to move away from the relegation zone. Consequently, the tackling was rather more fierce than might be expected from such a good footballing team.

In the fifty-seventh minute, I was involved in an incident with England captain Alan Shearer which neither of us is ever likely to forget. It would make headlines around the football world for many weeks afterwards and would bring me a degree of notoriety which I never sought, not least because I was the innocent victim in the case.

I was going for a ball near the touchline when I tried to get my body in front of Alan to hold him off so I could take the ball away from him. Alan got his arm across my chest and swung me around. As we went down his left boot came whirling round and caught me full in the face. There is a photograph which shows Alan standing on my leg with one boot while the other is moving to my head.

I was stunned by the pain of it and the next thing I saw was blood pouring from my nose and from a cut above my eye. It was pretty sore, I can tell you, and like a boxer who is hurt by a foul blow, I stayed down to recover as best I could.

When I looked up, referee Martin Bodenham had given a foul against me for the initial challenge. I could not believe it when he waved play on and took no action against my assailant. The linesman had only been about fifteen yards away from the action and must have seen what had happened.

As the game raged on, I was lying with half my body on the pitch and half off it. I was just concentrating on trying to stop the flow of blood when David Batty came running over, grabbed my legs and tried to throw me completely off the pitch.

Nobody realized afterwards that I was actually more angry at Batty for his activities than with Alan. I thought he was coming over to see if I was all right, but all he wanted to do was to get me off the pitch so that the match could carry on and there would be no question of any action by the referee against Shearer.

The television cameras had not missed the swinging boot, however, and the video replay clearly showed that Alan at the very least had been quite reckless.

Martin O'Neill had certainly seen everything that happened, and along with half the crowd, he went ballistic. Later he would say 'I do not care whether you are Alan Shearer or the Pope, you just do not do that. I saw Lennon get kicked in the face. Of course it was deliberate. He should have been sent off.'

I got a bit of treatment and was able to carry on but I was still incensed at what had happened. I just could not believe that the referee and linesmen could have seen Alan Shearer kick me and not take some kind of punitive action. I went up to Bodenham, who was usually a good and fair referee, and said 'Did you not see that?' He waved me away instead of giving Shearer a card. Had he done so, it might have saved Alan some grief as well.

Afterwards the incident was played time and time again on the television football shows, and even made the main news programmes. But then those were the days when Alan Shearer was just about the most famous footballer in England. I was alarmed at the way the story spiralled out of control, gaining its own momentum each passing day,

I was annoyed that Alan did not come to see me after the match to say he was sorry, but from the outset he maintained that it had been an accidental clash. It would therefore be unnecessary to apologize, he seemed to imply. A large contingent in the media and elsewhere detested Allen's goody-goody image and they were determined to make his life a misery now that he had gone so far out of line in such a public manner. In the days after that match, the phones at Filbert Street never stopped ringing. The newspapers were having a field day, but I soon got tired of all the requests for interviews, all of which I refused, though that didn't stop reporters turning up on my doorstep and badgering me for a quote.

I put his reaction down to the pressure that he was under at the time. After all these years at Celtic, I can understand what it is like to be underachieving in front of your fanatical supporters, and even though Newcastle had reached the Cup Final, their poor performances in the Premiership meant they were getting a lot of grief on Tyneside.

Under a constant barrage from the media, the FA decided to call an inquiry into the incident, saying they would use the video evidence. Now the balloon really went up, because if they decided to prosecute Alan and found him guilty of kicking me deliberately, then he would almost certainly be banned from the FA Cup Final. There was even speculation that his place at the World Cup finals might be at stake, as he had indicated that if he was banned from Wembley he might not go to France. I, for one, could not see the FA beaks being so stupid as to take any action which might lead to one of England's best players missing the tournament, though some pundits called for Alan to be stripped of the captaincy of the national side. I did not want anything of that nature to happen – all I wanted was for him to say sorry.

At that point, Alan gave his first on-the-record reaction. He issued a statement saying: 'I have now seen the television pictures of the incident and I am amazed how bad it looks by comparison to what actually happened. I was brought down by Neil Lennon over by the touchline and we both fell clumsily.

'As I tried to get to my feet I had to really tug my left foot free and the momentum of doing this looked on television like a kick. It certainly wasn't and the fact that Neil is virtually unmarked confirms this. If I did accidentally catch him, I certainly did not mean to. I would never try and deliberately hurt a fellow professional.'

The Newcastle manager was none other than my great hero Kenny Dalglish, who defended his player as you might expect: 'The two of them just fell, the momentum carried Alan over. There was no malice, no intention. I've never seen him do anything to injure anyone deliberately. He is competitive, not vindictive in any way, shape, or form.

'This is not the first time he has been criticized, and it's not the first time people have been wrong, is it? He doesn't want preferential treatment, but he doesn't want to be punished because of who he is.'

I had some sympathy with the latter viewpoint, but the fact remained that he had kicked me. But what was the point in pursuing him? Martin O'Neill said that he wanted to let the matter drop and my view was that if the match officials had not seen it then nothing could be done anyway, so what was the purpose of continuing to hound him?

What did annoy me was the way people came out and tried to make out that Alan was entirely innocent. Gary Lineker, a former Leicester player, don't forget, was at the match and he said that you could see that Alan hadn't meant it. England manager Glenn Hoddle joined in, saying that he did not mean to do it. Even the late Tony Banks, MP, who was then the Minister for Sport, came out and defended Alan.

I began to question myself. Had I imagined all this? Was it me that was in the wrong? Any minute I expected the Queen to issue a Royal proclamation saying 'Shearer is innocent'.

The only problem was that Alan had a bit of 'previous', having been accused by Leeds, Barnsley and Tottenham of unsavoury tactics. In the latter case, Ramon Vega, who would later join Celtic, said that a Shearer elbow had broken his nose.

Gordon Taylor, head of the PFA at the time, represented Alan at the hearing. Early in May, about a week before the hearing, Gordon phoned me and asked if I would speak on Alan's behalf to the FA panel. I told him that if Alan Shearer himself were to ask me then I might consider it. A few minutes later Alan called and I told him I would speak on his behalf.

My reasoning was simple. He had said it was an accident and I had to accept that. I also did not want to come out of the whole affair looking like the baddie, and I did not want to 'do in' Alan Shearer or anybody else in football – that was not why I went into the game. I was also getting heartily sick of the whole matter.

The hearing was at Hillsborough, and first in to be questioned was Alan, then the referee and linesman. While I was waiting in the ante-room to be called before the panel, I got talking to Shearer's agent, Tony Stephens. He told me that he had only five clients and I thought 'that's not a lot for a supposedly top agent'. But then he told me their names – Shearer, David Beckham, Dwight Yorke, David Platt and Michael Owen. With a golden handful like that, he did not need any more.

He proceeded to tell me about how great Alan was and what a nice guy he was, which was not exactly what I wanted to hear at that point. When I was eventually summoned before the panel, they showed me various angles of the video evidence – it looked even worse from some angles, and in one shot you could see a Newcastle player holding his head in his hands because he had a clear view of the incident and knew what Alan had done.

The three-man panel asked me for my reaction and I told the truth. I had been angry at the time, but had accepted Alan's word that it was an accident. I would have liked to have told them that I had accepted Alan's apology, but none had been forthcoming.

The panel cleared Alan of kicking me deliberately, citing new video evidence from a different angle. I never saw that and I couldn't believe their findings that 'The alleged incident of Alan Shearer swinging out with his left leg was a genuine attempt to free himself.'

Alan was free to play in the World Cup and I was just glad it was all over, though it all left a sour taste in my mouth.

Over the summer, there was a real possibility that Martin would leave Filbert Street – he had been linked with Celtic, among others. At Leicester, there was always a lot of talk about boardroom spats, but the manager always deflected that stuff away from us. We did know, however, that he had reservations about the chief executive, Barry Pierrepoint, though he never let it affect his role as manager. There was only ever going to be one winner in that fight, and Mr Pierrepoint didn't last long after Martin's 'clear the air' meeting with the board which also boosted his budget for the playing squad.

At the time there were more reports of clubs such as Leeds being interested in me, but once Martin indicated that he was staying at Leicester, I was happy to sign up for more years and more money. By this time I was on £10,000 per week which meant I earned nearly twice as much in one week than I did in a year when I first joined Crewe.

We had a mixed start to the season and once again I saw red – blood, that is – when my nose was cracked during the 0–1 defeat to Blackburn. Still the rumours persisted that Martin was going to leave. Back then, and seemingly ever since, every major high-profile managerial post which became vacant was immediately linked with Martin. He has always had a very blasé attitude about the rumours and reports predicting that he would be going to this or that job, though he did take false reporting seriously. He successfully sued one newspaper for reporting that he had breached his contract by talking to another club without permission.

Even though it must have been deeply annoying when he was so focused on his job at Leicester, he did deal with one report quite humorously. George Graham had just left Leeds United and just about every paper in the land was reporting that Martin was lined up for the job. As luck would have it, Leicester were next to play at Elland Road. When our bus reached the stadium, Martin had us all in stitches when he said to the driver 'Just park in the manager's space.' He had the last laugh as well, as we beat them 1–0. It was only later that we found out that Leeds had made an approach for Martin's services and he had been only half joking about that space . . .

That match was a bit of a turning point for us, as we went on a run that extended to nine unbeaten matches, including a memorable 2–1 win over Spurs at Filbert Street. The reason I recall it was Martin's half-time talk – he told us he had decided to stay with Leicester. It was all the inspiration we needed.

In the Worthington League Cup, we put out Chesterfield and Charlton before beating Leeds 2–1 at Filbert Street.

The quarter-final paired us with Blackburn. Not only did that match include the rarity of me scoring the winning goal, my first strike of the season, it was also a header – one of only a handful in my career.

Emile Heskey was on fire at that time. We called him Bruno because in size and build he really did resemble former world heavyweight champion Frank Bruno. As usual there were all sorts of rumours about him moving on, but Martin persuaded him to stay and he played a crucial part as we advanced to the final of the Worthington League Cup by beating Sunderland over two legs in the semi-final. Tony Cottee's excellent double in the first leg at the Stadium of Light set us up for victory, but Niall Quinn gave them a half-time lead at Filbert Street. That interval produced the single biggest bollocking Martin has ever handed out in his career – some fifteen minutes of non-stop verbals which had our ears ringing. But it did the trick as we got the equalizer through a Tony Cottee volley. We were off to a cup final again.

Our league form had dipped – Manchester United had beaten us 6–2 in a terrific game at Filbert Street – and we went out of the FA Cup to Coventry, but on 21 March 1999, we were back at Wembley with a chance not only of a trophy but also of getting into Europe once again.

The run-up to the final against Spurs was full of the usual hype and in the match before it I scored one of my best-ever goals, a curling shot which got us a 1–1 draw with Charlton. Of course my colleagues tried to make out that it was a cross that luckily went in, but what did they know about goal-scoring? Did they not know what a scoring sensation I had been as a schoolkid?

The final was like so many other big games that you lose – you tend to forget what happened and remove the details from your memory. I felt fine before the game and we were all up for it, but once we got out on the Wembley pitch there was a lot of lethargy in our side and we had no momentum, no fluidity about our play.

It wasn't our first cup final so nervousness could not be the excuse. We also had a good record against them, even though George Graham was managing a very good team with the likes of David Ginola – then at his very peak – Sol Campbell, Les Ferdinand and Darren Anderton in the side.

It's no excuse, but we were missing our first-choice left-back, Frank Sinclair. On the Friday night Martin had called a team meeting at 7 p.m. to discuss tactics, but Frankie turned up over an hour late and the manager was furious. The following morning Martin told Frankie he would not be playing and would not even travel with the squad, then told him to pack his bags and go home. Martin could be tough at times, though he was always fair.

Spurs didn't exactly play very well either, but we just had one of those days when nothing happened for us. Even with Spurs having to play most of the second half with ten men because Justin Edinburgh was sent off after cuffing Robbie Savage, we just could not impose ourselves.

There were very few chances in the game although we almost scored four minutes from time when Tony Cottee just missed the rebound from Robbie Savage's shot. It looked as though we were going to extra-time, but three minutes into injury-time, Steffen Iversen broke down the right and his low cross was knocked up by Kasey Keller straight to Allan Nielsen who bent low to head home the winner. At the end the overwhelming feeling was one of frustration, because we knew we had let ourselves down.

That final had a long and bitter aftermath. When cup finals come around, there are always touts looking for tickets from players. One of the Leicester boys knew a really professional tout in London who was happy to take your tickets and sell them on, no questions asked. I think we got to buy up to seventy-five each, with tickets going to touts for more than £100, so each person who sold their allocation could make £7,000 or more, tax free. At one time during the run-up to the final, one of the players came into the dressing room with a sports bag full of money and handed out big wads of cash.

I didn't get involved because I had so many members of my family and friends wanting to go to the game that I had no spare tickets in any case.

One of my very good friends was a Spurs fan who wanted to go to Wembley with his son. I knew them well and was sure they would not cause any trouble and nor did I think the people around them would be offended as I knew most of them. So I gave my friend two tickets, thinking nothing of it, not least because there had never been any trouble at cup finals that I could remember.

During the final, however, the actual ebb and flow of the match led to problems. There were Spurs fans in the Leicester end and with the build-up of excitement they could not contain themselves when their team scored. Though we could not see exactly what happened out on the pitch, trouble kicked off immediately and it was very unpleasant.

One poor woman was hit in the face and the photograph was in all the newspapers. Inevitably, there was an investigation by the FA and just about every player and member of staff was questioned, with twenty-five of us being involved at one stage or another during the inquiry which dragged on for many months. Indeed, it did not end until we were in the Worthington League Cup Final the following season.

Most of the squad members who were questioned said they had given their tickets to family and friends. I had lawyers in London at the time who advised me to ask for a personal hearing and put forward my case that I had done nothing wrong. The legal eagles did not come cheap, but I felt so passionately about the issue that I paid through the nose for their advice and went to the hearing.

I just did not want my name dragged through the mud when I knew that what I had done was perfectly innocent and I had not made any money. I went in front of the commission and said that I, too, had distributed my tickets solely to family and friends, except that I added that two of the recipients were Spurs fans. I thought I was being honest and helpful when I added that I could say exactly where they had been sitting and that there had been no trouble involving them. If I had just kept my statement to saying 'family and friends', I would still have been telling the truth and would have escaped any punishment. But it would not have been the whole truth. The fact that I could testify to my friends' good behaviour made no difference to the FA disciplinarians. All that mattered to them was that I had sold two tickets to Spurs fans to sit among the Leicester support.

When the guilty verdicts were handed down, seven players and staff members got fined a total of £75,000 with Andy Impey being hit hardest as his ticket ended up in the hands of the Spurs fan who hit the woman. I got a reprimand while others who had also been involved got off scot-free, leaving those of us who had been named as guilty parties to take the public rap for the whole shebang.

The FA had accepted that I could account for every one of my tickets and that I had made no money on the black market, but my name and that of Leicester City had been tarnished, unfairly in my opinion. I felt aggrieved that other, more guilty players, had walked away. The practice of players selling tickets to touts was widespread in the game at that time, and for all I know it still is. There were no official rules in place, though some were instituted after the scandal, but mostly I think the FA wanted to make an example of Leicester because of all the publicity.

Though I had been gutted to lose the Worthington Cup Final, in the next few weeks I went on to enjoy one of my best periods with Leicester.

As the season ended, I won the Midlands Player-of-the-Year Award, as voted for by the Midlands Football Writers' Association. It was a prestigious prize to win, not least because past winners included the likes of Paul McGrath. There were also some great players in the Midlands at the time I won the award, so I felt particularly pleased to be honoured. I also got to meet Brian Clough, as he presented the trophy – fearing his well-known caustic wit, I hardly said a word to him on the night!

The 1999/2000 season would bring massive changes for several Leicester players. Yet again there were rumours linking me with Celtic, Aston Villa and Liverpool, among others, but I was happy to stay at Leicester as long as Martin remained there – a lucrative new contract earning me £1 million a year helped to make my mind up as well.

Martin always said that if a bigger club came in for me, he would not stand in my way, and I took him at his word. Mel Stein had become my agent and he had it written into my contract that I could seek another club if Leicester finished below fifteenth in the Premiership, but that never happened in Martin's time.

Over the course of that long season, our league form held up well but it was our cup runs which brought us glory. In the FA Cup we would go to the fifth round before being put out by Chelsea, this after we had beaten Arsenal on penalties after two 0–0 draws.

I was absent from both of those games because in December I had suffered a serious hamstring injury in my right leg in a Worthington Cup match against Leeds United. We had earlier beaten Crystal Palace and taken revenge on Grimsby, our conquerors of the previous year, before edging past Leeds and then comprehensively beating Fulham 3–0.

Muzzy Izzet was injured at around the same time, which meant that our normal midfield pairing was missing for thirteen matches. We returned against Aston Villa in the second leg of the Worthington Cup semi-final, the team having gained a goalless draw at Villa Park in the first leg. We had suffered so many injuries that Matty Elliott had been moved up front to play alongside Emile Heskey. It was yet another of Martin's inspired choices, as Matty scored the winner in injury-time at the end of the first half.

For the second year running, we were in the Worthington League Cup Final and this time our opponents were from a league below us – not that we did not give plenty of respect to Tranmere Rovers.

Before the final at the end of February, a couple of connected events of some significance happened to the club. I say 'connected' because no sooner had Martin signed Stan Collymore, the so-called 'bad boy' of English football, than we were off to La Manga in southern Spain where a whole heap of trouble awaited us – and Stan got the blame.

Stan's time at Aston Villa had been pretty disastrous, and he had not played a Premiership match for eleven months. Later there would be all the reports about his problems with depression and I clearly recall thinking that he was making things up as he went along. It was only when I suffered from the illness myself that I realized what he had been going through.

The problem with Stan was that trouble seemed to follow him around. The manager had decided that a few days' break in La Manga would put us in the right frame of mind for the final, so leaving John Robertson and Steve Walford in charge, he waved us off to sunny Spain saying he would follow a day later.

The complex we were staying in was beautiful and included a golf course. Those of us who played the game were there within minutes of arriving on day one of what was supposed to be a four-day break. The rest just stayed in the bar and had a quiet afternoon. By the time we golfers returned at about 7 p.m., everyone was ready to party and the drink started to flow. Before midnight things were getting pretty raucous, there was loud banter and dancing on the tables and we were certainly the centre of attention.

There was a pianist playing during all this so I didn't hear what happened when a Scottish woman and Stan exchanged words. Whatever was said, she ended up stomping off, while her husband watched what was going on.

At that point Stan produced his weapon of choice – a small fire extinguisher. We urged him to put it away, but he couldn't resist it and let fly. It was one of those devices that uses chemical dust rather than water and the cloud went everywhere – including hitting the Scottish woman and her husband. There was bedlam after that, with lots of screaming and shouting, in the course of which Stan got slapped and beer was thrown.

Steve Walsh took exception to some disapproving people and dropped his trousers to moon at them – it turned out they were Norwegian journalists. Oops!

My abiding memory is not of all that bother but of our physio Mick Yeoman's face – he was covered in the white powder and all you could see were these two big eyes staring out.

We all got sent to bed and the next thing I knew was John Robertson banging on the bedroom doors and telling everybody to get packed as we were leaving for England right away. The Scottish couple had put in a massive complaint about our behaviour and the complex manager must have valued their custom highly as he asked our party to leave. Poor Robbo had the task of calling Martin O'Neill to say don't bother flying out here, we're on our way home. The 'break' had lasted less than twenty-four hours.

The press descended on us and La Manga and made hay with the story. Also staying at the complex were the players of Rosenborg FC, the Norwegian champions. Their coach Nils Arne Eggen said our group had drunk more beer in a few hours than his team did in a year and was quoted as calling Robbo 'Whisky' John Robertson – and I thought football coaches stuck together.

On the plane home, we all knew we were in trouble, so everyone kept their heads down. But trust Marshy to make a memorable wisecrack – 'I must have had a great time,' he said, 'because it only feels like yesterday since we were flying out!'

When we got back to Leicester Martin was absolutely raging. I remember his words to us all: 'You lot better win next week.' He fined Stan two weeks' wages and made the rest of us pay for the trip ourselves.

Stan had become known for being at the centre of so many

rows that the baggage just followed him around and was regurgitated any time something else happened. I would come to know how he felt after joining Celtic.

Stan was actually a quiet, likeable guy, and the shame of it is that he had got himself in shape and was playing superbly when he broke his leg playing against Derby just five weeks after the Wembley final. It was a horrendous break, his ankle having gone one way while the rest of his leg went the other. I was first to get to him and was nearly physically ill when I saw the extent of the injury. By the time he recovered Martin had left and Stan was never the same player again.

Despite everything that had happened at La Manga, nothing could shake our bond as a team and we returned to England full of confidence for the Worthington League Cup Final against Tranmere Rovers of the First Division.

Tranmere had enjoyed a fantastic run to the final and were at Wembley on merit. John Aldridge's men started the match well and it took us nearly twenty minutes to get ourselves into the match. It began to become a very good game indeed, and after twenty-eight minutes we went ahead. Matty Elliott had reverted to playing at the back, but he went up for a corner taken by Robbie Savage and his header came back down off the crossbar, hit the back of their goalkeeper Joe Murphy and went in.

They went down to ten men when Clint Hill fouled Emile Heskey as he broke on goal. He had already been booked but could have been red-carded for that professional foul anyway.

Tranmere galvanized themselves and David Kelly equalized, shooting low past Tim Flowers in our goal. At that point, I distinctly remember Martin coming out of the dugout to indicate to me that we should calm the game down as we were still in control.

It became quite scrappy but still exciting and twelve

minutes from time, Matty went upfield again to head home from Steve Guppy's corner. I should have made it 3–1 when a rebound fell at my feet, but in trying to direct the ball home, I managed to miss completely.

It made no difference as we held on for victory. I had my second major winner's medal, and we were in Europe again. For the third time in five years, we returned in triumph from Wembley, and what a party or two we enjoyed.

The following week Stan and Emile played together for the first time in the former's home debut, the result a devastating 5–2 win over Sunderland, with Stan scoring a hat-trick.

We were all massively impressed with our new strike force, thinking that if we could keep the team together we would be some side the following season, but a week later, Emile was sold to Liverpool for £11 million. The club could not afford to turn down that kind of money, but his departure and Stan's leg break cast a bit of a shadow over the end of the millennium season.

We had won another cup and were in Europe, but those were not the reasons why the year 2000 became utterly momentous for Martin O'Neill and myself. For by the beginning of 2001, we had begun our odyssey to Paradise.

CHAPTER NINE
A Treble in Paradise

After Celtic had sacked head coach John Barnes after a string of poor results, it was almost inevitable that Martin O'Neill and myself would end up at Celtic Park.

It was a certainty that Martin would go to Celtic if he was asked. As soon as I learned that Celtic had formally approached Leicester to ask to speak to him, I knew it was only a matter of time before he went north. When he asked my opinion I told him that he would be mad not to go to Celtic as they were a much bigger club than Leicester and were something of a sleeping giant in terms of Europe. He asked me privately if I would consider joining him at Celtic Park and I said of course I would.

Martin signed for Celtic on 1 June 2000. Over the summer he took John Robertson and Steve Walford with him, and Celtic paid Leicester something like £2 million in compensation. Wherever Martin goes, there is only one person in charge of football at that club, so my boyhood hero Kenny Dalglish left the post of Celtic's director of football not long afterwards. Typically, Martin got straight to the point: 'Everything is brilliant except for the team,' he was quoted as saying on his first day in the job. He knew how to build that team, he had been promised money to do so by the Celtic board, and I was on his shopping list.

Before he even took over there was speculation that I would immediately go to Parkhead. After all, I had been his first signing when he had taken over at Leicester. For once, the speculation was not wrong, but the timing was more than a bit out.

There are not enough pages in this book to re-enact the months-long saga of my signing for Celtic – *War and Peace* is a shorter story. I have no intention of rehashing every detail, suffice to say it was a long and wearing few months, partially for a reason which I have never revealed until now.

I had loved being at Leicester but I knew it was time to move on because the only person who had really been keeping me at Filbert Street was Martin. I knew it would be the end of an era as some of Martin's signings would not interest the new manager.

I watched with interest as Martin went after some of his targets and got them – Chris Sutton from Chelsea, Belgian international Joos Valgaeren from Roda in Holland and my old sparring partner from Aston Villa, Alan Thompson.

Had I not been waiting on Celtic making an offer, I could have gone elsewhere. John Gregory at Aston Villa, Walter Smith at Everton and Bryan Robson at Middlesbrough were all reported to be interested in taking me. Eventually Celtic put in an offer of £6 million for my services, but Leicester wanted more. It's a fact that after the initial approach by Celtic, Leicester showed they were determined to keep me. Peter Taylor had not long been appointed manager when he said he wanted to see me. I thought that he was an excellent choice for the post at Leicester and over the next few months he showed himself to be a quality guy, a real footballing man.

I made it clear to Peter and in turn to my agent, Mel Stein, that if Celtic came in for me then I wanted to go to Parkhead. Both Peter and the club chairman John Elsom did their best to dissuade me but my mind was made up. John was a jovial chap who always had the best interests of Leicester at heart, but even he couldn't sway my mind.

Peter told me repeatedly that he didn't want me to go and, with the backing of the board, said I could have a new contract. At a pre-season game against Gillingham, John Elsom made what he thought was a final attempt to persuade me to stay. I told him I was determined to go to Celtic, but would abide by the terms of my contract until such time as I did go.

I then told my agent Mel Stein that I thought the club would offer me a new contract and that he should ask for a ludicrous sum of money, thinking that Leicester would not be able to match my terms, so hastening my departure. Mel called me back a couple of hours later and said 'You've got the contract.' The salary was £32,000 per week, making me the highest-paid player at the club by far and one of the best-paid in the Premiership. I couldn't believe it.

I spoke to Martin who was over in Copenhagen. In improving my contract, Leicester had also let it be known that it would take something like £8 million to buy me. Martin wished me luck and explained that the desired fee was about £2 million more than Celtic plc was prepared to pay. However they later offered £6.5 million and more – bids which were again rejected. In those circumstances, I had little option but to sign the new contract, though it contained an 'escape clause' allowing me to leave the following summer if Leicester failed to flourish.

So I got on with the business of playing. I was in good form at the start of the season before I got injured in training before a match against Southampton. We were doing a simple routine exercise with the ball when I fell awkwardly and went down heavily. I felt the pain shoot from my shoulder into my neck and it was touch and go whether I would make the game.

I was passed fit to play as long as I wore strapping on the shoulder but during the match I was in considerable pain and had to come off at half-time. The following morning I woke up next to the beautiful girl I was seeing at the time, and I realized immediately that something was wrong with me. I could not even properly describe the symptoms to my girlfriend but I knew something was seriously wrong.

I should have been full of the joys of life as I had a fantastic job and a beautiful woman lying beside me, but all I could feel was a darkness inside. That was the start of my first bout of depression, although I did not realize what was wrong with me at the time.

Things spiralled from then on and in a matter of days I was feeling considerably worse and could do nothing to rouse myself out of an all-consuming torpor.

By then I was not eating properly either as I had lost my appetite and I was also unable to relate properly to people, so that when I was standing in the middle of a room full of my fellow players, I honestly felt as if I was on my own.

My sleep became so badly affected that I was waking up almost every hour, on the hour. Anyone who has ever suffered insomnia will know just what hellish feelings it brings. I am normally a happy-go-lucky sort, a confident and strong person, but within days I had become a miserable wreck and was rendered weak by it all.

I did not have a clue what was wrong with me and took to alcohol for some relief. I did not know that that was one of the worst things you can do when you are depressed as alcohol is not a stimulant but a depressant. I was ill and no one knew what was wrong with me for the simple reason that I did not know myself.

Eventually I went to the doctor who very quickly diagnosed depression. I was shattered by what he said – I just did not believe that someone of my strength of character could suffer from this form of mental illness. I soon saw that it was the only sensible diagnosis but because of the stigma of admitting that you're depressed, which people see as somehow being unable to cope with life, I could not tell anyone what was wrong. My team-mate Stan Collymore had gone public over his problems with depression and had suffered a lot of sneering comments not to mention outright disdain – I did not want that happening to me.

I agreed to go on medication, taking twenty milligrams of Seroxat daily. As my shoulder was still giving me trouble I was having pain-killing injections in order to play and train as well. The wonder was that I was able to play at all.

Without any doubt the depression affected my form. Peter Taylor had every right to drop me from the first team but he persevered because he felt that I would recover in time. I am sure he was tempted to leave me out a few times but he did not do so.

All the time people were looking at me and they could see nothing physically wrong with me, but inside I was suffering agonies. To friends and even to the press, I tried to explain away what was happening by saying that I had not got over the departure of Martin O'Neill. In a sense, I suppose I hadn't.

Plenty of people speculated that my loss of form was a deliberate effort to get away from Filbert Street, but that was just nonsense. During the early part of the season, I thought my transfer chances had actually already gone, so there were no ulterior motives on my part. In fact, there were no motives for anything, as I could not summon up any drive for life at all, not even when playing in a World Cup qualifier for Northern Ireland against Denmark which we drew 1–1.

Though I was playing adequately, I knew I was under-performing badly, especially as the club were flying. We were sitting on top of the Premiership until we met reigning champions Manchester United at Filbert Street who overtook us by winning 3–0.

My dad had come over to spend a couple of days with me that week. Apart from the overall feeling of malaise at the time, my most vivid memory was watching the funeral of Donald Dewar on television with my dad. I had no interest in Scottish politics and, though I knew the First Minister was hugely respected, I still do not know why I ended up watching the service on television. It's funny to think of it now – me sitting watching a funeral on telly. Maybe it suited my mood, so I watched the whole thing, sitting with my dad and staring at the television. I vividly remember I was trying to think of something to say to Dad, but the words just would not come out.

A few days later came a sign of how much things had changed for me and for Leicester when Liverpool beat us for the first time in four years. I remember thinking before the match 'Do I really want to go out there before 40,000 people in the state I'm in?' But I had a job to do, and I couldn't exactly throw a sickie, though I'm afraid I played like a schoolboy. Of all the people to score the only goal against us, it had to be Emile Heskey.

I could not even get excited about our brief foray into the Uefa Cup, where we played Red Star Belgrade. It was another one of those rare but terrific European nights for the Leicester fans. They snatched a lead through Milenko Acimovic after just forty-seven seconds of the first leg at Filbert Street, but

Gerry Taggart equalized in injury-time. The second leg was played in Vienna because of the civil unrest in Belgrade at the time, but it did not appear to affect Red Star who were the better team on the night and won 3–1 to end our European venture.

The most crushing disappointment was when we went out of the Worthington League Cup, beaten 3–0 by Crystal Palace. I actually apologized to the fans that night but still felt unable to say what was really wrong with me. Even now as I think back on that period, I still feel uncomfortable talking about it as it is not in my nature to fail to perform to the best of my ability. At least I know now why it was happening.

By mid-November, I had begun to recover and I remember playing against Newcastle thinking 'this is better' and then against Middlesbrough I was suddenly feeling on top of the world again. The depression had lifted as quickly as it had arrived and it was like the sun coming out from behind thick dark clouds. I was voted man-of-the-match and Peter Taylor was delighted to tell me that my performance had been the best I had played since his arrival. I remember feeling that even if I never went to Celtic I was just so glad to get my health back that I wouldn't really care.

At that time Martin was convinced that Leicester had managed to keep a hold of me permanently, so when the phone rang in his office and Peter Taylor came on the line, he thought his fellow manager was calling to see if he could offload Stan Collymore. But Peter had taken me aside a few minutes earlier to ask if I would still be interested in going to Celtic if the opportunity arose. I think he had finally realized my heart lay elsewhere.

Celtic had been going very well and probably hadn't needed me earlier in the season, but you never know your luck. Paul Lambert had broken his shinbone and Rangers had thrashed Celtic 5–1 at Ibrox, so Martin was able to say that recruiting me was necessary.

I was utterly delighted and this time I insisted there would be no going back – I would join Celtic whatever. However, there were one or two complications in the negotiations, including the question of who was due to pay Crewe Alexandra the percentage of any subsequent transfer fee which they had been promised when I left Gresty Road. Although that contractual arrangement caused me some grief as it delayed my move, I still believe that there should be a better system than the one we have at the moment for compensating smaller clubs when they develop players and sell them on to bigger clubs. Managers like Dario Gradi and clubs like Crewe should get genuine rewards for their efforts.

I played my last game for Leicester against Leeds and at least went out with a 3–1 victory. I was leaving them in good order as the team was then third in the Premiership. Afterwards, Peter Taylor would point to my departure as the moment when things started to go wrong for Leicester. That's a backhanded compliment, I suppose, and I was certainly upset when my former colleagues slipped down the league to fourteenth and were relegated the following season.

By the first Tuesday in December I was so certain I was going north that I spent most of our pre-Christmas club bash that night talking to our recent signing, the Scottish international Calum Davidson, about football in his home country. I made my farewells, some of them quite emotional, and flew up to Glasgow on the Thursday.

I was utterly amazed by my welcome at Glasgow Airport. Martin had told me that the attention from the fans and Scottish media would be entirely different from what I had experienced before, but I thought it would be nothing I couldn't handle. I didn't know how wrong I was until I walked through the arrivals door at the airport and was met with a barrage of television crews, press photographers and reporters. John Robertson was beside me and he was sent flying as media and fans crowded in.

I recognized former Celtic player Davie Provan as one of my questioners and couldn't resist saying 'the last time I saw you, you had a perm' – and he did, too, back in the 1980s when he starred on the wing for the Hoops.

The melee continued for the next twenty-four hours, with the media following me everywhere. Arriving at Parkhead, my emotions were stirred by my first sight of the stadium since it had been rebuilt. I had often thought of visiting Parkhead when I was at Leicester, but our games always seemed to clash. Now I just stood and savoured the sight of a magnificent arena, while thinking how proud my family would be and how I was at last fulfilling my ambition.

One of the first people I met at Celtic Park was youth coach Chris McCart, whose grandmother had been my landlady all those years before at Motherwell.

After the routine medical, I finally signed and was introduced to the world as a Celtic player on Friday 8 December 2000. Doing the press conference gave me a tremendous buzz, even if Martin did remark about my blond hair and said 'don't worry, he's a lot more clever than he looks', before adding 'I don't want to put ferocious pressure on him, but if he doesn't do well, I'll kill him.' I think he was kidding . . .

The fee was £5.75 million, somewhat less than had been offered in summer. I can confirm that I took a pay cut to join Celtic. I had been on £32,000 per week at Leicester but I went down to £28,000 a week. But hey, what price do you pay for happiness?

My chief concern was how would I continue to make my regular visits to see Alisha in Manchester, but we eventually got round that and she enjoyed visiting Glasgow. For the first few months I stayed in the Marriott Hotel where I eventually had a suite, but I soon bought the flat in which I still live in the West End of Glasgow – I had been told the area would be to my liking and by and large I have enjoyed my time there. I had been told the West End was the more cosmopolitan area of the city as it was near to the university and the bars around Byres Road. As Glasgow is a football city, everyone has a view on the game and they are not slow in letting you know it, but I suspect the attention would have been much worse for me in other parts of the city. I have grown to love Glasgow, though of course a few individuals have let the city down.

I met the squad and trained with them on the Saturday. I'll never forget going down to the training ground at Barrowfield and seeing it all lit up even in late morning – short winter days were another thing I would have to get used to in Scotland. There's been a lot of criticism of Barrowfield in recent years, but look at Celtic's success over the decades and you cannot say the old place has done badly for the club. However, I passionately believe Celtic must move with the times and the new youth academy and training complex being built at Lennoxtown will enable the club to attract the best young talent from across the world. That's why I invested some of my own money in the club share issue which is helping to pay for Lennoxtown.

I made my debut for Celtic on the Sunday against Dundee at Dens Park. Pulling on the hoops for the first time was a magical feeling, and taking part in my first huddle – when the Celtic players all gather round just before kick-off for a last exhortation – confirmed to me that there was no going back. 'This is it, you are here and it's not a dream' were my thoughts.

Dundee had a very good side under Ivano Bonetti at the time, with players like Gavin Rae, Giorgi Nemsadze, Steven

Tweed, Juan Sara and former Argentinian World Cup hero Claudio Caniggia. Practically my first action in a Celtic jersey was to stop him in the act of shooting. An early goal by Stan Petrov was cancelled out by a Tom Boyd own goal, but in injury-time, Didier Agathe popped up to score with a header at the back post from Stan's corner. We had won 2–1 and my Celtic adventure was off to a victorious start.

My first reaction was that I had landed in a somewhat different culture from the Premiership. The game was quite distinct in subtle ways, there was less time on the ball and the play was more rushed, and I had learned one important lesson – at Celtic you are expected to win every match and settling for a draw was a complete no-no.

I was interviewed after the match and said 'It's results like that which win titles.' That got me my first row at Celtic – the gaffer never wanted talk of winning titles or trophies until they were actually secured. Even though at that point in December we were already top of the league and looking good to win the championship, Martin still played down our chances. It was good psychology as we never fell into the trap of complacently thinking we already had things won.

Over the next few days I got to know the players and realized that Martin had once again created a happy dressing room full of winners. I soon went about establishing relationships with the likes of Chris Sutton, who has a terrific dry wit and a neat line in put-downs – a sort of cross between *The Office*'s David Brent and Simon Cowell of *The X Factor*. I had already mended my fences with Alan Thompson and our two great Swedes, Henrik Larsson and Johann Mjallby were particularly impressive from the first. Tommy Johnson and I quickly became friends and roomed together on trips. Tommy was a real jovial Geordie, a natural goalscorer whose career was blighted by injury and whose time at Parkhead was all too brief. I was in and out of hotels a lot at first, and Tommy and his wife Hayley would often invite me to their home for tea, hospitality I really appreciated. He has not changed a bit and we remain good mates to this day.

The Scottish contingent was led by peerless captain Tom Boyd and goalkeeper Rab Douglas, as daft as all the breed, while Bobby Petta and Lubomir Moravcik, the veteran Slovakian who was just a genius, were also in the team at the time. We were later joined by Ramon Vega, the Swiss international who had a brief but glorious time with us.

Paul Lambert was still recovering and there was a lot of speculation in the press that he and I would not fit into the same team – I don't suppose that after three championships and getting to Seville together, the pundits might admit that perhaps they were wrong.

One squad member I soon went to visit was Alan Stubbs, who I had played against when he was with Bolton's youth team and I was with Manchester City youths. Alan was then in Glasgow's Western Infirmary being treated for testicular cancer and he had just received a dose of chemotherapy. He was twenty-nine, the same age as myself, and I could only think 'there but for the grace of God'. Thankfully, he made an amazing recovery and has been playing as well as ever with Everton.

One of the few people who did not get much chance to make an impression on me was Eyal Berkovic. He just did not have the work ethic which Martin wanted and our midfield was full of good hard-working players, so I knew his days were numbered. At his previous club, West Ham, he had been involved in a nasty incident with big John Hartson, the Welsh international striker who was soon to sign for Celtic, so it's probably just as well that Eyal left when he did.

At that time I gave a very prophetic interview to the *Celtic*

View, the club's weekly magazine which had been the first proper club newspaper in the world back in the 1960s. I told them: 'Moving to Celtic has put me right in the spotlight and the gaffer warned me about that. But I never expected the attention I have received. If you play for Celtic, you're public property. I'm not too sure if I like that, but I'll have to get used to it.' Being honest, though, I wonder if I ever have.

I made my home debut against Aberdeen on a day when we were unstoppable. I was very nervous as I took the field in front of 60,000 people, but a couple of good early touches settled me down. We duly battered them from start to finish and won 6–0. It was my first real close-up look at Henrik Larsson in his pomp and he scored after about five minutes to institute one-way traffic towards their goal. I had already seen Henrik in training and was therefore aware that he was a truly special player, because he could do things with either foot that would make you gasp and he was also a terrific header of the ball. The way he played that day made me begin to believe that he was unique and of course he has since gone on to prove just what a one-off he is.

I was no sooner in the door than we flew to Orlando in Florida during the Scottish Premier League's midwinter break, a sensible 'time out' I had not experienced before. We stayed in one of the world's biggest hotels at the Disney complex and I recall thinking it was all a bit different from Crewe where there were never any overnight stays. At the Alex, we travelled there and back to matches on the day, no matter how far we had to go and dinner was often a ready meal cooked in the microwave on the bus. I had definitely moved up in the world.

On our return, the first big fixture was against Hearts at Tynecastle where Henrik scored all the goals with a hat-trick to send us nine points clear at the top and put him on the thirty-one-goal mark. I then made my Old Firm debut against Rangers in the CIS League Cup semi-final at Hampden in a match that would prove memorable. The atmosphere really was unique, I soon found. And it was tough on the pitch, too.

We had a very strong side at the time but so did Rangers, with Craig Moore, Lorenzo Amoruso, Arthur Numan, Jorg Albertz, Claudio Reyna, Tugay, Barry Ferguson, Stefan Klos in goal and Tore Andre Flo and Neil McCann up front.

Willie Young was the referee that night and he would be in charge of many Celtic matches from then on. I always got on well with him, as he was one of the few refs with whom you could have a bit of chat, and since in his day job he was a lawyer, he tended to win any verbal jousts. Willie had a very busy night at Hampden, as he awarded two penalties, booked four players and sent off three.

We went ahead after six minutes when Chris Sutton volleyed home after Ramon Vega's header had rebounded off the bar. Henrik skinned young Bob Malcolm for the second and after Albertz scored from a soft penalty, Henrik got another just-as-soft award at the other end which he converted.

There had been a lot of tough tackling in the second half in particular, with four bookings before two of football's more gentle citizens, Lubo Moravcik and Michael Mols, started a wee battle. Willie sent them both off and Claudio Reyna joined them for hacking down Bobby Petta. I was standing nearby and was accused of hitting Claudio, but it was more of a warning wave of a hand in his face than a smack.

It was deliberate on my part. I had felt that for far too long Celtic had allowed themselves to be intimidated by Rangers. I had noticed while watching the Old Firm matches on television that Rangers often bullied Celtic out of it, but I was determined that would not happen on my shift. Perhaps that did not endear me to the Rangers fans, but they do not pay my wages and I have always been determined to do everything within the laws of the game to ensure that Celtic win every match. The day that the Rangers fans stop booing me will be the day that I know I'm not doing my job.

That match was the first of a double-header against Rangers. On the morning of the league match at Parkhead the following Sunday, there was the first of many stories about me or colleagues which just happened to appear hours before a crucial match. This one concerned supposed death threats made against me by Loyalist terrorists because I was due to play for Northern Ireland. There were no names on the quoted sources and it was all rubbish. There have been many other similar situations over the years, sometimes with stories concerning the private lives of Celtic players, but it's funny how many of them break before an Old Firm match. Pure coincidence, of course.

Thanks to Alan Thompson's goal after seventeen minutes, my first home match against Rangers ended with a 1–0 win. Hugh Dallas was the referee and he is another of the men in black for whom I have great respect. Again, he would talk to you during a game, though I think he would probably tell you that I talked too much! He has been retired for a couple of years now and I think the authority he displayed has been missed. That day he sent off Fernando Ricksen for two bookable offences and he also ruled against Rangers' claims for a penalty.

I had enjoyed a quick and successful baptism into the unique world that is the Old Firm match. They really are games apart because so much is at stake. While winning against Rangers gives you a terrific feeling, losing one is horrible – in case anyone has any doubts, that feeling goes for every Celtic and Rangers player, as we all know how much it means. The only comparable matches in stature that I had played in before then were the League Cup finals at Wembley, but they had nothing like the edge an Old Firm game always contains.

Perhaps because of those wins, I was beginning to enjoy life in Glasgow. Being a Celtic player has its privileges, such as when I went to see one of my favourite bands, Texas, and was invited backstage to meet lead singer Sharleen Spiteri. She is a stunner and gave a great performance on stage that night.

By then we were so far clear at the top that it was a case of not if, but when, we would win the title – no matter how much Martin refused to admit it.

In the midst of our run to the title, I played for Northern Ireland against Norway – the match in which I was constantly booed. Upsetting though that was, I was determined not to let it affect my play for Celtic and, a few days later at East End Park against Dunfermline Athletic on 7 March 2001, I got my first goal for Celtic. Now you might think that having notched precisely three of them over the years that I am going to devote an entire chapter to each goal, but you would be wrong. Instead, I am merely going to say that, after quite brilliant strikes by Stan Petrov and Henrik Larsson in the first half, in the seventy-seventh minute I ran the length of the field, beat eight players on the run, dummied the goalkeeper and struck a magnificent third – actually, the ball came back off the post from a Tommy Johnson header and I stuck it away with the minimum of fuss, as any Lurgan schoolboy scoring sensation should do.

And what reward did I get? The manager promptly substituted me – the thanks you get for scoring goals! But the cheers I got from the Celtic fans as I left the field were very special to me. I felt accepted by the supporters from the first, and that has made all the difference to my time at Celtic.

Unfortunately, I damaged my shoulder again in the next match, against Dunfermline in the replay of our Scottish Cup tie, a game we won comfortably 4–1 after the initial 2–2 draw. This set us up for a quarter-final against Hearts who were then going strong but we won 1–0. It was during this match that the phenomenon of me being given sectarian abuse by non-Rangers fans began. In the previous match against Hearts there had been no such reaction from their fans, but all of a sudden I was a hate figure. This happened just twelve days after the bigots had abused me at Windsor Park and has continued ever since from a section of the Hearts support – need I say more?

To their credit, most Hearts fans do not agree with this nonsense and the club has repeatedly tried to do something about their lunatic fringe. Indeed, the following day their spokesman Douglas Dalgleish stated: 'Our fans have been calling and leaving messages on our website to name those responsible. We think about twenty people were involved in shouting sectarian abuse and it is very disappointing. We'll now take steps to identify them as best we can, then take the action we see fit. There's no place for sectarianism at Hearts. People can shout and chant but to single out individuals for their religious beliefs isn't on.' That was in 2001 – five years later, I still get 'the treatment' from Hearts fans. And all it does is make me and my colleagues try harder against them . . .

We suffered a real blow against St Johnstone when Stan Petrov broke his leg during our 2–1 victory in Perth. He would be out for months and the first match he missed was the CIS League Cup Final against Kilmarnock on 18 March 2001 – another diary date as it brought me my first winner's medal with Celtic. It was Henrik's day, as every Celtic fan who was there will remember. His hat-trick was simply sublime and we were victorious despite being down to ten men for much of the second half after Chris Sutton was rather harshly sent off.

I had won my first trophy with Celtic and the feeling was simply euphoric. The Lurgan Celtic bhoy was now a medal-winning Glasgow Celtic bhoy – dreams do come true.

Martin banned all talk of it, but we all began to think of the treble of League Cup, Scottish Cup and Premier League which Celtic had not achieved since the heyday of Jock Stein three decades earlier. The last-named title was the next to be achieved, with a run of three games in the first week of April.

A grinding 1–0 win at Pittodrie was followed by a midweek match against Dundee in which Johann Mjallby came on as a striker and scored a late winner as we deservedly won 2–1.

That set us up for the game against St Mirren. Two days before the match I was personally boosted by being named the Bank of Scotland Player of the Month for March – an honour I was delighted to receive as I felt it recognized the way the team had battled their way to victories in the CIS Cup and Premier League.

St Mirren were bottom of the league and we were expected to steamroller them. It is all very well thinking that, but doing it can be a different thing, especially as nobody had told the Buddies who put up a spirited fight. We created chance after chance but nothing would go in until the thirty-eighth minute when Henrik put Tommy Johnson – playing in place of the suspended Chris Sutton – clear in the box. His first touch let him down but he recovered to shoot under Ludovic Roy and the ball went in off Scott Walker.

We piled on the pressure but Roy did very well in their goal and at the end, it was Tommy's single goal which gave us the league title. No matter what my friend does in life, he has his place in Celtic history.

It was all over and we had won the league in the fastest time for twenty-six years. Looking from the pitch, the scenes of joy were quite incredible. Two legs of the treble had been achieved and Parkhead became one giant festival.

Some of us dashed out to a supporters' club in the north of Glasgow to be with the fans and on the way back through Robroyston we could see street parties getting under way. Back at Parkhead we had our own party and it was a fantastic night with which to celebrate the highlight of my career.

It is often the case that at the moment of your greatest triumphs, life has a habit of reminding you that nothing is certain in this world and success is a fleeting thing. We were due to receive the SPL trophy with a huge celebration at Parkhead on the night we played Hearts when I received word that my sole remaining grandparent, my nanna Margaret Moore, had died. She was my mother's mother, and had become the matriarch of the family around whom so much was centred. Championships and everything else suddenly became irrelevant.

My grandfather, Frank Lennon, had died in September 1986 and my other grandfather Cornelius Moore died four years later. My grandmother Jane Moore died in 1998 and now the last of my grandparents was dead. It was the passing of a generation and I thought back on them all.

Cornelius had been a top-class Gaelic footballer but he was perhaps better known in Lurgan for his part in organizing the annual pilgrimage to Lourdes. He helped get the sick and disabled to that holy place for many years until his failing health meant that he, in turn, had to take his place among the pilgrims rather than the organizers.

When I was helping in their shop in the summer, I could always count on a sweet or two at the end of the day and I can still smell the wonderful odour of fresh bread from the baker's shop that he used to send me to. He also supported me in my football – he paid £120 for me to go to Norway with Hillsborough Boys Club in 1982, a lot of money in those days.

Grandfather Frankie was a bull of a man and my dad always tells the story of how he and his brothers were fighting out in the garden one day when grandmother Jane shouted on him to do something. He just leaned out of the window and said 'Boys, I'm fighting the winner.' That was the end of the battling.

Both my grandmothers were wonderful, loving people, and my chief regret was that I never spent enough time with them or my grandfathers. All these thoughts flooded through my mind as I returned to Lurgan for my grandmother's funeral. I'm glad that she was alive long enough to see me settled at Celtic, but I know that whatever I had chosen to do, all my grandparents and indeed all my family would have supported me.

It was a sad few days, but when I returned to Glasgow I was able to throw myself into my work and occupy my mind that way.

And we did have some fun, such as when Frank Bruno came to open boxing promoter Alex Morrison's new gym shortly after we had won the title. What a character big Frank was, a real gentle giant and very funny with it. I just hope he has no recurrence of the mental troubles which afflicted him a couple of years ago.

Craig Moore from Rangers and Morten Wieghorst and I all attended the opening, a visit which was arranged by a mate who is a huge Rangers supporter. Andy Smiley is a Glasgow businessman who I often see above the tunnel at Ibrox wearing his blue shirt and orange tie and shaking his fist at me. But he is a Rangers fan who just wants his club to do well and we get on fine away from the football. He has a typically Glaswegian sense of humour.

I once got him some tickets for a Celtic-supporting client of his and he said he would return the favour. I returned to the Marriott Hotel where I was staying at the time to find Andy's present – a boxed set of videos of Rangers' nine-in-a-row league victories with a note from Andy saying 'watch this and learn something'. Funnily enough I haven't got around to watching them yet.

As the season drew to a close we were looking ahead to the Scottish Cup Final against Hibs, having beaten Dundee United 3–1 in the semi-final, during which Henrik had broken Charlie Nicholas's post-war scoring record for Celtic. The league did not exactly peter out as we still had to play Rangers at Ibrox. I did not tell anyone that I had been to the stadium before as a schoolboy and it was even more impressive on my second visit. I know this will probably amaze some Rangers supporters but – whisper it – Ibrox is one of my favourite stadiums. The surface is usually good and the intensity of the atmosphere on my many visits to Ibrox has always brought out the best in me.

It's just a great place to play. When we go there, the rest of the squad always get off the bus first. They move into the safety of the dressing room and open the windows so they can hear the boos when I alight. It's actually quite funny and I take it all in the intended spirit, of course.

It was certainly a fine place to be that late April afternoon as we destroyed Rangers. Before we had won the title, Rangers manager Dick Advocaat and just about everybody else at Ibrox had moaned about the injury list which had robbed them of key players for crucial matches. There was some truth in the statements but we got a bit fed up with them harping on, so without telling Martin, Tommy Boyd arranged for special T-shirts to be made. After we won the championship we all donned the shirts with the slogan 'No Excuses' on them. It was a barbed retort to Rangers, who had annoyed the Celtic fans with a mock huddle before the championship decider which they had won two seasons previously. Nor did Rangers take losing their title very well – Jorg Albertz came out with some sort of statement that we had won only because they had been 'so bad'. We decided to make Rangers pay for those words.

It was 0–0 at half-time and Rangers had enjoyed the better of the play, but during the interval Martin told us to start getting the ball to Henrik and especially to Lubo Moravcik. Lubo was in the twilight of his career at that stage, but he was still a bundle of energy around the place, a mercurial but magnificent footballer who lived for the game. I loved playing with him as you could give him the ball in any area of the field and he would do something with it. He also had a dynamite shot in both feet – I remember him hitting one from thirty yards against Hibs with his supposedly weaker left peg and I don't think I've ever seen a ball hit so hard.

That day at Ibrox, Lubo ran riot in the second half, scoring two fine goals and generally controlling play, but the icing on the cake came with Henrik's fiftieth goal of the season four minutes from time. In winning 3–0, our performance that day showed the gulf in class that had opened up between the two teams. The season before, Rangers had beaten Celtic by twenty points, and now it was the other way round. In truth, they really had no excuses.

Before the Scottish Cup Final we went out for a golfing break to Marbella. Perhaps the Spanish hospitality was too generous as we then lost our unbeaten home record to Dundee, who beat us 2–0 on a day when we just did not spark. It was my first defeat in the hooped jersey after twenty-one victories and two draws. You would think that having won the league and being in the Cup Final, Martin might have cut us some slack but not a bit of it – he gave us a real tongue-lashing.

But there were also plenty of congratulations going around. In Belfast I was presented with the Guinness International Player of the Year for Northern Ireland while Henrik unsurprisingly swept the 'Player' boards in Scotland before lifting the Golden Boot award as the top scorer in Europe. It was the King of Kings' year all right – he even scored a hole-in-one during Tom Boyd's testimonial golf day.

All that remained was the Cup. How our fans were desperate for the Treble! The Celts had last achieved that feat in 1969 and it had been a long wait.

My second cup final at Hampden was just as memorable as the first. Hibs were plucky but Henrik was superb. Lubo Moravcik went off injured after fifteen minutes and was replaced by Jackie McNamara who opened the scoring after thirty-eight minutes. Henrik put us two up early in the second half before making it three from the penalty spot with ten minutes remaining.

When the final whistle blew, Martin went round every one of us, and you could see in his eyes what the Treble meant to him. I just remember trying to take in the scenes of the cup presentation and the lap of honour, because it was the perfect end to the perfect season.

We were all winners in that strong team and I like to think I had played my part in bringing some drive into the side. Henrik had led us on the field, but above all it was Martin's commitment and intelligence which had inspired us to become champions and cup winners.

After a brief summer break we returned to a new situation in Glasgow. For the first time, both ourselves and Rangers were in the Champions League, but we both had to go through the qualifying stages.

Ramon Vega and Alan Stubbs had left Parkhead, but we had signed Bobo Balde, the captain of Guinea, from Toulouse and big John Hartson arrived from Coventry. Momo Sylla came from St Johnstone while Martin also brought my old mate Steve Guppy from Leicester. The basis of the team that would see us through the next two seasons was now in place.

As we faced Ajax of Amsterdam in the first round of the qualifying stages, we had been given deliberately tough pre-season matches against Sunderland, FC Porto in France and Manchester United in Ryan Giggs' testimonial. The Portuguese beat us 1–0, but we recorded the same score in our favour against Sunderland before winning a seven-goal thriller at Old Trafford. Celtic famously do not play friendlies and we owed them one for beating us 2–0 in Tom Boyd's testimonial, but I think United were stunned by the passion we showed in that match, in which I managed to score against Fabien Barthez as we ran out 4–3 winners.

All too soon we faced Ajax with a place in the Champions League proper at stake. This was our finest hour to date in my time at Parkhead. Their manager Co Adrieense said after the first leg that we had given them a football lesson, and indeed we had.

Didier Agathe was wonderful that night. He had been the steal of the year when Martin had signed him for £50,000, and against Ajax he showed all his electric pace to tear them apart down the right wing, while Bobby Petta did the same on the left. They both scored and Chris Sutton added another to give us a 3–1 lead in the tie. Back at Parkhead, we were perhaps a bit too complacent as we let them in too often and Ajax eventually won 1–0. But we had done the hard work in Amsterdam and would play in the Champions League.

We knew that we were in for six very difficult games when the draw put us into a 'group of death' with Rosenborg, Porto and Juventus, but we had never expected an easy ride at that level.

In Scotland, things were not so much easy as simple – we turned up to play and took home three points some ninety or so minutes later. From the start of the season to near the turn of the year, we dropped just two points thanks to a goalless draw at Livingston.

When Aberdeen finally beat us 2–0 on a poor day at Pittodrie, there were banner headlines because of the shock. We were soon back to winning ways, however, and had the title in the bag before the 'split' introduced by the SPL in which the top six and bottom six play each other in the last five matches. We rendered it redundant in a sense, but it has been a worthwhile venture in other seasons.

We romped away with the league – there is no other way to describe it. At the end of the season we had amassed 103 points, scored 94 goals for the loss of just 18, lost just one game and drawn only four. I even managed to score one of our goals, banging in the third in a 3–1 win over Hibs in December. Rangers were second, eighteen points behind us. In the league we had beaten them twice and drawn twice, but under new coach Alex McLeish they had become a better side in cup competitions, and the biggest disappointments of the season came when we lost to our biggest rivals in both tournaments.

The CIS Cup semi-final at Hampden was a terrific game of end-to-end stuff, even if Bert Konterman's twenty-five-yard shot in extra-time ended our hopes of a second treble. And I would rather draw a veil over the Scottish Cup Final of that year. Just twelve days before the match there had been an explosive encounter between us at Parkhead, the 1–1 scoreline concealing a real battle which saw Johann Mjallby, John Hartson and Fernando Ricksen sent off. The final continued in the same vein with the tackles flying in and five goals in all, one each from John Hartson and Bobo Balde for us and Rangers scoring through a superb free-kick from Barry Ferguson and two from Peter Lovenkrands, who headed the winner in the dying seconds.

We had been close to a second treble, but it was a case of 'so near and yet so far', and in any case we had the league championship to comfort us. But I suspect most Celtic fans will remember that season for our amazing adventures in Europe against the cream of continental football.

Our first Champions League match was against the might of Juventus in Turin. The opening match was supposed to have been against Rosenborg of Norway but the game was scheduled for 12 September 2001 and we all know what happened the previous day. Of course, no one wanted to play in the wake of the events in the USA. Like everyone else, we had all been stunned by the images from New York, Washington and Pennsylvania and agreed with Uefa's decision to cancel the matches scheduled for that night. I do wonder if things might have gone differently for us in the tournament had we started at home, but we will never know.

Juventus were expected to attack us and score at will, but for the first forty-three minutes, it would have been difficult for an observer to say which team was the home side. We contained them comfortably and might have scored after thirty-two minutes when I crossed to Chris Sutton. His downward header looked to be going in until their goalkeeper Gigi Buffon somehow got back to the ball to make an incredible save.

Against the run of play, they scored with a breakaway goal through David Trezeguet just before the interval and during half-time Martin told us just to carry on playing as we had been doing. They put us under pressure in the second half and Trezeguet scored a second, but we just would not give up and got one back from Stan Petrov's twenty-five-yard free kick.

Edgar Davids of Juventus was then sent off for a second yellow card, but he could have gone earlier for one of a rash of late tackles. With five minutes left, Alessandro Birindelli brought down Chris in the penalty box and Henrik made no mistake from the spot. We thought we had salvaged a draw but in injury-time Nicola Amoruso went down in the area after Joos Valgaeren got near enough for the Italian to be able to dive spectacularly. I couldn't believe it when German referee Helmut Krug pointed to the spot. It was the most blatant dive I think I have ever seen but he had fooled the referee. Instead of getting a yellow card, Amoruso was able to score from the spot and give his side a totally undeserved victory. Martin had remonstrated with the officials so loud and long that he was sent to the stand and his emotions were still boiling over some minutes later, as television viewers saw in a memorable interview.

In the dressing room there was just an air of disbelief. We had come so close to a result against the Italian legends, but had been robbed by a dive. No one blamed Joos at all, but he was inconsolable.

However, we had proven that we were able to match the best in Europe, and a week later we showed that at home we would always be a formidable test. Martin was banished to the stand for one match by Uefa, but he had done all his homework on Porto and we were more than ready for the Portuguese champions, including their cynical tough-tackling ways.

We had several chances which went astray before Henrik pounced on a loose ball in their box and put us ahead after thirty-six minutes. Celtic being Celtic, we went chasing a second when it might have been better to contain them. Several times we came close but their goalkeeper Sergei Ovchinnikov was outstanding and we did leave ourselves exposed at the back, Ibarra hitting the post.

However, we hung on for the win which put us back in with a chance of qualifying for the second stage. Our next fixture was also at home, although the match against Rosenborg was in doubt after the invasion of Afghanistan made every packed football stadium supposedly a terrorist target.

We were glad when the game went ahead, because even though it was no classic, we took all three points thanks to an Alan Thompson free-kick in the twentieth minute. With results elsewhere going in our favour, suddenly we were top of the group.

Suddenly it all went flat. We just did not get out of the traps in Portugal and Porto beat us 3–0, which meant we really needed a result in Norway. Rosenborg's striker Harald Brattbakk had spent a relatively unhappy eighteen months at Parkhead but had won undying fame as the man who scored the goal which clinched the 1998 SPL title, ending Rangers' run of championships.

We found Hell in Norway – literally so, as it's a village near Trondheim which we passed through. And Harald inflicted purgatory on us with two first-half goals which we just could not match. From topping the group we were now in third and would need a miracle to qualify.

Yet we so nearly gained that miracle. On one of the greatest of all European nights at Parkhead, we shared seven goals with Juventus in a match that had everything. Martin had reminded us how close we had come to beating them in their own Stadio delle Alpi and he instilled a fearlessness in us so that we attacked them from the start.

It nearly backfired as Alessandro del Piero put them ahead with a brilliant free-kick after nineteen minutes, but with Lubo Moravcik calling the shots we just charged at them incessantly and Joos Valgaeren was the most delighted man in Parkhead when he headed home Lubo's sublime chip after twenty-four minutes. No one had faulted him for the penalty in Turin, but he was still very glad to get his own back.

Some of our football that night was breathtaking, and we fully deserved to take the lead through Chris Sutton on half-time, his header from Lubo's corner firing in like a bullet. In the dressing room we were all exhorting each other to keep going, though we did not know that in Portugal, Rosenborg were giving Porto a real scare.

Juventus brought on David Trezeguet and the brilliant Frenchman almost turned the game in their favour, scoring a fine equalizer five minutes into the half. But we were still in control of midfield and Lubo was proving deadly in setpieces. When his corner found Sutty in the fifty-seventh minute, the Italian defence fouled him to prevent a goal chance and Henrik put us ahead from the spot. Our fourth was also set up by Lubo, his free-kick being headed out to Chris who hit a stunning volley on the turn. It was a fantastic goal, worthy of winning any match. Even though Trezeguet snatched his second and their third after seventy-seven minutes, we had won a brilliant victory over the Italian giants.

Yet even as the final whistle sounded we knew it had all been in vain. The subdued applause told us what we did not want to know – Porto had squeezed through against Rosenborg and we were out of the Champions League. Nine points would normally be enough to make the second stage in most groups and most years, but it was not enough for us in 2001.

But we were not out of Europe. As the team in third place,

we went into the Uefa Cup as consolation and found ourselves drawn against very tough opponents – Valencia of Spain.

Over there we were without Didier Agathe, Joos Valgaeren, Alan Thompson and Chris Sutton, but Rab Douglas had his best match for Celtic and pulled off save after save as we kept them to a single-goal advantage.

Back at Parkhead, we had to be cautious as they were very dangerous on the break, but we created enough chances to win the tie several times over, though we only took one – who else but Henrik, with a brilliant curling shot in first-half injury-time.

With the fans roaring us on, we almost snatched victory late in extra-time, when Santiago Canizares foiled John Hartson. The season before, Valencia had lost the European Cup final on penalties, but this time it was to be us who suffered that particular agony, losing 5–4 in the shoot-out. It was cruel and it was heartbreaking, especially as I thought we had done enough to justify victory. Celtic were out of Europe before Christmas again, yet I was sure that we had acquitted ourselves so well that we would do better in the following seasons. In fact, I gave an interview in which I predicted that Celtic 'would soon be winning European tournaments again'. I could not have known how close that prediction would come to being true.

I am not being greedy when I say that season should have seen us win more than the league. Had we qualified for the second stage of the Champions League, I believe we would really have made our mark in Europe. As it was, we had to be content with the league title, which of course meant we had qualified for the Champions League for the 2002/03 season.

During the summer of 2002, Henrik and Johann went off to star for Sweden in the World Cup, but I had to have an operation to cure a recurring problem with my left knee. I had first had an operation on the same knee about seven years earlier when I was at Crewe, which put me out of football for fifteen weeks. That was for tendonitis and afterwards the muscle on the medial side had not developed as well as it should have done. That can happen with operations of that sort and the effect is that the kneecap eventually gets dragged out of place. It had been giving me some pain and restricting my leg movement, so now I required some remedial work, known as a lateral release. As it was my second operation, I was a bit worried about the outcome but the operation went very smoothly with the kneecap being put back into place and various other things being tidied up. My recuperation went according to plan and most of the rehabilitation work was finished by the time we returned to pre-season training, but as with any operation of that kind you feel the after-effects for a month or so.

We had enjoyed our taste of the Champions League in the 2001/02 season and we were all desperate to be involved again. We had to qualify for the group stages first, however, and in our way stood FC Basel.

Before the first match we did not know a lot about FCB, as their fans called them. Obviously, we knew they must be a very good side as they were the Swiss champions and we knew that their manager Christian Gross had managed Tottenham so we were wary of them. They had also played ten or twelve games in their season and therefore had a fitness advantage over us.

Almost from the start of the first leg, what I noticed most of all was their excellent movement off the ball. The two Yakin brothers stood out. Murat Yakin was one of the best ball-playing centre halves I had seen for a long time, and his younger brother Hakan was a terrific playmaker with a cultured left foot. Christian Gimenez was a real handful up front and Ivan Ergic, an Australian international who was on loan from Juventus, was a tremendous athlete. But those were just four of an excellent team, full of international players including about a third of the Swiss national team. Gimenez gave them the lead early doors after a fine move, but we equalized after Stan Petrov was hauled down and Henrik Larsson made no mistake from the spot.

They continued to attack but we gave as good as we got. Early in the second half I hit a shot on the rebound but it was heading wide until Chris Sutton stuck out a leg to deflect the ball into the net. Now we were ahead and looking for more goals.

Rab Douglas made a magnificent save from Hakan Yakin before something highly unusual happened – Henrik missed a penalty. Their goalkeeper Pascal Zuberbuhler dived the wrong way but Henrik's shot hit his leg.

Our nerves were not settled until our two substitutes, Steve Guppy and Momo Sylla, won us the match. Steve's cross from the left was met with perfect timing on the volley by Momo, giving Zuberbuhler no chance.

It was a great strike which gave us a cosy two-goal lead, but we were not fooled into complacency. The way they had taken the game to us had been a real surprise. That did not happen very often in a European competition at Celtic Park, so we knew we were in for a tough time in the second leg.

But we also felt strongly that we had not done ourselves justice in that first leg and were determined to show the Swiss what we could do in Basel.

Between the first and second legs, the death threats incident took place in Belfast so it would be fair to say that my mind was not entirely on my job at the time. Apart from the fact that there might well be some nutter out there looking to shoot me, or else I had been the victim of dreadful phone hoax – remember, to this day I still do not know for certain which it was – there was also all sorts of speculation in the media that Celtic were about to hand me a new contract worth £5 million. I just wish that story had come from my agent!

At that time my representative was still Mel Stein. The contract story probably came about because the club asked to see Mel. I really don't know what Celtic's intentions were at that point and the discussions came to nothing. There was a rumour that an English club wanted to buy me, but it was complete nonsense.

I tried to put aside all these distractions in the run-up to what was a hugely important match for the club.

We knew that there was a jackpot sitting waiting for us, and all we had to do was get the correct result, which in our situation was not to lose by two goals.

Most of all we knew that our supporters would be ecstatic at the prospect of the biggest names in European football making their way to Parkhead again. It was a bit like the play-off games in which I had been involved in England, only in Celtic's case the stakes were much, much higher.

After the trouble in Belfast, my return to the dressing room at Celtic Park was always going to be an interesting experience. I wondered how the players would react, though I was always confident of their support. For me it was just a relief to get back to Parkhead and play for Celtic again.

Of course, as soon as I walked back in, the banter began, led by the manager. 'Ah, Neil, so you got my phone call, then?' said Martin. And big Chris Sutton joined in, having seen the interview with Adrian Logan which had been conducted at my parent's house.

'Where did you get that settee? *The Antiques Roadshow*?' Yes, it was nice to be back among friends . . .

After grinding out a 1–0 victory against Partick Thistle, we flew out to Basel on the Monday, where as usual we visited their stadium for training for an hour the day before the match.

I do not know if it was a reaction to all the events of the previous ten days, but on the day of the game itself I fell into a deep depression. It was as bad as I had ever experienced and I just wanted to lie in my hotel room with the curtains closed and keep the world outside. I had an overwhelming feeling of helplessness and just could not see how I was going to be able to leave the room, never mind play that night. About three or four hours before the match I called Dr McDonald to my room and told him what was happening and that I was convinced I could not play.

For the first time, my depression was so overwhelming that I simply could not face the prospect of doing my job and I was determined not to play. I said to him 'I just can't do it Roddy, I just can't go out there tonight.' Slowly and patiently he talked me round, eventually persuading me that I should play. After the match I was not sure that I had done the right thing in playing as I did not perform to my usual standard.

In fact very few of us played well that night. The St Jakob stadium was smaller than Celtic Park, but their fans made just as much noise as ours did at Parkhead. Although that did not affect us as we were all experienced players, the early goal which Gimenez scored most certainly did have an effect. We were stunned, frankly, and promptly conceded another so that we were 0–2 down after just twenty-two minutes.

The second goal by Hakan Yakin was a very poor one for us to concede. We had started with four centre-halves across the back four – Joos Valgaeren, Johann Mjallby, Bobo Balde and Ulrik Laursen – so to lose a goal from a corner was really not very clever at all.

After that we were chasing the game, but they were just as competent in defence as they were going forward and it was really difficult to break them down. Martin made changes for the second half, bringing on Steve Guppy and Didier Agathe and their speed down the wings certainly changed things for the better. And remember, we only needed one goal to go through.

We started pegging them back and Steve in particular gave the full-back a terrible time, getting in the crosses which were his trademark throughout his career. I remember us getting three decent chances, but the goalkeeper was in inspired form and saved at point-blank range on one occasion. Near the end, Chris Sutton almost pulled it out of the bag with a tremendous shot which looked as if it was going in, only for the ball to curl in its path and shave the outside of the post. We never did get the breakthrough, and that inch or so by which Chris missed a clinching goal almost typified our experience in Europe until then. We always seemed to get close to the finishing line but were never quite able to get across it, as happened in Turin and Lyon. If only we had got the breaks every team needs, I am convinced that we could have enjoyed a very good run in the Champions League.

At the end we all trudged off and we were on the chartered plane home a couple of hours after the final whistle. It was a very quiet aircraft which went back to Glasgow that night.

There was just a dreadful feeling of frustration that we had come so close to qualifying only to go out of the Champions League on the away goals rule. It was calculated that the club would lose at least £10 million because of our defeat by Basel and so it felt as if we had torn up the winning ticket in the Lottery. Basel were reportedly on £17,000 per head to beat us and qualify, but we were on good bonuses as well. As professionals you do know immediately that such a defeat is going to cost you hard cash. Players tend not to have too much to do with the business side of running a club, but we all knew how important a good run in Europe was to Celtic. Scottish clubs always start with a handicap because they do not have access to the funds which television brings to the English Premiership. The other clubs from the bigger leagues in Europe also generate vast sums from their national television deals, so it is vitally important for Celtic to be in the Champions League at every opportunity. When we lost to Basel we knew just how bad a setback it was to everyone at the club, especially those who had to deal with the financial side of things. But it was about much more than money – Celtic would be missing from club football's biggest show on earth and that was a massive disappointment to us all.

We did not know what lay ahead of us at that time other than the draw for the Uefa Cup, which would be our consolation for not making the Champions League. What a consolation it would be – worthy of a chapter all of its own.

CHAPTER TEN

I was in Seville

The Champions League is the Holy Grail in European football, the 'blue chip' tournament to which the best clubs always aspire. We very much looked upon the Uefa Cup as 'second best', though not quite the joke tournament some people called it. Funnily enough, even after everything that happened and all the fantastic events of Seville, the loss to Basel still rankles with a lot of us. If we did so well in the Uefa Cup, just how far could we have gone in the Champions League?

Back in Scotland there was the usual knee-jerk reaction that the team needed to be changed and Celtic should spend vast sums the club did not possess on players who would supposedly strengthen an ageing squad. It was just the usual hyperbolic punditry which we all dismissed as nonsense and certainly the manager, although obviously deeply disappointed, came out in support of all of us. As usual, Martin knew how to read the feelings in the dressing room and how to keep us together for the tasks ahead. There was also a sniffy attitude on the part of some pundits that if we could not beat the champions of Switzerland, what chance would we have against some of the more prestigious sides in Europe who were also heading into the Uefa Cup.

In a way it was comforting that FC Basel went on to do so well in the initial group stages of the Champions League. Indeed, they almost qualified from the second group stage as well, leading Liverpool 3–0 at one stage before the Reds came back to earn a 3–3 draw. Basel thus proved what we knew from our meeting with them, that they were an excellent side full of good players led by a fine manager. Of course, as we watched them prosper our feelings might have been 'that should have been us!' But by then we were well into a Uefa Cup adventure in which Liverpool would figure.

After we were drawn against FC Sudova of Lithuania, I remember saying that we would have to concentrate on doing our best in the league and go as far as we could in the Uefa Cup. The championship was always our priority, as that would gain us entry into the Champions League.

None of us really envisaged at that point just how far we would go in the Uefa Cup, but the philosophy of the manager was that we entered every tournament with the intention of winning it. The point was we were still in Europe and could still look forward to some of those great nights at Celtic Park which were the highlights of our season. The question was how many would we enjoy?

Our reaction when the name of Sudova came out of the draw was simply 'Who?' None of us had ever heard of them and I have to say that after playing them we were none too impressed. If they had been playing in Britain I suspect they would have been stuck in a part-time league and when they arrived at Parkhead for the first leg they seemed to treat the tie as a big day out.

At the time, there was a lot of nonsense in the media about Henrik suffering from a goal 'famine' – he must have gone a whole two matches without scoring – but he soon put that right. We actually missed five or six chances before Henrik scored after sixteen minutes. He completed his hat-trick before half-time and Stan Petrov, Chris Sutton, Paul Lambert, John Hartson and Joos Valgaeren all scored as well. Sudova nabbed one in the last minute to make the score 8–1. The tally of goals was a real confidence booster for all of us and gave us a lift just when we needed it.

The second leg was a stroll, David Fernandez scoring his first for the club and Alan Thompson grabbing the second in a game which saw eight first-team players rested. But we were not kidding ourselves about the quality of our opponents, as we knew that we had been handed the nearest thing to a 'gimme' that you will ever get in Europe.

There was certainly nothing easy about the next club we played in the tournament. I can remember the buzz that erupted when the draw paired us with Blackburn Rovers. There was just huge excitement all around Parkhead from the moment we learned who our opponents were to be. Whenever Celtic play an English club it is always going to be tagged the Battle of Britain and there is nothing our supporters like better than a trip south of the border to play one of the big English clubs. Drawing Blackburn Rovers at that time had an added spice to it because their manager was Graeme Souness, the man who had set Rangers on the road to their nine-in-a-row success. He was still something of a hate figure to the Celtic fans, which is part and parcel of life long after you play for, or manage, one or other of the Old Firm duo.

But Graeme was hugely respected by everyone in football for his tremendous achievements as a player and manager, and we knew that he would like nothing more than to put one over on Martin O'Neill's Celtic. At that time, Blackburn Rovers were going particularly well and were third in the Premiership, having won the League Cup the season before. With players like Damien Duff, Andy Cole, Tugay and

Dwight Yorke plus Brad Friedel in goal, they were a very impressive side. They came to Parkhead on the back of beating Arsenal, who of course went on to win the Premiership that season. The Rovers were very confident, perhaps too much so.

There was also in the background the much-discussed possible move of Celtic to the Premiership. All sorts of topics were raised in the days running up to the match. How good was this Celtic side in British terms? Would our players rank alongside theirs in terms of quality? Could Celtic cope in the Premiership? Were the champions of Scotland any match for the third-best team in England?

Like everyone else, we players had discussed exactly how we would fare if we moved to England and the Premiership. The consensus among us was that we would be a pretty good side and get into the top six at least. Now we would be handed a very good opportunity to prove that we could indeed make a go of it if the club ever played in England.

We thumped Kilmarnock 5–0 at home as a warm-up to the midweek game and as the match approached we were all in good spirits and very much looking forward to having a go at Blackburn. Graeme Souness tried to play a few mind games with us – praising us one minute, then damning us with faint praise the next – but Martin wasn't having any of it. He kept us very much on our toes and warned us about the Blackburn manager's tactics.

On the night, Rovers played very well but we did not perform half as badly as many people subsequently made out. We had quite a lot of possession, particularly in the second half, while in the first half Brad Friedel made a couple of excellent saves. I was particularly enjoying my jousts with Tugay in midfield, but it was not a classic match by any standards. We were getting worried that it would end goalless until Henrik popped up with the winner five minutes from time.

At the final whistle we had won the game, albeit narrowly, and most importantly, we had kept a clean sheet. Yet anyone reading the papers or listening to the pundits on television and radio must have thought that we had lost, as nobody gave much for our chances at Ewood Park.

I thought we deserved the result at Parkhead and we certainly did not deserve the verdict which Graeme Souness delivered on us. It was one of the most infamous statements ever made by a visiting manager at Celtic Park and I can assure you it cost him very dear. Their captain, Garry Flitcroft, came out of the dressing room after the game when feelings were still running high and made the fatal error of repeating what his manager had said in his post-match talk to the team. 'It was men against boys out there,' Flitcroft alleged Souness to have said. No matter what Souness had said, it was entirely his prerogative to say it but Flitcroft should never have repeated that remark outside the dressing room.

It was picked up by all the newspapers who used it in their headlines. We 'boys' were more than a little upset. It gave us all the incentive that we needed to go down there and give them a beating. In the run-up to the second leg we talked about little else.

I could not believe the way we were being written off by the press, not only in England but in the Scottish newspapers as well. It just made us all the more determined to prove everybody wrong, especially Graeme Souness.

We knew in advance that the match would be televized live in England as well as Scotland, so we wanted to show the football fans down south how far we had progressed. We had dominated the game in Scotland for a couple of years but had not been given the credit we deserved. Some of the English press were very dismissive of Scottish football, making such remarks as 'a Scottish medal has all the value of something you get free in a packet of cereal' or similar insults. It was an arrogant and small-minded view and not for the first or last time such haughtiness would backfire on the English.

It was also going to help us that the second leg would be more of a British-style match, not the slow, slow, quick, quick, slow routine that we so often came up against in Europe. I thought that it would have something like the pace of a Premiership match, which would not be surprising as we had several players in our side who had played in England's top flight, such as Chris Sutton, John Hartson, Steve Guppy and myself.

We were certainly fired up in the dressing room where Martin used Garry Flitcroft's faux pas to considerable effect. In his final speech to us, Martin said 'Are you going to let them talk about you like that?' He cast his eyes around the dressing room and said 'I am looking at the big players in here that I know are going to go out there and perform.'

As we came out onto the pitch we were very aware that Celtic fans had come to Blackburn in large numbers. We knew beforehand that many thousands had travelled south with no tickets and at that point were probably trying desperately to find a pub in which to watch the game. We could also see small pockets of supporters scattered around Ewood Park, which is not the biggest or best of stadiums and only has a very good atmosphere when it is full, as it was that night.

Martin had pulled a masterstroke with the team he set out that night. The intention was to take control of the midfield, so he left out Paul Lambert and put Chris Sutton in there alongside myself and Stan Petrov, leaving Henrik and big John up front. We were confident that we had the physicality to dominate Blackburn in the middle of the park.

There was a lot of nonsense written and spoken about the fact that Paul Lambert had been left out of the side, apparently because he and I could not figure in the same midfield together. This was despite the fact that we did indeed play many times together in the same team. Against Blackburn, the manager simply wanted to pick a team to play a particular way, and as nearly always happened, he was proven correct.

We knew we could not let our fans and Scottish football down, because we really felt that we were indeed representing Scotland and the Scottish game. Before the kick-off we were all totally focused and as soon as the whistle blew, we absolutely battered them. We were in almost total control for most of the match, especially after Henrik gave us the early lead with a typically brilliant finish, dinking the ball past Friedel.

At half-time Martin exhorted us to keep going, to keep doing the same things and above all to maintain our concentration. Early in the second half Chris scored a great goal with a near-post header. It was a typical Sutty goal, the kind he scored so often when we most needed them. It was game over at that point and we retained our control until the final whistle. Indeed we could have scored several more goals as we did have the chances, especially the one which fell to big John.

When we came off that pitch, the feeling was amazing. The bhoys in the dressing room were ecstatic, but no more so than our fans outside Ewood Park. We also knew that back home it would not be just our supporters who would be delighted that we had put one over on the English. I think we showed how pleased we were in the various interviews after the game. Of course Henrik had the last word when he said it had been 'men against boys' out there. It just shows you that you should always be careful with your remarks in football, because the game has a habit of coming back and biting you.

A few people were kind enough to say afterwards that it had been my best game for Celtic. They had perhaps forgotten that I had played in the Premiership for several seasons and that gave me an advantage when it came to playing English teams. I knew the way they played and it was the sort of game that suited me; the fact it was such an important match also helped me to retain my focus throughout the ninety minutes.

In the next round we were drawn against Celta Vigo, a crack outfit from Spain, so we knew we were in for a tough assignment, perhaps even harder than Blackburn. History was against us because no Celtic side had ever put out a Spanish side over two legs in a European knockout competition. There was also the fact that Celtic had not remained in Europe after Christmas for something like twenty-three years.

Vigo were going well in La Liga and of course in subsequent seasons would do very well indeed in the Champions League. They had an uncompromising streak in them, with three or four players who were hard and seasoned after years of playing in a top league. They also had some very skilful players, such as Lopez, Edu and Silvinho, and Luccin in midfield. We knew that we would have to take a lead to Spain as they had a very good home record.

On the night of the first leg we almost lost a goal in the opening seconds. I can still see Silvinho haring away down the right wing and sending in one of his lethal crosses but Lopez messed up his shot and Rab Douglas saved it. We settled down quickly after that and began to play some good football and boss the game.

I cannot recall them getting a real chance after that initial opening and our game plan worked almost to perfection as we gobbled them up at the back and pressed forward in midfield against their anticipated deep defence. Martin always liked us to play a pressure game and the pace of our play did not suit them at all.

Yet the goals would not come and I could sense the frustration in the team and among the fans as Vigo proved just what tough nuts they were. Martin was also getting upset, leaping about the technical area even more than normal. The referee on the night was a Frenchman called Claude Colombo and, in my opinion, he was a bit of a disaster who really could not cope at that level. He ended up sending Martin to the stands three minutes from time which of course attracted an automatic touchline ban later on in the tournament.

Once again we had Henrik to thank for our win. He popped up to score in the fifty-second minute with a vital header. Having made the breakthrough, I felt we would go on and score more, but though we could and should have scored at least another couple of goals, all we had to show at the end of ninety minutes was that solitary strike.

In the circumstances we were delighted to come away with a 1–0 win. More than a few pundits were ready to write us off, however, no doubt reckoning that Vigo would be too powerful for us in Spain, while our loss to Rangers a few days previously was also thought to be a crippling blow – but what did the pundits know about that Celtic side?

We might have anticipated some decent weather in Vigo, but when we got there we found it was a cold December evening. There had been some very heavy rain and the pitch had soaked it up so conditions were not exactly conducive to silky football.

Our main aim was to avoid losing an early goal, but even if we did concede a goal we knew that we only needed to score one and they would have to get three. It looked bad for us when Mora Nieto Jesuli scored after twenty-three minutes with a deflected shot. But we had no intention of giving up and nearly fifteen minutes later Ulrik Laursen hit a long free-kick to big John and he did his usual trick of shielding the ball from the defender and backing into him before turning and unleashing an unstoppable shot into the bottom corner. The Spaniards protested vehemently to the referee that John had committed an offence, but we had the away goal we needed and from then on it really was backs-to-the-wall stuff.

About ten minutes into the second half, I pulled a hamstring. Any footballer or athlete who has suffered such an injury will know the feeling – it's a bit like what you imagine the pain would be like from being shot in the back of the leg. You realize instantly what has happened and know that you will not be able to carry on. It probably happened because it was a cold December night and the pitch was so heavy and I had felt a touch of cramp just before the injury occurred. There was nothing I could do except lie there and wait for the medical people to arrive. There are few worse feelings in the game than being stretchered off the pitch. To make things worse, for some reason we were unable to make a substitution straight away. The ball was back in play and we just could not get Paul Lambert onto the field.

As I was being carried down the tunnel on the stretcher, I could hear the crescendo of noise from the Spanish crowd behind me and I knew that they had scored. Benny McCarthy's goal from a Lopez cross meant they needed just one more goal to go through.

Those players who have suffered an injury and have had to wait in the dressing room for treatment will know what an agony I suffered for the next half hour. Sometimes you are lucky and there might be a radio to tell you what is going on in the match that you have just departed, but mostly you have to rely on the noise of the crowd. The worst thing of all is the feeling of helplessness that you can do nothing to affect events outside, while you also know that you are going to miss important games in the weeks ahead. I was pretty certain I had a bad tear and that I was looking at about four to six weeks out, which was depressing enough, but I could also tell from the crowd noises that Celta Vigo were pressing for the third goal.

It was truly horrible to be lying in that dressing room with my leg swathed in ice. All I could do was cross my fingers and pray while the boys clung on desperately to our aggregate lead. Eventually the final whistle was blown and I could hear the noise of our supporters celebrating before the lads came pouring into the dressing room in a high old state. We were taking Celtic further in Europe than any previous squad had done for twenty-three years, and we had finally laid the bogey of being unable to conquer Spanish opposition. It was a very happy flight home to Glasgow, even if I was wrapped up and immobilized. I was in some pain, but I knew that at least I had more European games ahead.

Being in Europe after Christmas was a huge psychological boost to us, but there was no real feeling around Celtic Park that we could go all the way and win the trophy. We were confident in our own abilities but there were a lot of truly formidable sides left in the Uefa Cup at that stage, so a lot would depend on the luck of the draw.

Lady Luck seemed to have deserted us as we were promptly matched against FC Stuttgart, one of the top sides in Germany, who were well-known for their pace and flair and were not really a typical German side. Their manager Felix Magath had put together quite an accomplished side who were going well in the Bundesliga at the time. They had a big centre-forward in Kevin Kuranyi who was a real danger and in Alexander Hleb they had the best player to come out of Belarus, a terrific playmaker who of course is now with

Arsenal. He was a fantastic footballer, one of the best that I have ever played against and their top man by a mile. He had the ability to run at you with the ball or make the telling pass, as well as score goals, and he showed all of his skills against us.

We had suffered a real hammer blow earlier when Henrik broke his jaw playing against Livingston. We were certainly going to miss him against Stuttgart and big John was also out, but that gave the chance to Shaun Maloney to show what he could do on the European stage. He played up front alongside Chris Sutton while Stan, Paul and myself played in midfield, with Didier Agathe and Alan Thompson patrolling the wings.

Such was the reputation of the Germans coupled with the loss of our two main goalscorers that once again we were written off by the pundits. It did not bother us that we were the underdogs in many people's eyes. In fact, the role quite suited us.

On the night of the first leg, things did not seem to go our way at first, but gradually we got into the game, especially when their big centre-half Marcelo Bordon got himself sent off after seventeen minutes for a 'last man' foul on Stan Petrov. Referee Pierluigi Collina was the best in the world at that time and he didn't hesitate before making his decision.

However, Stuttgart shocked us with a classic counterpunch after twenty-seven minutes when Kuranyi headed low past Rab. Not only were we a goal down, but they had the vital away score.

It was then that we dug deep into the reserves of resilience we had developed as a team. Paul Lambert got us back into the match with an absolutely beautiful goal, Shaun Maloney chesting the ball down and Paul stroking it into the corner. Shaun had not played that much European football, but he showed what he could do on the big stage with a very good strike that sent us into the dressing room leading 2–1 at the end of an eventful first half.

We had our tails up and the crowd were behind us all the way as we dominated the second half. Stan scored a crucial third goal after seventy minutes with a well-taken effort which beat their goalkeeper at the near post. A 3–1 victory was all we could have asked for, especially after conceding the opening goal, and we were confident that we could score in the return leg in Germany, meaning they would have to score four against us. Little did we know that scoring would be the order of the night in Stuttgart.

Uefa had changed the system for the draw, so we knew that whoever got through would be playing Liverpool or Auxerre in the quarter-final, with Liverpool the hot favourites to qualify. It was a huge incentive for us, as we knew that a tie against the Reds would be titanic for everyone involved.

We were fired up from the start in Stuttgart and thoroughly deserved our magnificent opening goal from Alan Thompson who just threw himself at Didier Agathe's cross to head the pall past Timo Hildebrand with just twelve minutes gone.

Didier was on fire in that first half. He flew down the wing time after time and they had no answer to him. Two minutes after the first goal, on one of his rampages he rounded the full-back and cut the ball back to Chris Sutton who smacked it high into the net from five yards for our second. We were now 5–1 ahead on aggregate, but Stuttgart were not finished. They pulled one back just before half-time and then embarked on a rousing comeback.

At half-time we knew they still needed to score four more, so it was a case of telling each other to keep our heads. We did lose some of our concentration towards the end and you cannot afford to do that against teams in Europe, but their two goals from Hleb and Mutzel were never going to be enough.

Pundits said if the match had gone on they would have knocked us out, but the fact is we were too good for Stuttgart over 180 minutes. It was a tremendous scalp for us to take and showed how far we had come as a team, because they went on to perform very well in the following season's Champions League.

It was a remarkable feat for Celtic to make the quarter-finals of the Uefa Cup, but the real bonus was that we would meet Liverpool for Battle of Britain Mark II. They had beaten Auxerre and now we had another English team to face with all the attendant hype that would bring, only this time, with all due respect to Blackburn, we were playing one of the giants of football, a side with a great European tradition who had won the Uefa Cup two seasons previously in an unforgettable final against Alaves of Spain.

Liverpool were also in the middle of a terrific run, having gone eleven games unbeaten and won the Worthington Cup by beating Manchester United in the final. Most people wrote off our chances long before the first leg, saying it was a foregone conclusion, not least because they had players of the calibre of Steven Gerrard, Michael Owen and two of my former colleagues, Danny Murphy and Emile Heskey.

Liverpool were undoubtedly a very classy outfit, but we had no qualms about facing them, even though the tie came at an unbelievably tough time for us, which saw us play Rangers twice and Liverpool twice in the space of a fortnight. We beat Rangers convincingly on the Sunday, with big John scoring the only goal of a game we dominated. It was a terrific performance which set us up wonderfully for the first leg on Thursday 13 March.

The days leading up to the match were some of the most

extraordinary of my career. The media attention was unprecedented for a game outside the Champions League and the demand for tickets was such that I'm sure we could have sold out Celtic Park two or three times over. As it was, we walked out to a full house of 60,000, and when Gerry Marsden led the singing of 'You'll Never Walk Alone', the anthem of both clubs, the noise was deafening.

The Celtic fans were even more ecstatic when Henrik, back playing just five weeks after breaking his jaw, gave us the lead inside two minutes. I thought we would go on and score more, but Liverpool steadied themselves and showed what a good team they were by coming back at us and retaining possession. Emile Heskey's goal fifteen minutes before half-time was a sickener for us and the second half was a strange sort of deflated period in which neither side created too many chances, the best of them probably falling to Michael Owen with Rab Douglas pulling off a fine save.

There was a crazy incident late on, when El Hadji Diouf spat on one of our fans. I cannot abide footballers who spit on opponents; to lose your rag and gob on a fan is just beyond the pale and he was rightly prosecuted for the offence.

Liverpool were obviously the happier team having gained the away goal, but we were never anything less than confident that we could go to Anfield and get a result. But on the Sunday we suffered a real blow to our hopes for the season as we lost the League Cup Final to Rangers.

We were gutted to lose that match, so it is a testament to our mental strength that we were able to pick ourselves up in the days before the trip to Anfield.

Again all the questions were raised – would we collapse before a team with such a prestigious record in Europe? Could Celtic really match the Premiership's best and therefore be able to play in it?

Gerard Houllier tried a bit of psychology by saying that qualifying for the Champions League was more important than progress in the Uefa Cup, but he was not fooling anyone – everyone at Liverpool knew the game was of massive importance, a Scotland v England clash that was beamed live to all of Britain and beyond.

Compare Houllier's approach with that of Martin O'Neill. Everyone, but everyone, had predicted our demise, but at that point Martin showed his mettle. In the dressing room before the match he gave us an unforgettable talk. I personally do not think we needed that much motivation as we were all sure of ourselves and positive that we would compete and get a result. Yet Martin's words inspired us to even greater heights of determination. He looked around the dressing room and pointed out young Shaun Maloney. 'This is a European quarter-final and this boy is only nineteen, but he might never get this opportunity again.' He looked around the older guys and added: 'You guys in your thirties probably won't get the opportunity again to prove a point, to prove to England and Europe that you deserve respect, and that you are worthy of a place in the semi-finals.' He made his points tellingly in his usual manner and did so in only two or three minutes, yet by the time he had finished we were ready to go out and run through brick walls if we needed to.

Of all the European matches I have played in, this was the highlight. To go to Liverpool and not only win, but beat them convincingly, was historic for Celtic and all of us who played that night.

It was no surprise after Martin's team talk that we started the game really well, though watching the video of the match later, we seemed to take the commentators and pundits aback. Our display was not in the script, but by the time we scored our first goal just before half-time we were convincingly on top. Our goal was a strange one, scored from a free-kick by Alan Thompson, their wall all jumping up at the same time and the ball slipping under them and by Jerzy Dudek.

By then we had control of the midfield and throughout the second half we were restricting them to long-range efforts. I particularly remember Rab Douglas saving a thirty-yard effort from Steve Gerrard and thinking 'that's the nearest they'll get'. When John Hartson struck a magnificent goal from twenty yards out, we knew we had won the Battle of Britain II.

To be in that dressing room afterwards was to know that you had been part of something very special. Everyone was higher than kites and for the first time we were saying to ourselves 'We can do this, we can go all the way.'

I distinctly recall the looks on the faces of the English journalists when we came out into the mixed zone where the media interview players after European matches – they were absolutely gutted and it showed.

We had made most of them eat their words. I wondered if any of them would have the guts to explain to their readers why they had so confidently predicted a Liverpool slaughter of Celtic and how they had got it so spectacularly wrong.

Our fans were also beginning to believe that something wonderful was about to happen. They had packed Anfield – everywhere you looked around the stadium there were green and white scarves – and there were many thousands scattered across Liverpool, all of them determined to be there and be part of a unique occasion.

We particularly appreciated the fact that our huge travelling support all behaved themselves, the affinity between them and the Liverpool fans helping to make it an unforgettable night for everyone connected with Celtic Football Club.

We were now just two games away from the final and

we certainly thought we had the best of the draw in facing Boavista of Oporto, because the other semi-final featured Italian giants Lazio against the best team in Portugal, Boavista's city neighbours Porto FC.

We did not know much about Boavista at first, but we knew they were no mugs. There was a subtle difference in the run-up to the first leg at Parkhead. For the first time since Sudova, we entered a tie as favourites, and while it did not make any difference to our preparation, there was certainly increased expectation on the part of the Scottish media and our supporters.

Maybe we responded to that mood, because we started that first leg quite brilliantly. We could and perhaps should have been two up by half-time, not least because Belgian referee Frank van Bleeckere turned down two good penalty claims. However, Boavista were proving unexpectedly difficult to break down. From the first whistle they made their game plan clear, which was to defend in depth and boot the ball anywhere to clear their lines – up the park or into the stand, it didn't seem to matter to them. Sometimes such teams can be the most awkward to deal with and there is always the chance that a side playing in that style will break upfield and score.

Of course, it didn't really help matters that we gifted them the opening goal. Early in the second half a tame cross came in and Joos Valgaeren stuck out a leg as Rab came to collect it, the ball squirming into our net. It was just one of those things that happens in football and nobody was to blame, but it summed up the way the night was going for us.

Yet as often happens in football, the goal changed everything. We charged up the park a minute or so later, I swung in a cross and Stan laid it on a plate for Henrik to strike home. Surely now we would go on and win.

To my utter annoyance, I was booked when I gave away a

tame free-kick which was in range for Pedrosa, one of their specialists. I remember praying 'please God don't let them score from this', and somebody up there must have heard me as big Rab made a fine save, much to my relief.

We had another couple of penalty claims turned down and I couldn't help notice that our supporters were getting anxious. When we were finally awarded a penalty it looked as though we would at least take a lead into the second leg, but their goalkeeper made a superb save from Henrik's effort.

At the final whistle we had come from behind to gain a draw, but it did not feel like a normal 'escape'. We knew we should have beaten them and we were all intensely frustrated.

The most annoying thing was their cynicism – something which we would discover was not confined to one half of Oporto's old firm. Every chance Boavista got to waste time they took full advantage of it. They would put their foot on the ball and kill the tempo of the play, while every foul on them was a cue for a display of pain, grief and woeful acting that would not have been out of place in one of those awful Mexican soap operas which Chris Tarrant used to mock on television. The more they do it, the more frustrated you become and the harder you try, instead of just trying to stay relaxed and cope with their shenanigans. By and large, it is not in the nature of British footballers to employ such tactics, so we vowed that in the second leg we would make them pay.

The doom-and-gloom brigade were falling over themselves to say that our bubble had burst and the final was now beyond us, that we had blown our chance of making the final. But perhaps curiously, that was not the feeling in the squad. We knew that after seeing them up close, we were the better players and the better team, and it would be a matter of grinding out a result over there and getting an away goal as early as we could.

Apart from Boavista's cynical ploys, the most disappointing element of the night was that a small section of our support took to booing me – well, why should they be different from everybody else in Scotland? Seriously, though, it was depressing enough that the team had underperformed without taking some personal grief. In previous rounds they had got on Didier Agathe's back when he didn't go haring down the wing beating three or four players every other minute. It just wasn't feasible for him to pull off those amazing runs every time, yet a small group started giving him stick and then it spread – I suppose it's the mob mentality to join in and kick a man when he's down. Other players got 'the bird' too, so in that semi-final first leg it must have been my turn.

Afterwards I was incandescent with rage and couldn't hide it. Yes, I had made a mistake or two, but I was doing my best for the club in the semi-final of a European tournament – something which, don't forget, no Celtic fan under the age of thirty had seen the club in – yet I was given that sort of treatment. I felt like screaming 'Give us a break.' I know full well that I take criticism from fans for playing the ball sideways or backwards but I will not knowingly give away possession. As for that night against Boavista, most of the problem was that we had no choice but to play safety first because they were getting everybody behind the ball, kicking everything that moved yet remaining dangerous on the break.

In fairness, the jeers stemmed from the fact that our fans want us to attack all the time, but in the modern game against European opponents in particular, there are times when you just have to move the ball around and be very patient as you wait for the gaps to open up. Sometimes our fans want the ball up the other end of the pitch regardless of the niceties of a situation. It's the way they are and they are not going to change, neither would I want them to, but that night a small section of the crowd went too far in venting their displeasure at me when all I was trying to do was win the game for them. Having said that, there was a big section of the crowd who realized what was going on and they started cheering me and singing my name, which gave me a real lift.

In recent years at Parkhead, I've noticed that our fans can go quiet for long periods. Even if we are three goals up they will be restless and you can clearly sense it down on the pitch – it's almost as if they are bored waiting for something to happen.

That night against Boavista the crowd was rightly anxious as it was a semi-final, but the fans should realize that it is those times when players need their support most of all, instead of picking on individuals and having a go at them. Most Celtic fans do appreciate the need to get behind the players at all times, but it is painfully obvious when an individual player is being heckled and we can hear the discord in the support when others try to back the player who has been singled out.

Before the second leg, as usual we visited the stadium twenty-four hours before the match. I remember being unimpressed with the ground as it was being rebuilt in advance of the European Championships of 2004. Both ends behind the goals were empty and there were just the two main stands.

I knew immediately that it would mean a different atmosphere from the one we were used to in the big cup ties, but of course once again our fans seemed to infiltrate most corners of the ground.

In many ways it was a typical semi-final. They set their stall out to defend the away-goal advantage which they had gained in the first leg. Indeed, it looked as if they were going to settle for a 0–0 draw as they did not come out to play any sort of open football. It was all nervy, edgy stuff, with neither side wanting to risk giving anything away. But we knew we had to get a goal and as the game wore on we began to wonder where it would come from as it was really difficult to break down their defence.

Paul Lambert went off injured and Chris Sutton came on, just a few weeks after breaking his wrist. Then enter Henrik Larsson – who else? The goal in the eighty-first minute summed up the tie in many ways. Henrik tried to play a one-two with big John but the ball struck the defender before rolling into Henrik's path. He actually mishit his shot but the goalkeeper had already decided to go one way when the ball went the other.

It was one of those moments in a career when time seems to stand still. I was thinking 'is it in or not?' when the massive roar from our fans told us what we wanted to know. If I could have reached Henrik I could have kissed him. Over at the dug-out I could see Martin and Robbo and all our staff leaping about like mad things. It was an incredible feeling to know that we were just nine minutes away from a European final. It was a mixture of elation and apprehension as we knew we were nearly there, but we still had to survive to the final whistle.

Those nine minutes plus four of injury-time were the longest of my footballing life. Now Boavista tried to attack but it seemed that every long ball which they hit was headed clear by big Bobo or Johann Mjallby. When the final whistle was blown, we were all ecstatic but also drained and relieved that we had finally made it.

Asked afterwards how I felt, I told the press I felt like a boxer who had taken all the punches but was still standing. The football at times had been brilliant, but the events off the pitch had been overwhelming and in many ways I was just glad to have survived it all.

On the way back home we arrived at the airport to fly out

of Portugal to be greeted by scenes out of a Beatles movie. Porto were flying in from their success against Lazio in Rome and there were thousands of people there to greet them. It was crazy stuff, everyone singing and cheering, with the Porto fans – deadly rivals of Boavista – and some of ours all queuing up to congratulate us and pat us on the back. The plane journey home was the happiest any of us could recall, but there were only three days before we had to go to Ibrox to play Rangers.

The club had asked for the game to be postponed, as it was so close to the semi-final, but the police and the SPL said no. We just had to get on with things, but in truth we were already in the realms of fantasy – Celtic had made it to a European final for the first time in thirty-three years, after a long period in which it looked as if the club would never hit such heights again. All of a sudden the loss to Basel seemed an age away.

We were now looking at an incredible end to what had been a pretty traumatic season for me personally, but nothing could have prepared us for the utterly extraordinary experience which Seville became for everybody connected with Celtic Football Club.

It really started with that match at Ibrox. We knew our fans would come up with something to taunt the Rangers support, but the sights that greeted us that day were something else.

As the team bus approached Ibrox we came up to the roundabout near the stadium. Plonked in the middle of it was a Celtic fan sitting on a deckchair pretending to sun himself. Next to him was another of our fans using a foot pump to blow up a big green inflatable Li-lo crocodile. Inside the stadium, our fans produced a torrent of beach balls and quite a few of them were dressed in ponchos and sombreros. 'We're going to Seville', they sang and when we won 2–1 we also knew we were back in with a serious chance of winning the league title again.

The weeks leading up to Seville contained the most incredible mixture of excitement and anticipation that any of us had ever experienced. Everyone has a story to tell of that time, but I recall my overwhelming feeling was that we should try and stay focused on the match and try to ignore all the hype surrounding us, though that was well-nigh impossible.

All sorts of problems emerged. It soon became clear that big John Hartson was struggling to make the final because of his recurring back injury and indeed he was eventually ruled out.

It was a blow to us as we knew we faced a really tough task. Porto were favourites and deserved to be so after the way in which they had progressed through the tournament under Jose Mourinho's guidance. Beating Panathinaikos of Greece away and thumping Lazio 4–1 in the home leg was enough to tell anyone that they were a very good side indeed, and though we knew very little about Mourinho – he was not 'the Special One' at that stage in his career – we knew that he was a fine young manager who had already led his team to the Portuguese championship that season, his first full season in charge.

We had played Porto in the Champions League the season before when we beat them 1–0 at Parkhead but lost 3–0 in Portugal, so we knew that they were a quality side full of good players such as Capucho, Deco, Costa, Valente, Costinha and Vitor Baia in goal.

Derlei was new to us, but we knew he had to be good as he was equal top scorer with Henrik in that year's Uefa Cup. Basically it was the spine of the team which would go on to win the Champions League the following season, which puts our performance against them in some perspective.

We did not vary our preparations too much. In the days before the final we watched videos of their matches, particularly observing their setpieces. It was clear that Deco was their best player, the playmaker at the heart of the team, and he would have to be carefully watched. But by and large, we spoke about and rehearsed our own game plan, as our feeling was that if we could get things right on the night we would win, no matter who we played.

As the excitement among our fans grew to a fever pitch, it became clear that we were going to have a huge following in Seville, the one question we all heard incessantly was 'Any chance of a ticket?' But we were locked away in our own wee shell for most of the time, concentrating on the job we had to do.

The media focus on us reached new and sometimes bizarre heights – for instance, I found myself drawing the prize in a raffle, though it was no ordinary one. A week or so before we went out to Seville the *Glasgow Evening Times* asked me to pick the winner of a draw for which the prize was an all-expenses paid trip including two tickets for the final, courtesy of club sponsor ntl.

I pulled the name of David Brodie from Drumchapel out of the hat and for good measure I telephoned him to tell him he had won. 'This is Neil Lennon here,' I said. Not surprisingly he didn't believe me at first, but when I said 'Did you enter an *Evening Times* competition?' he realized it was genuine. He almost deafened me down the phone with his roar when I told him he had won. There was a nice touch to David's story – he was worried about getting time off, but a colleague who was a Rangers supporter agreed to cover for him and he made it to Seville.

So did about 100,000 other fans, many of them without tickets who just wanted to be in the city along with us. We

At the gates of 'Paradise': the fans look happy that I've signed for Celtic and have finally arrived at Parkhead in December 2000.

One third of the Treble in 2001– it's my turn to show the Scottish Cup to our fans.

Champions! With Martin O'Neill, Paul Lambert and that coveted Scottish Premier League trophy.

Getting stuck into one of the Old Firm games with Emerson of Rangers.

ABOVE: Chasing the brilliant Ronaldinho in a Uefa Cup match against Barcelona.

LEFT: Challenging Juventus's Del Piero in the air in the Champions League.

The King and I: Henrik Larsson celebrates yet another goal, this time in our Uefa Cup quarter-final home leg against Liverpool in 2003.

Celebrating victory in the Battle of Britain over Liverpool in the second leg at Anfield.

LEFT: Jorge Costa getting away from us in the 2003 Uefa Cup Final against Porto FC in Seville.

BELOW: The body language says it all: Chris Sutton and I turn away in despair after Derlei scores the winner and is engulfed by his Porto team-mates.

BELOW: So near and yet so far: Uefa President Lennart Johansson presents me with my runners-up medal while the Uefa Cup is within touching distance.

The doting dad – with Alisha on holiday.

The lads on a golfing day out. From left to right, my agent Mark Donaghy, good friend Joseph Taylor, my agent and big mate Martin Reilly.

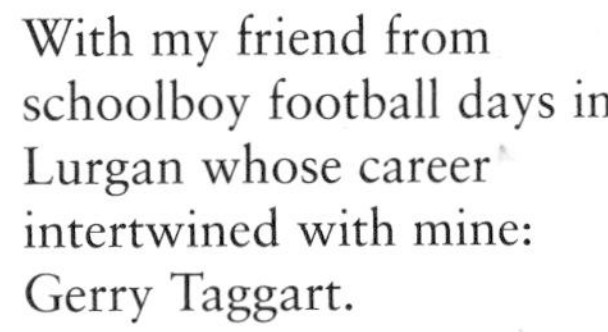

With my friend from schoolboy football days in Lurgan whose career intertwined with mine: Gerry Taggart.

Martin Reilly, myself and the rest of the tartan brigade at Martin's wedding.

ABOVE: Goodbye and thanks for everything, gaffer. Saying farewell to Martin O'Neill after the Scottish Cup Final win of 2005.

ABOVE: East End Park, Dunfermline, 19 February 2006. You'd celebrate, too, if you had just got your third goal in five years.

LEFT: Two fans who got to play for their favourite club: Roy Keane and I celebrate beating Rangers in February 2006.

ABOVE: My first trophy as captain: lifting the CIS Insurance League Cup after beating Dunfermline 3–0 at Hampden Park on 19 March 2006.

RIGHT: Gallagher, Irene and myself on the day Celtic were presented with the SPL trophy for 2005–06.

A title for the green-and-white redheads: with manager Gordon Strachan and the Bank of Scotland Scottish Premierleague trophy of 2005–06.

Champions! Billy Connolly looks on as I show the fans the Bank of Scotland Scottish Premierleague trophy.

players had no idea of the sheer numbers of people who were making the trip to Seville. It was only when we arrived in the city on the day of the final that we realized just what had happened – it seemed as though half the population of Glasgow had made it to Spain.

Among those who attended the final were my mum and dad. It was the first time they had been to continental Europe in their lives and they were accompanied by my daughter. I also paid back some of the huge debt I owed to Dessie Meginnis, the man who had started me off in football, by ensuring that he travelled from Lurgan to Seville.

Our club hotel was not far from the city, but all the wives, families and girlfriends were at a beautiful hotel a bit further out and we went down to see them the day before the match. It was all designed to keep things relaxed and happy.

The evening before the final we were taken to the stadium for the usual acclimatization visit which Uefa permits before any European tie. As we walked out onto the pitch at about 5 p.m. I was really shocked, almost physically stunned, by the sheer heat in the place. The sun was beating down and it was like standing next to a furnace. For someone like me with red hair and a pale complexion this was torture by fire. I remember turning to Steve Walford and saying 'I'm not going to be able to play in this', but he pointed out that the final would not be kicking off until 8 p.m. and it would be a lot cooler by then.

We were also disappointed by the state of the pitch which was quite firm with bald patches in places. We did our usual training routine before returning to our hotel where wee Jimmy Johnstone and Bertie Auld of the Lisbon Lions were on hand to greet us and wish us luck. Along with lifelong Celtic fan Billy Connolly they were doing interviews for television. Although it was nice to see them, we tried not to get caught up in that whole media circus – a quick drink and we were all off to bed.

We tried to keep things cool on the day of the match, though that is possibly not the most apt description of events that were played out in temperatures approaching 40 degrees centigrade.

On our arrival at the stadium a few hours before the kick-off we went out onto the pitch, again in searing heat. There were only a few fans inside at that time and Martin O'Neill came over and joked 'Lenny, there's a rumour going round that there might be a football match on here later' – as usual, his sense of humour was helping us through the events.

By the time we went back out for a warm-up, the stadium was about three-quarters full, and we were greeted by the amazing sight of our fans standing up and belting out 'The Fields of Athenry'. Every last man, woman and child was on their feet with their chests pumped out and singing for us. Even though it was still boiling hot, I swear I felt a chill run down my spine. Probably for the first time, I knew just how much this occasion meant to our supporters. And here was I, a lifelong fan myself, representing Celtic as a player. It all got to me then and it was difficult to suppress my emotions, but I had to do so as we had a final to win.

I have to confess that I was concentrating so much on the ninety minutes to come that I barely recall anything that was said to me in the minutes before the game. The pre-match ceremonies seemed to drag on but eventually the match got under way.

We did not play particularly well in the first half, but we still had a few chances. The most disappointing thing about all three goals we lost that night was that I felt that all of them could have been prevented. They opened the scoring just before half-time after Rab Douglas saved from Alenitchev but

Derlei reacted quicker than our defence to shoot home the rebound. Going in at the interval having just conceded a goal is never easy, but Martin went quietly to work, emphasizing the need to concentrate.

Cometh the hour, cometh the man, and two minutes into the second half we were level. Henrik played one of his best matches that night, taking his goals with aplomb. If you look at the first goal on video, it is all about the power and spin he generates when he heads Didier Agathe's inswinging cross. It looks as though the ball will go wide, but the curl he imparted with his head brings the ball into the goal.

Back they came and Alenitchev's goal after fifty-four minutes was a real sickener as he was given far too much space in the box.

But we only had to wait three minutes for Henrik to strike again. His second goal was all about his natural instincts in the box and his ability to seemingly suspend the laws of gravity and hang in mid-air. The header from Alan Thompson's corner flew by Baia. When Henrik got that second equalizer, we felt that things were going our way. We tired towards the end of the match, but roused ourselves as we prepared for extra-ime.

The referee, Lubos Michel of Slovakia, did us no favours. He was fussy and petty and did not deal with the antics of the Porto players. We knew they would play-act and make a drama out of everything, but we were all sickened by the extent of their cynicism, especially as extra-time wore on.

Even though big Bobo got sent off five minutes into extra-time for a second yellow card offence, we never felt that they were going to hammer us. They did not have the bulk of possession and to be honest, I felt that both sides were settling for a penalty shoot-out.

Their winner has been blamed on Rab Douglas, and even

though he did not collect Valente's chip shot as he might usually have done, I still felt we could have dealt with the ball better. Instead, Derlei nipped in and we were 2–3 down.

Walking back to the centre, I could see Alan Thompson was really down, his eyes almost filling up with tears. 'Come on,' I said, 'there's still five or six minutes left so let's just go for it.'

And we did, but to no avail. Their time-wasting became historic, but the referee just would not take action against them. I remember Ulrik Laursen brushing against their goalkeeper. He fell to the ground as if he had been shot and then got up before rolling over on the ground again. The incident had taken place in their penalty area but by the time Baia had finished rolling, he was a good five or six yards outside their box. Cue the usual rush by their players to square up to Ulrik, to try to get him booked and waste more precious time.

When Lubos Michel eventually did take action, it was to send off Valente for yet another cynical foul. That there were only four minutes of injury-time was a disgrace – their goal celebrations alone lasted two minutes.

At the final whistle we had lost by the odd goal in five. In the blink of an eye our great adventure had finished. I slumped to the ground, totally knackered. Inside I felt completely numb. The big screen in the stadium showed my face and it looked as though I was crying, but the tears did not come then, as I didn't have any in me.

'That's the end of it,' I thought. 'It's over.' There was nothing else to think or feel. I was shattered emotionally, just anaesthetized. I didn't know what to feel or how to feel it. I just wanted to get off the pitch and find refuge in the dressing room.

But then I saw Mourinho going over to shake a wee boy's hand and I was instantly raging. Their way of playing football had angered me intensely. It is nothing to do with a British stiff-upper-lip mentality but about the way football is heading – the play-acting, the time wasting, the sheer cynicism seems to have become normal behaviour for teams on the continent, and that's just not football in my book. Our fans were criticized in some quarters for booing Porto when they were presented with the cup, but our supporters were not being disrespectful. Rather, they were showing their disgust at Porto's disgraceful tactics which left a bad taste in all our mouths.

I'm still bitter about that aspect of their display. I couldn't help but give a sour laugh when I heard Mourinho criticizing Deco for his antics when Chelsea played Barcelona in the Champions League. Did the Special One not realize where Deco learned his tricks? And should he not have done something to remove that facet of Deco's play when he was his manager?

At the end, our fans then showed the world what true supporters of football are really all about. Their rendition of 'You'll Never Walk Alone' was so defiant, so proud, that even the Porto fans applauded them. There were no problems between the two rival supports in Seville, just a difference of opinion between the two teams as to how football should be played.

But the result can never be undone, and at the end I offered my congratulations to Mourinho and his men and then went off to receive my runners-up medal from Uefa President Lennart Johansson. Notice I did not say 'loser's medal' as I do not think Celtic lost much that night. In fact, we won back Europe-wide respect for a club which had not featured on the big stage for far too long. In the three years since that night, the reaction of the fans has shown that the team which took the club to Seville are now firmly in the pantheon of Celtic heroes.

Martin's reaction in the dressing room said it all. He told us 'You did not deserve to lose that match. I am so proud of you all. Let's do it again next year.' Even in the midst of a devastating defeat he was already thinking ahead.

Chairman Brian Quinn and director Dermot Desmond also came in to say how proud they were and to thank us all individually and collectively. It's been a habit of Dermot's over the years to pop in after big matches and the players do appreciate the fact that he is a fan who also has the best interests of Celtic at heart.

The rest of the evening was an anti-climax. We did the usual press interviews then got back to the hotel where my family were waiting for me. My mum and daughter gave me a hug – and I still didn't cry!

I sat up talking to my dad and Dessie for a while, but like most of the players, I soon headed for bed. We still had one last match of the 2002/03 season to play . . . and only then would the tears flow.

Looking back on that Uefa Cup run now, I wish more than anything that we could have beaten Porto that night, but I suppose I am like any other Celtic fan who made that journey to Spain. Sometimes memories are more important than trophies and at least for the rest of my life I will be able to say proudly: 'I was in Seville.'

CHAPTER ELEVEN

Trouble in the Streets

The rest of the 2002/03 season was just as much of an anti-climax as Seville. At the start of it, many people had thought that FC Basel would not be able to live with us, given our experience the previous season. As we had been doing so well domestically I can understand why people were shocked at our Champions League exit.

We were a pretty awesome side physically in those days with a real winning mentality, hammering Aberdeen 4–0 and Dundee United 5–0. It was not just Henrik who was scoring goals either. Against United, for instance, Jackie McNamara, Chris Sutton, Stan Petrov and Ulrik Laursen joined him on the scoresheet.

I remember one victory at Dens Park in September for another reason. At Croke Park in Dublin that day, my home county Armagh was playing in the All-Ireland Gaelic Football Final. My friend from my days as a Gaelic footballer, Anthony Tohill, had managed to get me a ticket so you can imagine my chagrin when our match against Dundee was switched to the Sunday. As soon as the game was over (we won 1–0), I dashed off the pitch and my dad was soon on the mobile to tell me that Armagh had won its first-ever All-Ireland title – that was a very good night!

We had a solid defence and there was also a great spine to the team. I remember saying at the time that I felt that we were as good a side as the one that had won the treble. Of course, I couldn't possibly have known how close we would come to emulating the feats of Martin's first Celtic side. It just seemed that whenever we needed a result that team could produce it, so maybe that's why there was such a feeling of dismay at our loss to Basel.

Personally speaking, however, it had been a pretty disastrous start to the season. I could well have done without the baggage of the events that happened off the field. I was still not happy with my personal fitness and sometimes when you have an operation during the close season, however minor, there can be a hangover of sorts which lasts well into the new season. That was the case with me in the latter half of 2002 and the attack of depression in Basel did not help my overall mood over a number of weeks.

It was around that time that Martin became aware of my illness. Dr Roddy McDonald explained to him exactly what was happening to me. The doc was a great help and gave me every support and understanding in my time at Parkhead with him. I was very sorry to see him leave Celtic at the end of the 2005/06 season.

I always tried to play on while ill, but one match which I did miss because I was so unwell with depression was a midweek game against Motherwell at Fir Park in September 2002. Martin had told me to take time out to get my head sorted but as we were beaten 2–1 I went straight back into the team on the Saturday when we beat Hibs 1–0.

Other occasions on which I played while suffering from depression included the very first Champions League game against Juventus. I played reasonably well in Turin after discovering that I could function on the park adequately almost by playing from memory. It was as if my body could do the necessary even though my mind wasn't always on the job. For the avoidance of doubt, I have played at least one Old Firm match while diagnosed as depressed.

I am quite sure that there are a lot of footballers and sports people who have suffered the same symptoms without actually realizing the cause. Perhaps it is caused by our adrenalin-charged lifestyle, or something else to do with the fact that we are sports people in the public eye. At the very least there should be some research into this phenomenon.

I realized during that 2002/03 season that there are times in life when you just have to knuckle down and get on with work and the basic tasks of everyday existence, no matter how bad you feel. Professional footballers are no different from the rest of the population in that respect and the good thing about playing for a club like Celtic is that there is never a dull moment around Parkhead.

There was certainly plenty of excitement for me off the field. Back in December 2001, I had had a bit too much to drink at our annual party in a Glasgow restaurant. Upon leaving, I tripped over a kerb and split my head. My girlfriend and I then went to the Western Infirmary together where I was stitched and bandaged up. A long and rambling account of my supposed activities duly appeared in the newspapers the following day. The accuracy of the reports would have been less open to doubt, and indeed might have been more entertaining, if they had stated correctly that I happened to be wearing a Robin Hood outfit at the time!

A fortnight afterwards I was in a nightclub in Glasgow when a guy started speaking to me. I was minding my own business but tried to be friendly, only for him to go on and on. Eventually one word led to another and things got out of hand. The bouncers moved in and I left for the sake of peace and quiet but next day it was reported that I had been in a brawl and been thrown out of the nightclub.

This time Martin summoned me, but after hearing my side of the story, he merely told me to watch myself and try to stay out of trouble. His words were something like 'You're thirty now.' As if I needed reminding . . .

The furore over my travails led directly to the most infamous incident in the recent history of Celtic.

In order to avoid a repeat of my troubles the previous Christmas, in 2002 we decided to get out of Glasgow and go down south for our Christmas party. Alan Thompson suggested his home city of Newcastle and organized the hotel and a restaurant for us to visit a week before Christmas. While we were on the bus heading out of Glasgow, we noticed another bus just behind us with some familiar faces on board – it was the Rangers squad, who were also heading for Newcastle for their party. On board their bus, Neil McCann used his mobile to call Jackie McNamara and warn him that the Rangers players had been tipped off that the *Daily Record*, Scotland's biggest-selling newspaper, had learned what was going on and would be in Newcastle, so they were diverting to Liverpool.

We had made firm arrangements, however, and were not prepared to break them. Perhaps naively, we thought that the old rule that newspapers left players alone on their private Christmas outing would still apply. We also thought everything would be all right if we just behaved ourselves, which, more or less, is what we did.

We had a pleasant dinner and a few beers, but when we looked back on it later we realized there had been 'plants' all over the place. For example, there were two girls with disposable cameras who asked Steve Guppy and I to pose for a picture with them – we were tipped off too late by a Newcastle United official that those girls were to be avoided. Sure enough, the snaps appeared in a newspaper the following day, making it look as if we had been out on the town with them. As for the guys pretending to be Celtic fans who kept asking loads of questions about contracts: they were just a bit too obvious.

Late in the evening, we ended up in a bar called Buffalo Joe's where there were scantily clad girls dancing on the tables. At that point we were joined by a few more lads who were known to a couple of the players. Those guys were buzzing but they weren't causing any problems.

Suddenly there was a minor altercation with a bouncer. Words were exchanged and a couple of the players were asked to leave. This annoyed the rest of us so much that we all decided to make our exit.

Outside there were photographers waiting – the whole thing was obviously a set-up. Some of the lads, including those who were not players, were so annoyed they chased the photographers and caught one on a bridge over the Tyne.

It was reported that I had run and chased people, so I must have been to Lourdes or somewhere for a miraculous cure of the hamstring I had torn against Celta Vigo just a few days before. It was still causing me pain and I was limping along most of the time.

The truth is that I walked up behind the lads and told them to make sure they didn't do anything stupid. All they did was to take the memory discs out of the photographer's camera and throw them in the river. No one was beaten up, though the photographer was so scared he dropped one of his cameras, which was then given back to him.

One of the party who wasn't a Celtic player grabbed his

other camera, but Jonathan Gould took it off him and handed it in to the police when he got back to the hotel.

A few of us carried on to another club near the river, where the police arrived about thirty minutes later. They brought the photographer with them and he picked out Johann Mjallby, Joos Valgaeren and Bobby Petta as the men who had supposedly assaulted and robbed him. Now anybody who knows Joos and Bobby will be aware that they would run a mile from trouble, while if big Johann hit you – well, you wouldn't be in a fit state to go running to the police.

The officers came over and arrested the three of them. I had seen everything that happened and told the lead police officer that they had done nothing wrong. I said that if they went outside, there would be press waiting and there would be huge trouble. But the policeman was having none of it – 'it's his word against theirs and we are arresting them so you keep out of it', was the gist of what he said.

When I tried to protest again the officer immediately put his handcuffs on me. I was stunned as all I had done was protest my friends' innocence. I was then frogmarched out of the club and guess who just happened to be up on the bridge with cameras ready? A battery of flashguns erupted and it was obvious that we had been set up from start to finish.

In the police station, Johann, Joos and Bobby were put in cells where they stayed until released on bail twenty hours later. I warned the police officer who had cuffed me that if they did not let us go, there would be a media circus outside in the morning and all sorts of questions would be asked. He said the police were just doing their job, but after about twenty minutes he put me in the squad car and took me back to the hotel.

The damage had been done, however. The next morning I was all over the front pages in handcuffs and my new

Christmas shirt – that was what really bugged me, as the shirt I thought was damned smart actually looked pretty dreadful.

The media went crazy over the story. All the television channels covered it and the newspapers all tried to outdo each other in the hysteria of their coverage. The *Daily Record* went completely over the top with a front-page headline 'Thugs and Thieves' and page after page of one-sided opinion masquerading as news. We were not so much denied the presumption of innocence as condemned without trial and executed in public.

Record editor Peter Cox then went on television and made some very uninformed comments. That was the straw which broke this camel's back – I called my lawyer. I had been suffering biased reporting ever since I arrived in Scotland and had grudgingly accepted it as part of the job, but Cox had gone way too far.

My lawyer felt I had a pretty good case, especially if we took Cox and the *Record* to the courts in England where we would get a fairer hearing. In the High Court in London, I was granted leave to sue for libel in England as the incident had taken place in Newcastle, my daughter lived in Manchester and I had the right to protect my reputation as a former Leicester player. It was still going to be a huge risk, however, but I felt I had to make a stand.

My case was considerably helped when, on the night we beat Liverpool at Anfield, Celtic's then chief executive Ian MacLeod came in to the dressing room to say all the charges had been dropped against Johann, Joos and Bobby.

The club issued a statement: 'The players are taking legal advice concerning the vicious personal attack launched by the *Daily Record* and by its editor, Peter Cox, who went on television to repeat in graphic detail what have now been found to be grossly unjustified allegations.' But for various reasons, I was the only one to continue with my case.

Meanwhile, a lot of Celtic fans organized a boycott of the *Record* and its sales fell. The real miscreant, Peter Cox, was later sacked and many commentators pointed to the 'Thugs and Thieves' reports as the start of his downfall.

In August 2004, the High Court in London was told that the *Record* had settled out of court with me. My counsel, William Bennett, said their articles were highly likely to suggest that I had robbed the photographer. The solicitor for the *Record*, Patrick Swaffer, said the paper never intended to make that suggestion against me.

The allegation was 'without foundation' and he added, the *Daily Record* offered 'sincere and unreserved apologies'. They also paid me a sum of money in damages and picked up the costs of the case. As part of the settlement, I am not allowed to disclose the amounts involved.

The money was not important, however. It had taken twenty months but I had been vindicated and could at last put that sorry episode behind me. I have no hard feelings towards the *Record*, but Mr Cox is not on my Christmas card list.

More trouble came my unsolicited way. After we had played at Motherwell in early May 2003, just a fortnight before the Seville final, I was on my way home after midnight when I stopped to pick up the girlfriend I was seeing at the time. I was parked on Great Western Road when I saw three lads walking up the street towards me. They were a bit boisterous but I thought nothing of them as they went into a fast-food shop. They came out and hailed a taxi, which swung around to face me so that the lights were shining into the car.

One of them spotted me and I thought 'Uh, oh, here we go.' Two of them came over to my car and leaned in at the window which was slightly open.

The first one said 'You're Neil Lennon, aren't you? You're shite, you are.'

'Nice people', I thought. Not.

One was a local but the other's accent gave it away that he wasn't from Glasgow. The first one made it clear he was a Rangers supporter and they then challenged me to a foot race over fifty yards – the usual wee boy nonsense you have to put up with from time to time. As my girlfriend came out to get into the car they started slagging her off, so I told them to pack it in.

One of them called me 'a f****** scumbag', so I replied 'I might be a scumbag but in the morning I'll still be a millionaire.' This witticism was lost on him – he spat on me through the window. As soon as the door was shut on my girlfriend's side I drove off, furious with rage as I cleaned up the spit.

As bad luck would have it, just a short distance on, the traffic lights had turned to red, so I had to stop. As I looked in the rear-view mirror I saw the three of them chasing after me. I knew I was in for real trouble.

They came up behind and started kicking the car, so I got out and said 'F*** off, I don't want any trouble.' To be fair, one of the three did back off, but the other two were clearly drunk and they began shouting 'Fenian b******'. As I tried to push them away from the car the Glaswegian head-butted me – the infamous Glasgow kiss.

The pain sparked me into action. I grabbed my assailant, put him down on the ground and sat on top of him. I was about to smash his head in when I noticed the blood running down from my nose onto his face and that brought me to my senses.

I also had a vision of the newspapers with banner headlines saying 'Lennon beats up Rangers fan', and that is really what made me hold back from punching him silly. My girlfriend had got out of the car to help, but the other lad pushed her over and she fell to the ground, jarring her wrist.

While all this was going on, cars were continuing to drive past us as if it was the most natural thing in the world to see a man and a woman being beaten up in the middle of a busy Glasgow street.

One woman passer-by did come over and urged me to keep cool and get away as she had seen everything and would testify on my behalf to the police. Grabbing my girl, I got into the car and drove home so we could patch ourselves up. The cut on my face wasn't too bad and I was more concerned about my female companion who was badly shaken. The witness was as good as her word and her statement and our testimony was convincing. They both pleaded guilty when the case came to court six months later.

And here's the rub. Were they neds from a sink estate out to beat up someone for cheap kicks? No, Neil MacLeod, the one who head-butted me, was a law student while Gregg Miller from Aberdeen was a medical student. Both were at nearby Glasgow University.

In Glasgow Sheriff Court, the crown accepted their pleas of not guilty to sectarian crime, but MacLeod pleaded guilty to assault and breach of the peace and was fined £700. MacLeod's lawyer Peter Watson told the sheriff it was 'a classic misjudgment involving young men and alcohol'.

Miller pleaded guilty to breach of the peace and was fined £200. His father turned out to be company director.

Sheriff John Montgomery said: 'This may have started off in good humour, but it deteriorated to the extent that it ended up in an assault. Neil Lennon was simply minding his own business, until you both proceeded to get involved.'

In court Miller was said by his lawyer to have been 'horrified' by his own behaviour. Oh, really?

The previous weekend I had reacted to being abused by Dundee fans by flipping them the bird and of course my gesture was all over the newspapers. Miller showed how real his remorse was when he told the press outside the court: 'You saw a perfect illustration at the weekend of Lennon's temperament and his intelligence.'

That was pretty rich coming from an eejit who had just been convicted of a crime in which he got drunk, chased someone along a busy city street in full view of witnesses, kicked a car, screamed sectarian abuse, was involved in an assault, frightened the wits out of an innocent woman and put his career at risk by doing so.

As there had been a suggestion that the two students could be expelled I had decided to write to the dean of the faculties at the University and ask that they be allowed to carry on with their studies in the hope that they had learned their lesson. After I read Miller's words I changed my mind.

I have no idea what happened to them, or where either of them are now. Perhaps as they have grown up they have come to see things in a more mature light and might even regret their actions that night, while I suspect their criminal records have haunted them. To me their involvement and their status was just proof that, in Scotland, bigotry knows no class barriers.

That was the worst assault committed on me, but in some ways the most frightening incident involved only curses.

I was taking Alisha and a friend of hers to Edinburgh for the day when I was slowed down in roadworks on the M8. The motorway through Glasgow is a nightmare at the best of times, so you always have to concentrate – you certainly don't need what happened to me next.

In the lane next to me I spotted a man in his mid-thirties making signs at me. Then he rolled down the passenger window and started shouting at me, calling me a wanker and making the usual accompanying gesture. Even as we got up to 50 mph he tried to spit at me.

Alisha, who was just twelve at the time, and her friend were upset by his actions so I decided to get off the motorway at the next exit. However, he cut right across me, still gesturing madly, forcing me to take evasive action. If I had not been alert, there might well have been a nasty accident.

I got his car make and number and, as soon as possible, I got off the M8. I was not bothered about myself, but he had frightened Alisha. My daughter has been raised in England where none of this religious stuff happens, and here she was in Glasgow for a holiday, having to listen to all that guff from a grown man. I wasn't going to stand for it and I called the police.

The police came and took statements from us, and later charged thirty-five-year-old Thomas Ferrie of Uddingston. In court, he pleaded guilty to breach of the peace and was fined £500. Sheriff James Friel ordered that Rangers be told of the conviction, while his lawyer told the court: 'The total stupidity of it all is not lost on him.'

Too right. Ferrie was banned indefinitely from Ibrox. He also lost his job with Arnold Clark motor dealers although he later got it back on appeal.

I can only conclude that Ferrie took momentary leave of his senses. For surely no sane man would risk lives and frighten children just to shout some bigoted nonsense? But then bigotry knows no sense, especially when mixed with the mindlessness of a football mob.

I reported that incident to the police but there have been so many others that I don't usually bother calling the police as they have more important things to do.

Once I was getting into a taxi in Royal Exchange Square in the centre of Glasgow when I head the shout of 'Fenian bastard' and two bottles came flying over. One hit the taxi and the other went whizzing by my head, while my 'fearless' attacker ran off up the street still calling me 'Fenian' this and that.

The bigots surface in the most unlikely places. On one occasion I flew up to Inverness with the team. As we were making our way from the aircraft into the terminal, Chris Sutton and I got the verbals. We just ignored it, but the heckling had been heard by Celtic's security officer – it turned out the heckler was an airport fireman and he was sacked for his pains.

I have had to change my mobile phone number from time to time because somehow it has been given to bigots who have left seriously unpleasant messages on my voice mail. On one occasion these were so bad and so specific I had to inform the police, but they were unable to trace the sick caller.

The 'death threat' graffiti in Northern Ireland was not an isolated incident. In May 2004 the police came to my door early one morning to tell me that death threats had been painted on the road outside my house. It was the usual stuff – 'You are a dead man Lennon' and a reference to a banned Ulster loyalist paramilitary group. However, my main concern was that innocent people had suffered, because paint had been daubed on a car similar to mine but parked in the street next to ours – bigots, by definition, are not the smartest people.

The car had been painted with the words 'Fenian b******'. As it turned out, the car owners were Catholics and the man thought someone at his work was out to get him. Since his wife was six months pregnant, they were both frightened. I told them it was nothing to do with them and sent some flowers but that was scant consolation for the fright they endured.

A newspaper helpfully printed a photograph of our street explaining where my flat is – and also pointed out those of several Rangers players nearby. In fact, it was an attack on some Rangers players in Uddingston which made me speak out against the mindlessness of the bigots and seek action from both clubs to battle the problem.

'When you look at what happened with the boys in Uddingston, it is clear something has got to be done,' I said.

'You don't want things getting out of hand and reaching a stage where players can't walk down the street. At the end of the day, we are only football players. We all have a life to lead outside of the game.

'People don't know footballers as people, but they have an idea of what they represent and despise that. It is unfair on the individual.'

Those were my views then and I stand by them. The work that is being done by Celtic and Rangers to eradicate sectarianism is slowly paying dividends, especially now that Uefa have decided to join the clampdown. This work must continue, but in the first instance we must get the safety of players and staff and their families absolutely ensured.

It's only since I moved to Glasgow that I have received such opprobrium in public. The only real trouble I suffered in Leicester was when some swine stole the wheels of my BMW. My neighbour alerted me to the theft early one morning – there in the drive was my beautiful new motor on eight bricks. I called the police and the insurance company but there was nothing they or anyone could do, so I went back to bed.

The postman then came to the door. 'Lenny, they've nicked your wheels,' he said. It seemed as though the whole street now knew.

Shortly afterwards a smartly dressed man with a briefcase

arrived at the door. I thought it must be the CID or the insurers reacting quickly so I went downstairs and opened up.

'I see you have had a spot of bother this morning,' he said.

'You could put it like that,' I replied.

'Well, would you like Jesus in your life?' It was one of the God Squad touting for business. I was livid.

'Not just now,' I said, 'but if you're talking to him later could you ask him who stole my wheels?'

That was about the sum total of my trouble in Leicester, but things have been very different in Scotland. I know that I have not always reacted well to problems on the pitch, but does any player deserve to have coins thrown at him, as happened to me at Aberdeen? A two-pence piece can take out your eye if thrown hard enough, so I firmly believe anyone caught doing that in a stadium should be charged with assault or something similar, as well as being banned from all football matches for life.

Being linked in the newspapers with all sorts of shenanigans is another frequent problem for me. A businessman friend of mine was once being tailed by the police in Glasgow. He was wrongly suspected of being involved in some skulduggery, but that didn't bother the cops or the press – I woke up one Sunday morning to see myself plastered over two pages in pictures with the 'suspect'.

I was once even questioned in a murder inquiry. Alexander Blue was a millionaire businessman who was murdered in the West End of Glasgow in June 2002. The police are still hunting the killer, but at one point Bobo Balde, Momo Sylla and myself were all questioned as apparently a taxi driver had seen three people fitting our descriptions all together near the scene of the crime. It was bizarre – I wasn't even in the country at the time and it is hard to imagine that there are three people hanging around Glasgow together who resemble us. Of course, the fact that we were questioned made the newspapers.

Some of the stuff which has been posted about me on the internet is beyond belief. At various times I have had death threats and there have been supposedly intimidatory warnings such as cartoons of me being hanged. The sickest was when someone posted on a Rangers fans' website that I had been killed in a plane crash. That website was later closed down because of the abuse I was given.

I used to think that the internet abuse was perpetrated by sad adolescents with nothing better to do with their time, but an expert later told me that much of it was the work of grown men, hiding behind the web's anonymity. I wonder if their families know what they are doing.

The problem for those who think that they can intimidate me or upset me by posting this sick rubbish is that they are wasting their time – I am the original technophobe. I think there's a computer in my house somewhere but I wouldn't know how to start it up and I have never actually used the internet. The only way I find out about the nonsense is when the press call me to tell me about it. There's the funny thing – the same newspapers that give me grief all the time are the first to condemn the website trash.

The Irish newspapers have tended to be kinder to me. In early 2003 there had been some talk in the Belfast newspapers of me returning to play for Northern Ireland. I did think about it, and indeed took time to reflect on an international career which had begun at primary school and had seen me progress to become captain of my country.

My full international career began in 1994. I had been playing well all season at Crewe when Bryan Hamilton drafted me into the squad for a short tour of the USA prior to the

World Cup which was taking place in America that summer. Before we left, I was selected to play for the Northern Ireland B team against England B, whose squad included the likes of Chris Sutton, Paul Merson and Alan Stubbs. I enjoyed the match even though we lost 4–2, and joining the rest of the national squad for the tour to Boston, New York, and Miami made me think that I might get that all-important first cap, even though I was only a Fourth Division player.

I was not involved in the first game against Colombia in Boston, which we lost 0–2, but I did not think that Bryan Hamilton would have dragged me across the Atlantic for nothing, and sure enough, I made my debut in the second match of the tour, against Mexico on 11 June 1994.

I first pulled on the full International jersey in, of all places, Miami's Orange Bowl – Old Firm fans will get the irony. I played half the match against Mexico on a blisteringly warm day which suited them much more than it did us.

It was only two years since I had been sitting in the sweat-box at Crewe, working my way back to fitness. Yet here I was playing for my country just a few days before my twenty-third birthday.

The ironic thing was that no one had really expected me to make my debut on that tour so not a single member of my family or any of my friends were there to see me on my big day. Speaking of sweatboxes, that's exactly what we encountered in the Orange Bowl, as the heat soared to well over 100 degrees Fahrenheit. The official attendance was 8,498, but it looked to me like 30,000 Mexicans had somehow got into the Bowl.

The American referee Helder Diaz must have been affected by the heat as he gave a foul just about every time we breathed in the vicinity of a Mexican. Their first came from a dubious penalty and their second from an equally soft free-kick.The referee also disallowed a perfectly good goal by Iain Dowie who towered over the Mexican keeper Campos.

The final score was 0–3, so my international career was off to a less than brilliant start.

Just after that tour, I had my first operation for tendonitis and was not involved with Northern Ireland again until the end of the following season, when we toured Canada. I did not participate in the match against the host nation but played the whole game against Chile which was a whole new experience even though we lost 1–2.

It was unusual working with Bryan Hamilton as he was so different to Dario Gradi and certainly nothing like Martin O'Neill later at Leicester. He talked a lot about the game and could be a bit over-fussy, though he was a decent man and an underrated manager because under him we actually gained the best results in my time as a Northern Ireland player. We won eight and drew nine of his thirty-two games in charge – and believe me, every win for Northern Ireland is a massive achievement given our tiny population.

After I missed out on a dreadful loss to Latvia at home, I was recalled to the squad for the away match against Portugal in FC Porto's stadium. This was a European Championship qualifier and I had never played at anything approaching this level. They had a fantastic team at the time with Paulo Sousa, Figo, Rui Costa and Fernando Couto all in the side. I had never encountered football like it before – we were lucky to get a touch of the ball for three or four minutes at a time. It was real backs-to-the-wall stuff but we defended very well considering that they won twenty-one corners. The equalizing goal for us was scored by my old Manchester City colleague Michael Hughes from a free-kick and unbelievably we had gained a result against a team filled with quality players. I didn't think that I had done very well, but I realize now that it was all part of the learning process for a man then playing in the Fourth Division.

The draw against Portugal gave us a big lift and after beating Liechtenstein 4–0 over there, we then played our last qualifier knowing we would not be going to Euro 96 in England. Nevertheless, the match against Austria turned out to be a tremendous game. The rain hammered down but we still played some good football and deserved our 5–3 victory. It could have been six because I remember missing a good chance quite near the end.

We had not been very far away from making the play-offs, but in retrospect it was the defeat at home to Latvia which cost us most dear, and I am not just saying that because I was left out of the team for that match. In international competition, you need to win your home games and we did not manage that. Had we got a result against Latvia we might at least have made the play-offs and I think Northern Ireland could have gone on to greater things at that time because we had a young squad who were learning fast. We finished the group well, though afterwards we never seemed to get going again. Sadly, our poor home form continued into the World Cup qualifiers which we started by losing 0–1 to Ukraine in Belfast.

I remember watching the draw for that World Cup qualifying group on television and my reaction was two words which rhyme with 'clucking bell'. It was a really tough group, as we had Germany, Portugal, Ukraine, Armenia and Albania with only two certain to qualify for France 98.

In our opening match against Ukraine, it looked as though we were heading for a draw until their substitute Sergei Rebrov arrived. We had been playing well but when he scored with a header at the back post it took the wind out of our sails.

It often seemed as if we could turn it on against the big

teams only to struggle against lesser sides. We also seemed to have a problem with winning games at home, for example against Armenia in the next qualifier, although at least I got my first international goal in that match – a shot that was deflected and then went in off a post – in a dire 1–1 draw.

By contrast, we then achieved the best result of the early stage of my international career in a memorable encounter with Germany. It was their first home match after winning Euro 96 and they were hot favourites, so for us to get a 1–1 draw was quite remarkable. My mate Gerry Taggart scored the opener but Germany struck back within two minutes through Andreas Möller. Tommy Wright was in goal for us that night and he pulled off a string of marvellous saves which were the main factor in our clinching a truly surprising result.

The game was played in Nuremberg and afterwards, unsurprisingly, we had a good night out in the city. You could say we had a wee rally at the Nuremberg bars . . .

Our real problem was a lack of consistency. For instance, we lost a friendly in Palermo, Sicily, against the might of Italy – I was back in Leicester on Coca-Cola League Cup duty that night – but then we came out and were quite brilliant in a home friendly against Belgium, winning 3–0, before holding Portugal to a 0–0 draw in a World Cup qualifier.

That Portugal match was the first of a double header with the Belfast game being followed by a trip to Kiev to play the Ukraine. Now it was well known that we players enjoyed a good time when playing for Northern Ireland, and most of the lads stayed on before leaving for the second game the following Wednesday. As luck would have it, Bryan had organized a golf tournament at Royal County Down, one of the world's finest courses, on the day I had arranged to go home to Lurgan to see my parents.

The course is very near to the Slieve Donard hotel in

Newcastle, County Down, where the team were staying, and also close by is a well-known pub called the Percy French. The golf was ignored by most of the lads who went down there for a drink and stayed most of the afternoon. Bryan was stalking about the hotel trying to find out where his squad had gone. The lads eventually returned after 4 p.m. only to find they had been called for a team meeting at 6 p.m. Quite a few of the players could hardly stop themselves falling asleep at the meeting.

Words were exchanged between Bryan and a couple of players, but it all blew over and we did well against Ukraine, equalizing after losing an early goal and giving them a real fright before Shevchenko scored late on to give them a 2–1 victory. But a goalless draw in the following match in Armenia meant that our chances of qualifying for France 98 looked very slim indeed.

The annoying thing was that we had some good players at the time, with the likes of Taggs, another old friend – and occasional sparring partner – Steve Lomas, and Keith Gillespie of Newcastle United. We also had strong characters who were not afraid to speak their mind. Jim Magilton of Southampton was one of them, and he had once paid for his forthrightness by being left out of the team. He and Iain Dowie were friends who had played together for Southampton. They both knew football inside out but also had a great sense of humour. I am not surprised that both have gone on to become managers, with Iain going to Charlton Athletic and Jim recently appointed at Ipswich Town. Back then, they were the leaders of the Northern Irish team and if anything needed to be said, one or other of them would usually say it. They had also talked about going into coaching and I am sure both of them will succeed as managers as they have the personality and the ideas for the job.

One of the best 'free' holidays I have ever had was our end-of-season trip to Thailand to play that country's national side in Bangkok at the invitation of the Thai FA. It was just a marvellous experience to visit such an exotically different place. The people of Thailand are incredibly hospitable and there was a huge welcoming party for us at the airport. They were very warm and friendly and could not do enough for us.

We had four days in Bangkok followed by six days in the resort of Phuket. Although we all said we would try to experience the culture of Thailand, by the time we got to Phuket we were exhausted and mostly sat by the pool enjoying a glass of the amber nectar. We were knackered largely because the match itself took place in quite extraordinary heat and humidity which we had previously avoided by training at 8 a.m.

Perhaps it was a reaction to all that hospitality but we did not take the many chances we created and the match ended goalless. It had been a learning experience to play in such conditions, but not one I cared to repeat.

Our hopes of qualification for France 98 evaporated with another very disappointing result, against Germany in Belfast at the start of the 1997/98 season. We played quite brilliantly for an hour, before their coach Berti Vogts brought on substitute Oliver Bierhoff, who promptly rattled in a hat-trick in the space of seven minutes. It was his first hat-trick in senior competitive football at any level and he chose to do it against us.

Our next match was to provide one of my worst experiences in international football. I still cannot believe that we lost to Albania of all nations. The match was played in Zurich because of some civil unrest in Albania, so that should have given us an advantage, but we were missing six key players and they played well above themselves to snatch a 1–0 victory. Nevertheless, we should have beaten them as we had a total of eight players from the Premiership and First Division.

Beforehand, we were all aware that Bryan Hamilton's job was on the line as the media had taken against him and pressure was building on the Irish FA. Unfortunately, football is a results-driven business and the fact was we were not getting the results we should have. A 0–1 loss to Portugal in our last qualifier sealed his fate and Bryan went, to be replaced by Lawrie McMenemy.

Bringing in a big-name English manager had worked for the Republic of Ireland with Jack Charlton and for a while it seemed as though Lawrie would do the same for us. In March 1998, we won our first match under his charge against Slovakia, Lubomir Moravcik and all, thanks to a brilliant Steve Lomas goal which was the only strike of the game. That match was played at Windsor Park, and when we beat Switzerland at home a month later by the same score, it looked as though we were starting a revival.

Even when we lost 4–1 to Spain in Santander, Taggs getting our goal, nobody really cared as it was a warm-up game for them before the World Cup in France.

However, at the start of the following season we went to Istanbul and were well beaten by Turkey at the start of our European Championship campaign. The 3–0 scoreline was a fair reflection of the play, with their young and athletic team just beginning to become a real force in world football.

Beating Finland in Belfast got us back on track, with Keith Rowland, then of Queens Park Rangers, scoring from a move I started with a quick free-kick.

Our old problems surfaced in the next qualifier, when Moldova came to Belfast and twice went ahead, before I managed to shoot home the second equalizer after sixty-four minutes. We returned the compliment by drawing in Moldova, after a 3–0 defeat at home to a rampant German side had just about snuffed out our qualification hopes.

My next two matches were memorable friendlies. The first was against the Republic of Ireland in a charity match to raise money for the victims of the Omagh bombing. It was brilliant to play for the first time at Lansdowne Road, especially we won 1–0. That was also the scoreline, only it was against us, in our next match, at Windsor Park against the world champions France. It was a fantastic occasion for us and the quality of their team shone through, with the likes of Patrick Vieira, Lilian Thuram, Bixente Lizarazu, Robert Pires, Marcel Desailly and Lauren Blanc all in their pomp. Willie Young of Scotland was the referee and I'm sure he recalls the occasion when he had charge of the world champs – what's more, he did a good job when things got a little niggly.

Our Euro 2000 campaign promptly collapsed. Turkey hammered us 3–0 at Windsor Park and Germany put four past us in Dortmund. It was a nightmare because we were simply outclassed and could not compete. Lawrie McMenemy was a decent manager, but the paucity of playing resources meant he could do little to stem the tide.

In our final qualifier against Finland in Helsinki, Lawrie made me captain. It was the first time I had captained any side since the day I had been sent off when playing for Leicester against Norwich. What should have been a great night for me turned really sour because we got hammered again – losing 4–1 to the Finns really hurt, though they did have players of the calibre of Sammy Hyypia of Liverpool, Jonatan Johansson of Rangers and Joonas Kolkka of PSV Eindhoven.

Our self-belief was non-existent and our confidence was shattered, so it was no surprise that my first match as captain was Lawrie's last as manager, as he was replaced shortly afterwards by Sammy McIlroy.

At least we had two easier matches to open Sammy's account, beating Luxembourg 3–1 and Malta 3–0 away, before losing to Hungary 0–1 at home – I played only in the latter two matches. One or two players such as Iain Dowie had retired, but we had bright young players coming through the ranks such as David Healy and the future looked good.

I then missed a couple of games, against Yugoslavia and Malta, through injury. Apart from the way it ended, the thing which annoyed me most about my international career was the criticism I took for not being able to play in a couple of matches. This was somehow viewed as a lack of commitment to the cause on my part. The truth is that I always wanted to play for my country and I think a record of forty caps in the space of eight years proves that. It got to the stage where the Irish FA sent a doctor to examine me after I pulled out of one game, but their medical expert found that there was indeed an injury which prevented me playing.

I can reveal now that there were several times when we came back from receiving a real beating when I seriously though of quitting the international game, but each time I went back to my club, picked myself up and waited for the call for the next match. How can anyone possibly question my commitment, when I would have been within my rights to walk away from international football after the Norway game in which I was booed? I stayed on and played in the losses against the Czech Republic and Bulgaria, and came on as substitute against Poland in a friendly in Cyprus, only to receive the death threats when I was asked to become captain again.

That last straw came against Cyprus and cast a long shadow over my career as a Northern Ireland player. I was proud to play forty times for my country, but at the end it all turned very sour indeed and a lot of happy memories have been permanently blighted.

When reports surfaced in 2003 that I was considering returning to play for Northern Ireland I was able to say with certainty that my retirement was permanent. While I don't miss trips to places like Moldova, I would love to have played against England on that famous night in September 2005 when Northern Ireland won by the only goal of the game scored by David Healy.

In any case, I had a job to do with Celtic, and as 2002 became 2003, we were going along nicely in the Uefa Cup and looking good to win another domestic treble.

Even though we were doing well, there were still people prepared to criticize Celtic. The main bone of contention appeared to be that our average age was creeping ever upwards, and that we had several players now on the wrong side of thirty or fast approaching that supposedly landmark age. Here we were, just having beaten the third-best side in England and having steamrollered most of the teams in the SPL, but apparently we were too old. It was just so much rubbish and really annoyed me. With the advances in sports science, better diet and the increased professionalism and dedication of most modern players, there is nothing to stop most footballers from playing into their mid-thirties at a high level. Players are looking after themselves much better both on and off the field and the days when you almost automatically retired on reaching thirty-four or thirty-five are long gone. It doesn't matter how old you are or indeed how young you are, if you are good enough to play then your age should not be a consideration. At that time the Celtic squad all felt that there was no one out there better than us. Had there been, then Martin would have had no hesitation in going out and getting them.

We had also grown together as a team. There really was

a warm and friendly atmosphere in the dressing room. It could not be anything else when you had characters like Chris Sutton, Alan Thompson, John Hartson, Henrik Larsson, Stilian Petrov, Johann Mjallby, Paul Lambert and Jackie McNamara in the squad. All of us grew so close together that sometimes we developed almost a siege mentality. I have no hesitation in saying that I cannot recall working with any group of players who were as mentally strong as that Celtic side. We really never did know when we were beaten. And so much of who we were and what we became emanated from Martin.

In early 2003 I needed all my own mental strength as I focused on recovering from my torn hamstring. After the initial shock of the injury, I was able to look at matters with a bit more optimism. That season there was a winter break in the SPL, so I only missed a few league games before I had four weeks in which to recover before matches started again. I knew from my long period out of the game with my back injury that it was just a question of getting through each day doing what I could to assist the healing process. I just concentrated on getting fit again, as I was desperate to be involved in the remainder of our European campaign.

The break also meant that I was able to take a proper holiday to Orlando in Florida. With Alisha and a few friends, we stayed at the Disney World complex. For ten days we had a whale of a time in the sunshine. It was the best holiday I had ever had, and because it was January, Disney World was relatively quiet and we could get on the rides – everyone's a big kid at Disney World and I was no exception. We visited the Gator Park and like every other tourist, we marvelled at these giant creatures. It was also not too hot, which suited me as I don't really enjoy searing heat and my skin doesn't take too kindly to the sun. But all too soon I had to rejoin the squad who were in Florida to train and play a couple of friendly matches.

One of my most vivid memories of that stay in Florida was watching, with the rest of the team, the launch of the shuttle spacecraft from the Kennedy Space Centre. It was on the bright and clear morning of 16 January, and though we were many miles from Cape Canaveral, we could clearly see the shuttle and its rocket boosters tearing up through the atmosphere and heading for outer space with astronauts and scientists on board. Little did we know that there would be a tragic end to their voyage, for that soaring spacecraft was the shuttle *Columbia* which broke up on re-entry into the Earth's atmosphere sixteen days later on 1 February, killing all seven people on board.

The benefits of that time in Florida convinced me once and for all that the winter break should become a permanent feature of life in the SPL. I know that winter can be a moveable feast in Scotland and that severe cold spells can happen in April – as happened in 2006 – as well as January, but the idea of taking a break then has so many advantages that I really feel that it should become an accepted part of Scottish football. Players and coaches get a chance to recharge their batteries, the pitches are given a respite from being churned up and fans do not have to brave the worst of the weather to follow their team.

At one time, it looked as if there might not be an SPL from which to have a break. We players tend to let chief executives and chairmen do their thing while we concentrate on playing but we did follow very closely the saga of the possible breakaway by ten clubs in the SPL, which fortunately was resolved after long and tortuous negotiations.

At that time and subsequently, I have been asked if Celtic should move to the Premiership. My own personal feelings are that both Celtic and Rangers should be allowed to play elsewhere. Celtic are one of the biggest clubs in the world and we would more than hold our own financially in the Premiership, as well as in a playing sense as we showed with our wins over Blackburn and Liverpool. The fact that Celtic and Rangers are the two giant fish in a very small pond will always work against them when either club tries to compete at a higher level such as the Champions League.

I know from personal experience how restricted Celtic are financially because we play in Scotland. You only have to look at a club like Leicester when it was in the Premiership. City's gates at Filbert Street were on average about a third of Celtic's at Parkhead. Yet Leicester benefited to the tune of £20 million from television rights annually when Celtic were getting between £1 million and £2 million per year.

Celtic always have to work very hard at sponsorship and marketing to try to make up the shortfall, but both clubs in the Old Firm know that there is little room for expansion in Scotland for them. They need a bigger stage and the Premiership provides that. It would mean more revenue for the Old Firm and for the English clubs as well because I am confident that Celtic's fans would fill every stadium in the country, not least because we have supporters in every area of England as the list of fans' clubs shows.

Both clubs are well-known worldwide brand names and have been able to market themselves outside of Scotland, but as long as they both play in the SPL they will always be limited in what they can do, if only because they have to share a tiny television income with the other ten clubs.

Having said that, you cannot enter a league unless you are invited to join and I do not see chairmen in the Premiership waving the welcoming flags. If I was the chairman of Charlton or Portsmouth or indeed any of the clubs outside of the big half dozen, I would not exactly be falling over myself to invite Celtic and Rangers to join the party. Directors at the smaller clubs have quite rightly pointed out in the past that it would be like turkeys voting for Christmas as the two Scottish giants would threaten their survival in the Premiership.

As for the other clubs in Scotland, it is really up to them to get their act together to mount a challenge to the Old Firm. They always say that Celtic and Rangers are now too big to compete against, but surely that has always been the case, and it didn't stop Hibs and Hearts in the 1950s or Aberdeen and Dundee United in the 1980s from winning leagues and cups.

Hearts have shown over the last season that it can be done and Brooks Mileson's investment at Gretna has been rewarded with a march up the leagues and a memorable Scottish Cup run all the way to penalties after extra-time in the final at Hampden. If the right investors, the right management and the right players come together, there is nothing to prevent other clubs from challenging the Old Firm.

In March 2003 we underwent the most extraordinary fortnight of my time at Celtic. We had been going well in the league, but Rangers were still on top, largely as a result of beating us 3–2 in December which we followed by dropping points against Kilmarnock and Aberdeen. After the break we had won every league and cup match, even after Henrik broke his jaw and was out for weeks, and had reached the final of the CIS League Cup by beating Dundee United in the semi-final. On 8 March, we met Rangers at Parkhead, where I played well in a 1–0 victory secured for us by big John Hartson – the first time we had beaten them under Alex McLeish. Five days later came the 1–1 draw at home to Liverpool followed by the CIS Cup Final against Rangers at Hampden.

I wish I could blank out that afternoon, but the record books will always be there to haunt us. They played well in the first half, scoring through Claudio Caniggia and Peter Lovenkrands, but the second half was all ours. Henrik got one back with a typical bullet header before he set up John Hartson for what looked to be the equalizer. But the linesman flagged for offside as John thumped the ball home. Television replays showed that the goal was perfectly sound.

As we tried everything to get that second goal, Chris Sutton fell and broke his wrist in a collision with Bobo Balde and then Stefan Klos pulled off a sensational save from Henrik. We were all willing each other to make a dramatic finish when I jostled with Fernando Ricksen off the ball and was booked. I have to say that Fernando was not my favourite player at that time and I personally thought he was a bit of a liability for Rangers in Old Firm games. He made a meal of things but it was me who got booked and then with three minutes left, I tangled with Shota Arveladze and was shown a second yellow card which meant I was ordered off for the first time as a Celtic player.

Even then we could have come back as Lorenzo Amoruso brought down big Bobo in the box. John Hartson tried to pick his spot but his shot went past the post. Our dreams of a second treble ended a few second later with the final whistle.

There was no sense among us of having lost an unimportant final. Every match against Rangers is important for Celtic and we always want to win every tournament in which we compete. I was devastated to have been sent off, as I felt that I was not due at least one of the cards, and I think it says something that I was not disciplined by the club.

There was real gloom at training early in the week, yet somehow we picked ourselves up to beat Liverpool before travelling north the following Sunday for a Scottish Cup quarter-final against Inverness Caledonian Thistle.

It was a cup defeat against Thistle which had ended John

Barnes' management career, and if it had been any other manager than Martin, the same thing might have happened again. Only three of us – myself, Henrik and Joos – were retained from the side which beat Liverpool as Martin tried to rest players for the busy time ahead.

But the tactic backfired, as Martin admitted after a poor match in which we had all the pressure and none of the luck. We just could not equalize a single Dennis Wyness goal scored before the interval.

Going out to Inverness Caledonian Thistle was a huge blow. Obviously we were going great guns in Europe and were doing well in the league as we were within catching distance of Rangers, but to lose in such a fashion to a club in the division below us, albeit a side which would soon be joining us in the SPL, was not something we took lightly. Only three of us who had played against Liverpool were picked for that match, but we should still have been too strong for them. As it was, they scored in one of the very few attacks which they mounted that night, but it was enough to finish any thoughts of a dream treble. The gaffer was absolutely livid and we had gone from the real high of beating Liverpool to the lowest point of the season by far.

But worse, far worse, was to come at the end of the season. Somehow, despite all our distractions in Europe, we managed to keep going in the SPL, and a 2–1 victory over Rangers at Ibrox set up a remarkable run-in, in which it was nip and tuck all the way.

Rangers drew 2–2 with Dundee the following week, but neither of us dropped a point thereafter and we put four past Dunfermline and Motherwell and beat Dundee 6–2 to claw back some of the goal difference between us.

It meant that as we left for Seville, both teams sat on ninety-four points and were level on goal difference. For the first time, the new 'split' SPL would be decided on the last day of the season.

Coming back to Scotland from Seville we were proud and delighted with the welcome we received, but we knew we had to get ourselves up again for the last league match against Kilmarnock at Rugby Park on Sunday 27 May. Rangers had the advantage as they were at home to Dunfermline.

The tension, the ebb and flow and the final outcome of that afternoon will never be forgotten by anyone connected with the Old Firm.

We could tell from our fans' reactions how things were going at Ibrox. Chris Sutton put us ahead after sixteen minutes and doubled the advantage just before the interval. When Alan Thompson scored with a penalty, we were suddenly champions elect. But at Ibrox, Rangers dug deep and though Tommo missed a penalty before we got a fourth through Stan Petrov, it was not enough to counter their 6–1 defeat of Dunfermline.

It was all over. Rangers had won the league and would add the Scottish Cup a week later for the treble. For all our efforts, we had won nothing.

Most of us sank to the turf in bitter exhaustion.

We couldn't have done any more, and once again our fans proved magnificent in defeat. The Kilmarnock support exited, but our fans just would not leave Rugby Park until we came out to receive a last ovation.

They sang their hearts out at both ends of the stadium. As I watched the scenes I had a huge lump in my throat and could not contain my emotions. I just felt so sorry that we had created such expectations and almost lived up to them, that we had enjoyed such a fantastic season but at the end of it we had nothing to show for all our efforts.

As we walked off Rugby Park, I could see that Henrik

was deeply moved too and the tears came to both our eyes. We had played in a brilliant team, which I firmly believe was one of the best Celtic sides ever, yet had not won a thing. It was a travesty, the proof that football can be the most cruel of games.

At least we had given our fans some wonderful times and those who had been brought up on the stories of Lisbon in 1967 now had their own tales to tell of Seville 2003.

Thanks to our previous efforts in the Champions League, Scotland's Uefa co-efficient had improved to the point where both the first- and second-placed teams in the SPL gained entry to the top tournament, though we would have to play through two qualifying stages at the start of the 2003/04 season.

Over the summer, there was all sorts of talk about new contracts but it came to nothing, while the one man who everyone wanted to extend his contract, Henrik Larsson, remained adamant that it was to be his final season at Parkhead. When Henrik made his mind up to do something, he almost always did it.

The problems I had faced with the assault also led to a lot of speculation that I would leave, but I am no quitter and loved being at Celtic too much to be forced out by idiots.

Since we were once again having to play early matches in Europe, we played some stiff pre-season friendlies, including a less-than-successful tour to America during which we lost 4–0 to Manchester United in Seattle but came back to beat Boca Juniors of Argentina 1–0 in Cleveland.

Fortunately, our first match in the qualifying stages was against FC Kaunas of Lithuania, Vladimir Romanov's 'other' club. We beat them comfortably 4–0 over there before taking the foot off the pedal when winning 1–0 at Parkhead.

That 5–0 aggregate victory put us into the second and final

qualifying round against MTK Hungaria, known in the past as MTK Budapest. Once again it was 4–0 over there and 1–0 at Celtic Park.

We had qualified for the Champions League again, and we were all pretty confident of doing what no Scottish club had done previously, i.e. making the second stage. The group was tough, as it included Bayern Munich, Olympique Lyon and Anderlecht, but we felt our experience in the Uefa Cup would see us improve again.

We also knew that we would need to improve because playing in the Champions League takes you to a whole new level in football. In the days before a game everything around the club – training, preparation, the usual sense of anticipation that you get before any match – all of it goes up a few notches from the norm. The media interest grows by the hour, sometimes the foreign press invade, and you know from the daily gatherings around Parkhead – every day there are supporters looking for autographs after training – that the fans are looking forward to the match as much as you are.

The evening of a big European game is always very special. To walk out onto Celtic Park with the stadium full of light and colour and 60,000 people roaring their heads off is just a sensational experience that every footballer should be able to savour at least once in their life. When you hear that Champions League theme music, it sparks an electric feeling inside you. You know you are on the biggest stage in club football and you would have to be a statue not to feel energized by everything surrounding you.

I'm not just being sycophantic to our fans when I say you do not really get that kind of atmosphere at other grounds. Our supporters really do generate an overwhelming noise and I know that a lot of visiting players are intimidated by the atmosphere at Parkhead – you can see them visibly wilt and shrink at times – though there are others who thrive on it. We Celtic players always appreciate and react to the support we are given, particularly at Parkhead, and it is no coincidence that we have done so well in Europe when playing at home – don't forget that remarkable record of seventy-seven matches unbeaten at Parkhead under Martin O'Neill.

It was those fantastic European nights at Parkhead which made us desperately want to be in, and do well in, the Champions League so that we could consolidate Celtic's restored reputation in Europe. Under Martin, we had a settled team with a couple of young stars in Shaun Maloney and Liam Miller both knocking on the door to get into the side, and we really had strength in depth with, for instance, three international goalkeepers in Rab Douglas, David Marshall and Magnus Hedman in the squad.

Our league form was more than holding up – after a disappointing draw against Dunfermline on the opening day, we went on a barnstorming run which saw us win every league match from August until December, including an all-important victory at Ibrox. At times our football was sensational, as when we went on a run of five matches against Hearts, Aberdeen, Kilmarnock, Dunfermline and Dundee United which saw us score twenty-four goals for the loss of just one.

We had laid the foundations for another SPL championship. The question was how would we fare in the Champions League?

CHAPTER TWELVE

Farewell to the Kings

The 2003/04 Champions League campaign was one of the most exciting but ultimately most disappointing series of matches that Celtic have played during my time at Parkhead.

It began with what might have been a famous draw, but turned out to be a costly defeat. Bayern Munich had won the Champions League in 2001 and were many people's favourites to repeat the feat.

Even so, we were not afraid of them and went to Germany determined to get a result. We were by far the better side in Munich, even though we were missing a couple of players through injury and had Magnus Hedman in goal in place of Rab Douglas. Against a team which included world-class footballers such as Michael Ballack and Oliver Kahn, we dominated much of the play but failed to take any of the chances which fell our way. I had my own moment of glory when I nutmegged Ballack, and to be honest I thought we were in complete control of the match, especially when Alan Thompson dived to head home and give us the lead early in the second half. But defensive blunders cost us dear. When we failed to clear our lines after seventy-two minutes, Roy Makaay pounced to equalize. Even then I thought we would still get a draw, but four minutes from time, Magnus misjudged Makaay's cross and the ball ended up in the net. Once again we had been the better team but had failed to gain even a point.

The next game, at home against Lyon, was one of the best European matches in my time at Parkhead. Lyon had players of the calibre of Vikash Dhorasoo, Michael Essien and the Brazilians Edmilson and Elber, and were under the management of Paul le Guen who was to take them to four successive championships before joining Rangers.

They came roaring out of the traps, playing with power and pace while it took us a little time to get going. Alan Thompson missed a first-half penalty – he later swore that he would never take another one. But Liam Miller came off the bench to score our first, and though Gregory Coupet was absolutely brilliant in the Lyon goal, Chris Sutton wrapped up the points with a towering header.

Young Liam went on to enjoy a good first half to that season and had another excellent game in our next Champions League home fixture, against Anderlecht. Before that, however, we had gone to Belgium and maintained our dismal record of never having won a Champions League match on foreign soil.

I nearly missed that match because I had a terrible toothache. Dr McDonald gave me a couple of cocodamol tablets which knocked me out so much that I slept through my alarm call. I had to run for the team bus, but was four or five minutes late. I was hoping that Martin would not be on the bus but unfortunately for me, he was there and was extremely displeased with my late appearance. As he read out the team list, he told me I was lucky I was still playing.

I wish he had left me out as I was mentally off-kilter and did not play well at all. But then the rest of the team had an off night as well.

We should have won that match as they lost Glenn de Boeck after twenty-six minutes when he committed his second yellow-card offence. Unfortunately, we could not string two passes together and their ten men were inspired, Dindane Aruna scoring the winner for them with eighteen minutes left.

In the return at Parkhead, Sir Alex Ferguson was in the stand, though no one realized at the time that he was there to watch Liam. He played very well that night as we took the Belgians apart with one of our best performances. I felt I owed the club a big game because of what had happened in Belgium and I think I delivered. We were 3–0 up within half an hour thanks to goals from Henrik, Liam and Chris Sutton, with John Hartson making a major contribution throughout. They got one back from the pernalty spot, but in truth we were cruising.

Liam Miller later signed a pre-contract agreement to join Manchester United which was not calculated to endear him to the Celtic support or indeed Martin O'Neill. Things have not worked out for him at Old Trafford, but he is still young enough to make an impact in the game. After all, I did not play in the Premiership myself until I was twenty-five.

We knew that a win against Bayern at home would virtually guarantee us a passage to the second stage. On the night though, the German side showed great resolution in a defence featuring two great French full-backs, Bixente Lizarazu and Willy Sagnol, presided over by Oliver Kahn at his imperious best in goal.

It was end-to-end stuff at times as they were always a threat on the break. In terms of possession and territory we were well ahead but we could not create clear chances and I think they were happy to go away with a 0–0 scoreline.

Our task at Lyon was quite simple. As long as we did not lose we would go through to the second stage, but such was the closeness of the 'group of death' that we could also finish bottom and go out of Europe altogether. We were very confident in the run-up to the game as we were sweeping all before us domestically, but we gave Lyon a lot of respect.

It turned into a disappointing night, especially because I felt that each of the three goals we conceded could have been avoided. The dead-ball skills of Juninho Pernambucano were already well known and when his free-kick rebounded off the crossbar, we did not respond quickly enough and any one of three Lyon players could have scored, although it was Brazilian striker Elber who got there first. Big John Hartson pulled one back for us as we upped our game considerably, but Juninho struck with a thirty-yard effort which we felt Magnus Hedman should have saved.

With fourteen minutes left, Chris Sutton grabbed an equalizer and we knew that if we could just hang on we would make history as the first Scottish club to progress beyond the group stages of the Champions League. But with less than four minutes to go, an innocuous chip was nodded on into the box and Bobo Balde rose to clear it. His arm was raised, to be fair, but it looked more like a case of ball hitting arm than the other way round. I could not believe it when referee Urs Meier pointed to the spot. Juninho smacked the ball into the corner and we were out of the Champions League.

At the final whistle I told the referee exactly what I thought of him in language that needs only basic Anglo-Saxon to understand. His decision had cost the club millions of pounds and while it was obviously no big thing to him, it was massive for Celtic. With the stakes so high, a referee really needs to be certain about such important decisions. Mr Meier took exception to my advice and gave me a second yellow card, sending me off after the game. The Swiss referee later went on to earn the undying hatred of England's fans when he disallowed a perfectly good Sol Campbell goal in their European Championship quarter-final against home side Portugal. As a sufferer of them myself, I could never condone the death threats to Meier which followed that match, but I could understand the English fans' frustration.

That little incident earned me a two-match ban so I had to sit out the 180 minutes of our opening tie against Czech side Teplice in the 'consolation' Uefa Cup. After the experience of the previous season, we knew that the Uefa Cup could be something special and the fact was that by the time we came to resume European competition in late February 2004, we were already on the brink of winning the SPL.

The defeat at Lyon had knocked us out of step for a week or so, during which time we went out of the CIS League Cup to Hibs, but in the league we just couldn't be caught. Henrik knew it was his last season and wanted to leave Parkhead on a high, so his own contribution was immense as always. But right throughout the team there was a determination to win every match.

The key game, as usual, was against Rangers in the traditional New Year derby. Stilian Petrov, Stan Varga and Alan Thompson all scored as we romped home 3–0 to put us eleven points clear at the halfway point of the season. We went on a rampage in early 2004, winning every match until the second leg of the Uefa Cup tie against Teplice which we lost 1–0 in the Czech Republic, though it didn't matter as we had beaten them 3–0 in the first leg at Parkhead.

In the Scottish Cup, there was a real test for me at Tynecastle when things got a bit rough. Paul Hartley and Alan Maybury were both red-carded after clashing with me. Somehow I kept my cool apart from a bit of afters with Phil Stamp and we won 3–0 to set up a quarter-final with Rangers. We knew that the winner of that tie would almost certainly make it to the final, and so it proved as we beat them 1–0 and advanced to the final by beating Livingston 3–1 in the semi.

We were now looking at the possibility of a treble of League, Cup and Uefa Cup. While the first of these was virtually guaranteed, the latter contained an obstacle called Barcelona.

The first match at Parkhead was unforgettable. The level of skill they showed that night was out of this world, but we matched them and they did not like it.

I hadn't noticed any real nastiness but at half-time, as we were walking down the tunnel, I noticed Thiago Motta lurking with a strange look in his eyes. He had clashed with Bobo Balde a few seconds before the break, but I thought no man in his right mind would tackle our giant African.

Wrong. As I made my way to the dressing room, I heard the smacks behind me as Motta, Oleguer and a Barca official laid into Bobo. They were punching lumps out of him so I just took off and landed on Oleguer's back, got him in a headlock and tried a few rabbit punches for good measure as he tried to grab me in a place where the sun doesn't shine. One of the security stewards said 'let him go, Lenny', but I called back 'only if you grab him first'. The steward then intervened and restrained Oleguer.

As I was having my private battle, big Rab Douglas came to Bobo's rescue, breaking up the fight. Our big goalkeeper was as brave as they come and would always assist any of his team-mates in a rammy.

Eventually it all calmed down and the referee, Wolfgang Stark of Germany, had seen nothing. But he had to do something and he decided to send off Motta and big Rab. We needed a goalkeeper, and cometh the hour, cometh the bhoy. Craig Beattie came off and young David Marshall, who had celebrated his nineteenth birthday a week previously, took over in goal. His performance that night and in the Nou Camp a fortnight later have entered Celtic legend.

When Javier Saviola was sent off for a wild kick we put our numerical advantage to good use, Alan Thompson netting the winner with a lovely scissor-kick after a headed knockdown from Henrik. We had beaten one of the best teams in the world, on a night when our young stars like David Marshall and Stephen Pearson excelled themselves.

We travelled to Barcelona more in hope than expectation, and I am happy to say we prayed for a result – literally so. Didier Agathe and I were walking through the stadium when we noticed a room halfway down the tunnel. It was a small grotto, almost an indoor chapel, and when we realized what it was, we knelt and said a prayer. I don't know what Didier said, but I just prayed for a result of any kind. As we were praying, the manager came in and said 'what's this?' When we pointed out that it was a chapel, he too got down on his knees.

Our prayers were answered as we duly gave arguably the best defensive performance in Celtic's European history. David Marshall was outstanding as was young John Kennedy who replaced Bobo Balde in defence. John would later be terribly injured while playing for Scotland and has now been out of the game for two years, but it looks as though he is finally mended and we all hope he can return and fulfil his great potential. Didier Agathe was assigned to mark Ronaldinho and the man generally reckoned to be the best player in the world struggled against the bargain buy of the century, a £50,000 signing from Hibs who repaid that sum many times over in his years at Celtic.

How we survived I do not know, but we did and the 0–0 draw was enough to put us in the quarter-finals of the Uefa Cup.

Three days later we played Rangers at Ibrox and I had one of my best games there, as we won 2–1 with goals from Henrik and Alan Thompson. We had now gone nineteen points clear at the top of the SPL and it seemed that nothing could stop us.

Except, that is, for another Spanish side, Villareal. Unfashionable, small by comparison with giants such as Barcelona and Real Madrid, they nevertheless were very tough opponents in the quarter-final.

At Parkhead, they gave us a real scare with their possession football, taking the lead in the first half through Josico. Henrik got the equalizer after sixty-four minutes, so at least we had a draw to take to Spain.

Villareal had shown they were a classy side, something they were to go on to prove in the Champions League. But we helped them out that night, Bobo making a mistake to allow Sonny Anderson in to score. When Roger notched their second after an hour, we knew it was a massive task and try hard though we did, we were beaten by a better team on the night.

We still had the double of championship and Scottish Cup in our sights, and everyone was determined that Henrik would leave Parkhead as a winner again, no one more so than him.

We had lost the league fixture at Rugby Park a year previously, so there was a certain poetry in the fact that when we played Kilmarnock with six matches left it was with the chance to win the title outright.

It wasn't much of a game, but Stan Petrov's goal meant the celebrations could start in earnest. For the third time under Martin, we had won the league by a landslide, and during the season had set a British record of twenty-five consecutive wins. Henrik had also become Celtic's top scorer in post-war football, so we had plenty of reasons to celebrate as the squad went off to Gleneagles Hotel for a whale of a party.

Of course, the end of the season was dominated by the departure of Henrik. His achievements at Celtic have been lauded so much that I don't think I can add anything other than to say it was an utter privilege to play with him.

A natural-born footballer and a great athlete, he had one interesting habit, which was that he always took great care of his feet. I learned only recently that another footballer who went to great lengths to do the same was George Best.

Henrik could get annoyed, but it was mostly with himself as he was a perfectionist, like all the great players. This laid-back, highly intelligent man also has a very strong will, and no matter what incentives he was offered, he would not go back on his decision to leave. The King of Kings, as the fans called him, duly said farewell with extraordinary performances.

We were presented with the trophy at Parkhead after losing to Dunfermline on an afternoon when the children of all the players and staff, including Alisha, came onto the pitch to join our celebrations. We then completed our historic whitewash of Rangers – it was the first time Celtic had won all four league games against our rivals – before the Henrik saga drew to a magnificent close. In his last competitive match at Parkhead he scored both goals as we beat Dundee United 2–1. I remember thinking 'you couldn't make it up'. The emotions ran high and it all got to Henrik that day. His floods of tears were heartfelt, I can tell you, and quite a few of us had lumps in our throats at the incredible scenes.

How could he top that? By winning the Scottish Cup a week later at Hampden, that's how. Dunfermline threatened to spoil Henrik's party by scoring first through Andrius Skerla, but that only made the finale even more special as

Henrik scored two sublime goals and Stan Petrov got the third to bring the cup home to Paradise.

It was a fitting end to seven years of perfection from Henrik. His record of 242 goals from 315 matches stands comparison with all the great goalscorers. Yet he was much more than a striker, as likely to pop up in defence as attack. Remember also, he was out for many months with a broken leg and broken jaw.

With all the amazing moments in his final competitive matches, Henrik's testimonial match against Seville was not as emotional as it might have been, but the 1–0 victory was enjoyed by us all, especially Chris Sutton who scored the goal.

So it was farewell to the king, and it was no surprise when Barcelona signed him shortly afterwards, which in turn would bring an encounter replete with irony the following season. Johann Mjallby also left at the end of the season and he was another big loss to us.

That summer Euro 2004, in which Henrik starred for Sweden, dominated football's proceedings, but it also meant a very short close season for many players.

In the 1966/67 season, the year when Celtic won every tournament they entered and became the first British club to win the European Cup, Jock Stein took his squad on a team-building tour of the USA. We also needed match practice against top sides before the Champions League of 2004/05, so our pre-season tour was to the USA to take part in a tournament called the ChampionsWorld series. Martin could not accompany us at first because Mrs O'Neill was seriously ill and he had to stay by her side.

There was a disastrous start to the trip. We had to stop in Iceland, Greenland and Canada en route to Seattle and in total the journey lasted about eighteen hours. When we eventually got to the USA it took ninety minutes to clear security because of the heightened concerns at the time. At one point we were all trying to fill in boarding passes but they were in German, so we had to get Magnus Hedman to translate them for us. Not surprisingly, we were all exhausted by the time we came to play Chelsea.

We lost 4–2 but actually played quite well in the circumstances, but when we lost 5–1 to Liverpool in Connecticut – another exhausting journey away – the headlines blared about a crisis. After two pre-season games following the double, we were supposedly in trouble – we all thought it was a joke.

Martin returned to the squad and we duly managed to get back on track, beating Manchester United 2–1.

We had not made any big-name signings over the summer but Martin soon acted to strengthen the squad. He brought in the Brazilian Juninho Paulista who had been such a star with Middlesbrough. His idea was to reinvigorate the Brazilian so that he would show the kind of form he had displayed in his first spell in Britain. Juninho was a World Cup winner who was not yet at veteran stage and it looked like a very good signing after he made a brilliant debut against Rangers. He fitted into the role previously filled by Lubo Moravcik and that was part of the reason why we dominated the game, victory being achieved by another fine Alan Thompson goal five minutes from time.

Sadly for us, Juninho never fulfilled that early promise. Perhaps it was the pace of the game or the more physical nature of the way it is played in Scotland, but I don't think he ever adjusted to life here. When we lost 2–3 up at Aberdeen he was totally out of sync with the rest of us and that spelled the beginning of the end of his short stay at Parkhead. He might have done better with a longer run, but such is the pressure on Old Firm managers that you cannot afford to carry any passengers. He is now back in Brazil and playing well.

Early in that first Ibrox match I went into a tackle against Alex Rae and unfortunately he emerged with quite a bad injury. It was just one of those things that happen when you have two committed midfielders going for a ball. I have a lot of time for Alex, who went through hard times in his life and came out the other side to have a good spell at Wolves and then play for Rangers. You always knew where you stood with him as a player and, off the field, not many people know how much work he does for the Second Chance foundation. He asked me to attend a fund-raising dinner for the charity last year and I was delighted to do so. I sincerely wish Alex all the best in his new role as player-coach at Dundee FC.

The biggest talking point of the early part of the season came when we played Inverness Caledonian Thistle up there. Juanjo came in a bit late on me, so I pushed him and he reacted by poking his head into my face. Referee Dougie McDonald didn't see it, but the fourth official did. Alan Freeland is an experienced referee and he saw what happened, as did everyone on our bench who were sitting only yards away and were incensed. Freeland called over the referee and told them what had happened and McDonald decided to send off Juanjo.

The television cameras were at the other end of the ground and had not captured the incident clearly, so I do not know on what basis the pundits decided that I had been feigning injury. They completely ignored the fact that it was the fourth official, Alan Freeland, who had the best view of the incident and it was he who called over the referee. Freeland does not strike me as the sort of official to take action unless there is something to go on.

It was made out that I had tried to get Juanjo sent off, on the basis that the Inverness player said that he had not touched me – well, he would say that, wouldn't he? In all my career I have never tried to get a fellow professional a card, and let's face it, I have been involved in a rather more high-profile case. If I did not try to get Alan Shearer banned – remember, I spoke in his defence – then why would I start with Juanjo?

When the Scottish FA let him off, I couldn't believe it. I wonder if that would have happened if the card had been shown to me.

I had another 'clucking bell' moment when the draw was made for the Champions League. It could hardly have been worse when we were drawn with Barcelona, AC Milan and Shakhtar Donetsk. It was immediately termed a 'group of death' because everyone knew about the Spanish and Italian giants, yet the supposedly weak team were the champions of Ukraine and had just spent 14 million Euros on the Brazilian player Brandao – a sum that Celtic could only dream about spending.

Barcelona were probably still miffed that we had knocked them out of the Uefa Cup the previous season and they were definitely the better team when they came to play us at Parkhead. They had added Deco of Porto to their already world-class line-up and of course they now had Henrik.

We went a goal down, but we hung in there and Henri Camara set up an equalizer for Chris Sutton. Henri had joined us on loan from Wolves and I personally think he took a lot of unjustified criticism in his time with us. He has gone on to show what a fine player he is at Southampton and Wigan.

Barcelona went ahead and the script was written for you know who. Henrik came off the bench and showed his quality with a typical Larsson goal, intercepting Alan Thompson's header back and rounding David Marshall to score. It shows the class of the man that even though a few Celtic fans booed him, he did not celebrate his goal or rub it in. He had a job to do and Celtic were no longer his club, but I guess he went through a welter of emotions that night.

Before the AC Milan match in Italy I was paid one of the greatest compliments of my career when their coach Carlo Ancelotti singled me out for praise, saying I reminded him of himself as a player.

It was the first competitive match in which I captained Celtic and it was a memorable moment for me to lead out the team in the San Siro against one of the greatest clubs in the world. I was delighted that my dad was there to see it. Andriy Shevchenko gave them the lead but we weathered the storm and dominated play in the second half, Stan Varga scoring with a header.

Momo Sylla came on as a substitute but unfortunately he went to sleep for a second, which is all the time that a player like Shevchenko needs. He got in behind us and set up Filippo Inzaghi to score. Their third goal by Andrea Pirlo was academic and the feeling was one of total deflation that we had come so near to getting a result only to lose 1–3.

Having played so well against Milan and come away with nothing we then went to the Ukraine and totally underperformed. That 0–3 loss to Shakhtar Donetsk was arguably the most disappointing result we had suffered in the Champions League. We lost Jackie McNamara and Chris Sutton but did not have the strength in depth to replace them. I was beginning to think we might have a longer-term problem . . .

The home game against the Ukrainians was won by just a single goal, which meant that unless we could pull off a miracle and beat both Milan and Barcelona, we would be out of Europe before Christmas, as the Ukrainians would enter the Uefa Cup instead of us.

I had a falling-out with our director and major shareholder Dermot Desmond after the Donetsk game. I suggested in the press that it was time for the club to spend serious money. Dermot then came on the phone to me to tell me a few home truths about Celtic, which was basically that if the club had any money, they would have spent it. He put me right on a few things about the way Celtic is financed, which included a few details I had not appreciated. It appeared that I had been criticizing him on unfair grounds and I acknowledged that. I had also never heard of a director who was prepared to fight his corner in that way and tell a player the whys and wherefores of a club's finances. That conversation increased my respect for him as well as my understanding of how Celtic functions as a club.

I have also always had the greatest of respect for our chairman Brian Quinn. He is a true gentleman and a great ambassador for Celtic, as well as being a fan to his boots.

More evidence that we were not progressing came when we lost 2–1 to Rangers in the CIS League Cup after leading 1–0, Arveladze bagging the winner for them in extra-time.

The league match at Ibrox ten days later was pure bedlam from start to finish, full of passion on both sides. Alan Thompson was sent off after Peter Lovenkrands went down rather too artfully for my liking and Chris Sutton was also red-carded.

We were two men and two goals down and I was being vilified everywhere I went on the pitch. I had never known the abuse to be so bad and it reached a crescendo when I went to chase a ball that had gone out of play. I was bombarded with Rangers scarves, so I thought it would be funny to pretend to spit and polish my boots with one of them. That only endeared me further to the Rangers support, but what happened after the match sent them apoplectic.

As usual after the final whistle, I went over to salute the Celtic fans in the Broomlooan Road stand when all of a sudden I saw Martin coming towards me. I really didn't know what he was going to do, but then he put his arm around me and walked with me towards our fans. In full view of the public and the cameras, he was saying 'this is my team and these are my players, and I back them to the hilt'. When I realized what he was doing, the Celtic fire within me flamed up and I, too, gestured my defiance to our support.

The press and broadcasters went crazy. There were calls for Martin and I to be disciplined, but as usual the reactions were all over the top.

One of the more bizarre interventions came from the normally sensible Rangers Supporters Trust who paid a lip reader to 'prove' that I had called the fans 'Orange b******' during the game. Leaving aside the fact that you didn't need a lip reader to hear thousands of Rangers supporters abusing me, I categorically deny shouting that at their fans – but you should have heard what I said to Alex McLeish and their bench!

It was after that game that Martin made a much-publicized remark: that I had been subjected to racial and sectarian abuse, i.e. I was being abused for being Irish and Catholic.

He was criticized in many quarters for saying that, but I could see the point that he was making and certainly I now know how players like John Barnes, Ian Wright and Viv Anderson must have felt when they first encountered racial abuse. When you are the victim of abuse, the football pitch can be a very lonely place and in a sense you are not really one of the twenty-two players on the field. I have played in games in England in which players were racially abused, and it is extremely unpleasant, not just for the poor guy who is being subjected to the jeers or monkey chants or whatever, but also for his fellow players. No player minds if he is being booed or jeered because fans don't like his performance, but to be abused simply because you're black or because you are Irish or a Catholic is surely beyond the pale in any civilized society.

It has been going on for five years now and to be honest I am quite used to it. Although it gets annoying from time to time, it is just something that I have to tolerate. Curiously, the abuse did not take place when I first arrived at Celtic, it really only began to happen on a regular basis after I was booed and jeered while playing for Northern Ireland. Since then, it has happened to me so often that it is really a matter of little concern to me. If anything I have used it to spur me on, with a feeling of 'I'll show you . . .'

My team-mates also rallied round me and felt the same way about one of their number being abused. So if you are reading this and you are one of the people who booed or jeered me, how does it feel to know that your contribution helped to inspire me and my fellow Celts to play even better against your team? And since I have been in a team which has won more trophies in the past five seasons than any other Scottish club, how clever does that make you?

Why have I been singled out for 'the treatment'? Some people say it is because I am combative, but as far as I know, I have never changed my style and, as I say, no one booed me incessantly before the Northern Ireland situation erupted.

I think it is fairly obvious that in places such as Ibrox and Tynecastle, it is because I am an Irish Catholic who plays for Celtic. I am not saying that I have received sectarian abuse in every stadium in Scotland, but undoubtedly the motivation for some people to boo me is bigotry. In a twisted view of the world, they think they can express their sectarian outlook by abusing me, picking on me because I am the highest-profile Irish Catholic in Scottish football. That appears to me to be the principal reason why I have been subjected to this long campaign of abuse at so many grounds. I have said it before and I will say it again – bigotry is a problem in Scotland and too many people are quite happy not to confront the issues involved. The vast majority of the population are decent folk who abhor sectarianism, but there is a sizeable minority who express their anti-Catholic feelings at football matches, and one way of doing so is to abuse me. Put it this way, if I was a captain of Celtic who hailed from somewhere in Lanarkshire, does anyone really think that I would be booed and jeered every time I touch the ball? I think that people who carry out this activity should take a long, hard look at themselves, but I won't hold my breath waiting for them to do so.

I have to say that I am disappointed with the number of journalists who have acted as apologists for the abusers. They have written that I am abused because of my aggressive manner, or because I have an arrogant style. So why is it that other players who have been aggressive or arrogant over the years have not received the same constant, continuous abuse as I have? Some people in the press have depicted me as someone who could not control himself on the field, and that, too, in some way excuses the abuse I have received. So why is it that my disciplinary record is actually nowhere near the worst, and I have only been sent off once in a league match in nearly six years in Scotland? All I have done on the field of play is to stick up for myself and my fellow Celtic players and defend ourselves from our opponents. I have done no more than Roy Keane did at Manchester United or Terry Butcher did for Rangers in his heyday.

Yet many people in the media do not see it that way and actively go out of their way to ignore the abuse I have suffered or act as an apologist for the abusers, instead of having the guts to say what is really going on. I get booed from the second I walk onto the pitch at Ibrox and Tynecastle in particular, yet there are journalists who are happy to sweep these things under the carpet and pretend that it is all happening because I wind other players up. For all the logic in that journalistic argument they would be as well writing that people jeer me because I have red hair.

What really annoys me about those who give me personal abuse is that none of these people – not journalists, not fans, nobody except my family and friends – really know what I am like as a person. Do they know, for instance, that I am hopeless at buying clothes for myself? I will often take the advice of the assistants in the shops that I visit. They will often come up to me and say 'we've got just the thing for you' and I am quite happy to take the recommendation.

I certainly don't consider myself a fashion plate, not least because I have the sort of body shape – long trunk and short legs – which is difficult to outfit. I do like to wear sharp suits with a smart shirt, perhaps colour co-ordinated with the suit, but I am not a great fan of ties and I tend to leave the top button of my shirt undone. Usually by the end of the night the tie will be off anyway and I can't see the point of putting something on which will only come off again shortly afterwards.

I am not into designer labels and I will not go out to buy something just because it has somebody's name on it. I like to wear jeans and trainers when I am going into training, but if I'm going out at night I like to look semi-smart. Of course, if I am on club duty it is expected that I dress appropriately. If I am representing Celtic then I want to make the best possible impression, and I will certainly always wear a shirt and tie to such things as football dinners. I've even worn a kilt and Highland dress on occasion, such as at the wedding of my friend and agent Martin Reilly – it was the first time I'd ever worn one and I looked pretty good in it too, even if I say so myself. I have to say that Martin looked even better in a tuxedo and a black kilt, though nothing could outshine his beautiful bride Gail.

I bet only my immediate family and several bootmakers know one secret about me – I have one foot that is bigger than the other. I have really long big toes and the one on my left foot is bigger than on my right. This means that I usually have to buy a pair that is bigger than I would like and hope that the right one isn't too roomy, or buy two pairs of shoes and discard half of them. When I am being measured for my football boots I have to get one boot at size 9 and the other at 8½.

I do like to have tight-fitting boots but I have never been able to find any kind of insert to ensure that my right boot fits as tightly as my left. At one point the sports goods manufacturers Reebok made me special boots and I stayed with them for several years as I really liked their footwear.

What else would people like to know about me? How about the dull part of life as a footballer? You spend a lot of time travelling and resting while you recover from the exertions of playing and training. I like to read books, mostly fiction and usually either crime or thrillers. For instance, I love Ian Rankin's Rebus series about the world-weary detective solving all sorts of gruesome crimes in Edinburgh. I have read them all and would love to spend some time in Edinburgh seeing all the places and settings. When I mentioned in a newspaper interview that I had read all the books and might visit the Oxford Bar where Rebus is supposedly a regular, Ian sent me a postcard saying 'Watch out, it's a haunt of Rangers fans.'

Another series of books which I loved was Roddy Doyle's trilogy set in Dublin – *The Commitments*, *The Van* and *The Snapper*. I was actually sore from laughing at Doyle's brilliant wit and humour.

Recently I've started to read memoirs and biographies – well, if you're going to write one, you had better see how it is done – and I was particularly impressed with some of the recent works about Che Guevara. I have always been fascinated by this Argentinian doctor who helped lead the Cuban revolution and became such a hero to people around the globe. I have to say that I am still trying to get to the bottom of what it was about Guevara that made him such an iconic figure, but there's no doubt that he was a brave man of principle who died for his cause, and that is very attractive to young people in particular.

Like most footballers I am prone to watching football on television if it is on live, but as a way of relaxing, I would rather socialize than watch telly. Even when I do watch something it's usually the old classics like *Fawlty Towers* and *Only Fools and Horses*. One of the best cop shows I have seen recently was the new version of *Rebus*, starring Ken Stott as Ian Rankin's detective – Stott was born for the part.

I do like to watch a good movie, however. One of my favourites of recent years was *Scent of a Woman* starring Al Pacino, in which he plays a former army officer who was blinded in action and who wants one last weekend of fun and games in New York before committing suicide. With his young nephew as a guide he ends up driving a Lamborghini and of course there's that famous dance scene when he does the tango with the beautiful Gabrielle Anwar.

Pacino was brilliant in the role and he remains one of my favourite actors. That film made a terrific impression on me when it first came out, so much so that I even went for tango lessons. I had about four or five sessions with an expert but I could never quite master that fiendishly difficult dance and I lost interest after a while.

As a youngster my favourite film was *The Quiet Man* starring John Wayne, and I grew up on the Duke's great Westerns such as *The Searchers*. I used to think that my grandfather bore a resemblance to John Wayne, as he, too, was a big, tall, larger-than-life character just like the Duke.

I also love my music, and I'll do a turn on the karaoke if pressed – 'Teenage Kicks' by the Undertones is my best number. I have been an avid follower of bands like U2 and Oasis for years. Of the newer bands, I know and like Kasabian as they are big Leicester City fans and I think El Presidente from Glasgow will be big stars. They are a very talented band who are already well known abroad.

Some more personal details – I am no great fan of fancy food. I like plain dishes cooked well but if I have any particular preference then it is for Italian and Japanese food. The best meal I have ever had was when I was on a cruise in the Caribbean and we stopped off at Puerto Rico. In the hotel in San Juan there was a Japanese teryaki bar where the chef cooked everything in front of you. He made a concoction of shrimp and scallop and then he made me the best steak I have ever had in my life – It just melted in the mouth. I have to say that I've never had anything since which came close to that meal. Perhaps one day I'll go back to San Juan and find the bar again.

There are a few restaurants, mainly Italian, in and around Glasgow which I frequent, and I like some bars – especially those where I get left in peace.

What other recreations have I tried? Well, I suppose I have been a sports fiend all of my life. I think I tried just about every sport I could, except for swimming – I was hopeless at it.

I loved to play but I also loved watching – any sporting event that was on the television would see me perched in front of the screen with my dad.

I have always loved boxing. Not for nothing is it called the noble art, and I have so much admiration for boxers, for their skills and athleticism, and for the sheer courage it takes to get into the ring. When the fighters are in the ring, all the talking has to stop and it comes down to a referee and two people who have to go at each other, man to man, to see who has the bigger heart for the fight.

I am too young to remember Muhammad Ali in his prime, but can recall a couple of his later fights such as when he won the title for the third time against Leon Spinks. Ali's natural successor was Larry Holmes and I remember my dad getting me up to watch him defeat the Irish-American hope Gerry Cooney. Then along came Mike Tyson, and though his career has nosedived, people forget just how awesome he was as world heavyweight champion. There was no dancing around from Iron Mike in his early days – nothing flash, just deadly punching. He would turn up in the ring with his black robe, black shorts and boots and once he had taken off the robe and the fight had started, it was usually a question of how quickly he would knock out his opponent. He was a real throwback to the era of Jack Dempsey and the other maulers of yesteryear.

Nigel Benn was similar to Tyson in that he always went forward throwing punches. I was at his fight against Gerald McClelland in Manchester which ended so tragically with the latter man badly injured. What a fight that was, with McClelland throwing such heavy punches that it could have gone either way.

Like everyone in Northern Ireland, I followed the career of Barry McGuigan very closely. The Clones Cyclone was a truly great champion who united the country behind him as he won and defended his world title. I have never met Barry but I hope to do so one day. Steve Collins was another Irish boxer I admired and I followed the fortunes of his long and distinguished career.

Prince Naseem Hamed was one of the best boxers I ever

saw. I was at his fight in Manchester when he beat Wilfredo Vazquez in the seventh round, and he was brilliant as usual. On the undercard that night was the best boxing match I've ever seen, a battle between Chris Eubank and Carl Thompson for the world cruiserweight title. It was toe-to-toe stuff for twelve rounds and both men must have been incredibly fit to maintain the pace they did throughout the fight. They were throwing bombs at each other, so they must have had strong jaws as well. The crowd were on their feet at the end and anyone who did not have admiration for Eubank before that fight certainly did so afterwards. On the judges' cards he lost that contest but I and many other observers felt he had won, and he showed great dignity in defeat.

Of the current crop of very decent boxers on the Scottish scene I particularly admire Scott Harrison, the world featherweight champion. I have met Scott and his father Peter, who trains him, several times and I've also been ringside at four of his world championship bouts. He has had his troubles recently but I am sure he will bounce back. When he puts his mind to it there is no more determined and focused boxer in the land. What I like most about Scott is that he doesn't shirk anybody, unlike quite a few of the so-called champions who have avoided fighting him. When he was defeated in the ring by Manuel Medina, Scott showed his courage and class by getting back into the ring and regaining his title from Medina at the very first opportunity.

I've also seen European super-featherweight champion Alex Arthur from Edinburgh a few times and I think he is a certainty to become a world champion.

Another Scottish sportsman that I greatly admire is racing driver Dario Franchitti who is based in the USA. He came to a match and it was a pleasure to meet him and his missus – better known as the Hollywood actress Ashley Judd.

One of the best things about living in Scotland is that I am never more than a short distance away from some of the greatest golf courses in the world. I have always enjoyed golf, which I first started playing when I was about fourteen, but it's really since I came to Parkhead that I have acquired the bug. It has been a privilege to play the likes of Turnberry and Gleneagles. At the time of writing my handicap is twelve, but I am sure that I could get it lower if I had more time to play. There are a few good players at Celtic and it helped us to bond when we came together under Martin O'Neill, who is no mean player himself. Paul Lambert loved a game, big John Hartson could hit a mean drive and Tom Boyd and Henrik Larsson also enjoyed a round. With that lot playing, the sledging could get a bit fierce at times, but I wouldn't dare repeat the insults.

The best golfing footballer I've seen is Paul Telfer who could be a scratch golfer if he put his mind to it. He hits the ball for miles and his short game is brilliant as well.

Gaelic football is the sport which I have played and enjoyed most aside from football. It's a great community game and I started playing almost as soon as I began to play football. I was pretty good at the Gaelic version, too, and have the medals to prove it. After I left school and joined Manchester City, I returned home briefly and was picked for the Armagh team which contested the Ulster Minors Final against Derry in 1989. We were well beaten that day by Derry who went on to win the All-Ireland Minors Final. They had in their ranks Anthony Tohill who became a real superstar in Gaelic football and won a senior All-Ireland title with Derry, and who I am proud to call a good friend. I still like to watch Gaelic football and particularly the Armagh matches. But I am no great fan of hurling – I wasn't mad enough to play it as a boy!

So there you are – you now know almost all there is to know about me as a person. But let's get back to football and the 2004/05 season.

The aftermath of that nasty Ibrox match almost overshadowed the fact that we had to play Barcelona three days later in the Nou Camp. We played superbly that night and showed all our defiance of those who had criticized us by gaining a 1–1 draw against a team which many rated as the best in the world at that time.

Unfortunately, we could only match that draw against Milan at Parkhead on a night when Shakhtar Donetsk triumphed over Barcelona to deprive us even of a consolation place in the Uefa Cup.

One of the highlights of that Milan match was the performance of Aiden McGeady. He is a terrific talent and people forget he is still developing physically and as a player. Some days he is unplayable, but sadly last season he picked up a bad knee injury, though I'm sure he'll be back and become an even better player.

As the season progressed, our domestic form was as good as always. We put Rangers out of the Scottish Cup just as they had beaten us in the League Cup. But in February there came what in hindsight proved to be a very notable defeat for us, when Rangers came to Parkhead and won 2–0.

It was the first time we had lost a home league match to them under Martin. Victory was a psychological boost for Rangers, no doubt, but there was very little between the teams except for a couple of defensive clangers by us. We just had a bad day at the office, as was the case against Hearts at the beginning of April when we lost 2–0. Big Bobo had made a couple of mistakes and was at the centre of a real rammy in the dressing room – you don't want to get on the wrong side of Bobo, and it took four people to hold him down! At least we got our revenge by beating Hearts in the semi-final of the Scottish Cup a week later.

Craig Bellamy joined us on loan to the end of the season and what a significant short-term signing he turned out to be. Craig had a fair amount of baggage from his time at Newcastle including his several high-profile fallouts with former Rangers manager Graeme Souness – which ensured that the Celtic fans were on his side from the start!

He is a bubbly personality, the sort of character we needed in the dressing room, and nothing at all like the demon he has been painted. Sure he can be cocky and display a bit of devilment, but that is part of his personality and he means no harm.

After we had beaten Aberdeen 3–2, the squad went over to Donegal for a break and let's just say a good time was had by all. It helped us to bond for the run-in and against Rangers we were quite brilliant – Craig Bellamy had been a star in Donegal and he starred against Rangers, too, as we beat them 2–1 at Ibrox.

We were five points clear with three matches to go and you would not be human in that situation if you did not think the title was in the bag. But complacency was no excuse for the perfomance against Hibs, where we just never got going. Ivan Sproule made the difference for them when he came on, and the late goals we lost in a 3–1 defeat meant that we were now just two points clear.

The match against Hearts at Tynecastle assumed huge significance. After Paul Hartley equalized we had to throw everything at them and Stan Petrov got the winner.

To be fair to Rangers, they stuck at it, too, and won three matches on the trot to ensure that the championship race went to the wire once again.

The whole season had come down to ninety minutes, just

as it had two years previously. The difference this time was that the destination of the title was in our own hands – we could only lose it.

Before the game against Motherwell at Fir Park, there was a funny atmosphere around the dressing room. There were whispers around Parkhead that Martin might be thinking of standing down as Mrs O'Neill was quite ill. But far from concerning us, those rumours only made us more determined to win the match as we thought that winning the league might persuade him to stay.

Motherwell were up for it and Fir Park has always been a difficult place to visit, but I felt before the game that we had done all the hard work and I was quite confident that we could see it through. We played well for much of the match but we just could not put them away.

There was an incident early on in which Craig Bellamy was clean through and from where I was standing it looked a definite penalty. A goal then would have turned the game in our favour.

Chris Sutton's goal looked to have set us up and then we had several chances to finish it off. But the goalkeeper, former Celt Gordon Marshall, made at least four wonderful saves to deny us.

Leading 1–0 is always difficult. I remember asking Hugh Dallas how long was left and he told me five minutes. I turned to Stan and said 'just five minutes left, let's keep it going', but then their striker Scott McDonald intervened.

He had his back to the goal with big Bobo on his case. The ball bounced up onto McDonald's chest and he turned and volleyed it into the top corner for a peach of a goal.

There were eighty-eight minutes on the clock. I just could not believe it had happened. We were two minutes from the title and now it was being snatched away from us.

We did not know that Rangers were in the lead at Easter Road, so I went over to the dugout and Robbo told me that we needed a goal, which meant that Rangers must be winning. We had to go for broke, but as we charged upfield they hit us on the counter. Their winning goal was a bit of a fluke, but they all count, though some hurt much more than others.

The feeling was one of utter numbness, just as I had felt in Seville and at Kilmarnock two years previously. What was really galling was the way Motherwell celebrated as if they had won the league. They had won a match, but their joy at depriving us of the title left a bitter taste in our mouths.

We were so down that we just could not wait to get out of Fir Park, but we had to analyse what had happened. Martin went ballistic with us – no wonder. We had lost the league in the space of a few minutes, undoing all the hard work of the season, and none of us could believe what happened.

I believe Martin's decision to quit Celtic was sealed at that point. We knew Mrs O'Neill had not been well the previous summer when the manager couldn't come out at the start of the American tour, but we did not really know how seriously ill she had become.

Losing the league was bad enough, but when Martin came in on the Wednesday and announced that he was going, it felt as though we were looking annihilation in the face. I had an inkling he was about to leave, but it still came as a hammer blow to hear the words.

Later he took me aside and gave me some advice for the future, and he thanked me for my efforts for his teams. Of course, I told him the feelings were mutual.

With Martin went his two lieutenants, John Robertson and Steve Walford. There was a remarkable chemistry between the three men, who are markedly different but complement each other so well.

Robbo was the buffer between the manager and the players and it was he who would come in each morning and gauge the mood of the dressing room. I always thought he looked like a university lecturer the way he dressed.

Wally is a laid-back character, who takes everything in his stride. The two of them were a great double act. Wally would wind up Robbo and nine times out of ten he would take the bait.

Working together for nine years, you get to know people and we came to trust each other implicitly, so their triple departure was a devastating blow to me personally as well as the club.

It sounds bizarre to say so, but the Scottish Cup Final against Dundee United was a total anti-climax. We went out and won it for Martin's sake, but it felt like a hollow victory because we had lost the big one. Craig Bellamy was outstanding but the match lacked passion, possibly because we scored after five minutes through Alan Thompson and Dundee United never really looked as if they wanted to risk attacking us.

At least Martin got the send-off he deserved, picking up the trophy in front of the fans who adored him. It was the end of an incredible five years which had been amazing for the players and fans alike. The scenes as he walked around Hampden were unforgettable, all of us going through a maelstrom of emotions at the end of a rollercoaster week.

The following day was Jackie McNamara's testimonial and it was fitting that Lubo Moravcik and Henrik Larsson came back for the match against the Republic of Ireland. It was a great day for the fans to be able to say goodbye to Martin, though they did not know that Jackie would be leaving too. With Henrik and Lubo there, it was a genuine end-of-an-era moment, a farewell to a period which had been the best for the club since the time of Jock Stein. With Martin in charge, a new generation of Celtic fans had seen what their club could achieve, and perhaps now they understand why their fathers and grandfathers had raved about the Lisbon Lions and their successors.

In time, those fans will be able to tell their kids about the Celtic of Henrik and Martin, of Paul Lambert, Jackie McNamara, Johann Mjallby, Joos Valgaeren and all the others who served the club at that glorious time. It was a time when we were kings, but even monarchs must leave the stage and make way for others. At a club like Celtic, there is always change and renewal and so a new manager soon arrived to take charge. And the club got a new captain, too.

CHAPTER THIRTEEN

Captain's Log

The best thing that happened to me during the 2005/06 season had nothing to do with football. A couple of years ago I met a beautiful woman who ran a popular bar in Glasgow called The Room. Irene McCloy now shares my life permanently and, while we have had our ups and downs, we are happy together, not least because our son Gallagher was born in December 2005. He has my red hair and his mother's good looks and is a healthy baby who is growing fast. He is the joy of our life and I like nothing better than just to sit with him on my knee at night. His sister Alisha adores her wee brother and my parents are delighted with their grandson.

Sadly, just a few days after Gallagher was born, Irene's father Alec died after a long battle against cancer. I liked him a lot and we had some good verbal jousts, not least because he was a Rangers fan! He is very much missed.

Back in the close season of 2005, there were pressing concerns facing me. I had reached the end of my contract and didn't know if Martin's successor would want me to stay on. Obviously, I had a long-standing professional relationship with Martin, so I did wonder whether a new manager would want new blood around the place instead of older players who had been loyal to the former gaffer.

One of them had already gone after a contractual dispute. Coming as it did so soon after his testimonial, club captain Jackie McNamara's departure was genuinely shocking, especially as I felt from talking to him that he wanted to stay. He was only in his early thirties, he had made a success of the club captaincy and he had been a tremendous player for Celtic over his ten years, so I was sure he would be made a suitable offer. I was not privy to the negotiations, obviously, but clearly Jackie finally decided to act in what he thought were the best interests of himself and his young family – security is important for footballers.

Craig Bellamy also wanted to remain at Parkhead and the rest of us would have loved him to stay, but Newcastle wanted much more than Celtic could afford and spending so much on one player would have meant that the new manager could not have brought in the players he wanted.

That new manager was something of a surprise. As with every other player, I had no idea that the club was even talking to Gordon Strachan, who had enjoyed a glittering career as a player with Dundee, Aberdeen, Manchester United, Leeds and Coventry, becoming the only person to win both the Scottish and English Footballer of the Year Awards, as well as winning a host of medals. He had played until he was forty before managing Coventry and Southampton, but in 2004 announced he was resigning from the latter club to take a break from football. He had been out of management for a year and working as a media pundit when Celtic came calling.

At the same time as I discovered that Jackie McNamara had left the manager was on the telephone to tell me the news while I was on holiday in Portugal. He emphasized that he very much wanted me to stay, outlined some of his plans, adding that he wanted me to take over as club captain.

I was still in the latter stages of negotiations with the club at that time. It has been well publicized that Celtic have been revising their wage structure over the past couple of years and I did agree to a cut in my basic wages, but that was less of a concern to me than the future of the team. However, after Gordon had spoken to me, I felt reassured and had no hesitation in signing up for a year.

I was so confident in the players that we had that I said in my first press conference as captain that we would win back the league title. Now it's one thing to say it, but quite another to do it, but with the likes of Chris Sutton, John Hartson, Alan Thompson, Stan Petrov, Didier Agathe, Bobo Balde and Stan Varga around, I felt sure that this happy band of brothers could rise to the task once again.

The manager had a lot of work to do over the close season, especially as he wanted to vary our playing style. He also brought in some players who would prove to be very influential over the coming months.

Polish international Maciej Zurawski was signed from Wisla Krakow where he been Poland's top scorer. The man the fans call 'Magic' is an easy-going type, a laid-back character who has quickly become a favourite at Parkhead. When you think that he was out through injury for a chunk of the season, you have to say he's made a very impressive start at Celtic with twenty goals in twenty-seven matches. And there's more to come, I'm sure.

Around the same time, his fellow Polish international Artur Boruc joined from Legia Warsaw on loan, though he later signed permanently. Big Artur is just like every other goalie – eccentric. On the field, however, he has brought composure and presence to the defence and after his recent performances in Germany in the 2006 World Cup, a lot more people have taken note of his ability. Alan Shearer compared him to legendary Manchester United goalkeeper Peter Schmeichel and I would not disagree.

Shunsuke Nakamura signed for us in late July from Reggina in Italy. He made an immediate impact at Celtic, not least because it seemed that every time you opened a cupboard, a Japanese reporter would fall out. That's because Naka is a genuine superstar at home in Japan, a mainstay of the national team which has a devoted following. While some people accused Celtic of signing him only with a view to the Japanese market, his performances throughout the season proved that he was worth much, much more to the club than the yen from the sale of shirts.

Other signings such as Jeremie Alladiere from Arsenal and Du Wei from China didn't work out for various reasons and they have left the club, while Adam Virgo and especially Mark Wilson have done their bit and are good long-term prospects for Celtic.

There were times at the start of the season when I had to pinch myself because I really was living a dream. Me, captain of Celtic – what an accolade, the first Irishman to hold the post since the legendary Bertie Peacock five decades ago.

One newspaper said I had lost weight and must have done special training over the summer for my new responsibilities as captain. All very flattering but the truth is I did nothing extra over the summer, and the promotional photographs which apparently showed me as having shed weight in the close season were actually taken in April!

I didn't just want to be captain, I wanted to be a winning captain. To have the captaincy and not win anything would have seen me quickly dismissed as a failure in the job.

At the start of the season there were plenty of people in the media only too quick and too happy to write me off as we made a disastrous start. Our pre-season matches had not gone well because of the number of changes taking place around Parkhead. They made us even more disjointed than usual at that time of year.

Then came one of the worst nights of my entire career, in the qualifying round for the Champions League in my first competitive match as full-time club captain. Even now, looking at the scoreline sends a chill down my spine: Artmedia Bratislava of Slovakia 5, Celtic 0.

That night in Bratislava we were quite simply caught cold – even the warm-up beforehand was poor, it just wasn't the sort of thing you do before a Champions League match. As each goal went in, I just could not believe what was happening to us and by the end we were dumbstruck with embarrassment. To make matters worse, I accidentally clashed with Chris Sutton and my big mate was carried off with a broken cheekbone.

It was like the last-day defeat in the league at Motherwell all over again, accompanied by the same feelings of shock and disbelief. Gordon said it was the worst night of his career and he was clearly gutted by what he had seen, as were we all. It was the worst performance by Celtic in my time at Parkhead, and I remember swearing to myself that 'this must never be repeated'.

The SPL fixtures computer must have a perverse sense of humour, because in our first league match of the season we had to go to Motherwell to play the team which had beaten us on the last day of the previous campaign. We hadn't forgotten how they had celebrated our loss of the league, so we saw this encounter as a chance for revenge. When we went 3–1 up it looked as though we were going to get that vengeance. However, they came back with three headed goals and that showed we had a problem defensively, not least because we were missing Bobo Balde who had been left out as punishment for missing the bus on the morning of the Artmedia game. At 3–4 it looked as though Motherwell had mugged us again, but Craig Beattie came on to scramble the equalizer. At least we had gained a point and in training we were able to work on things as we prepared for the return leg against Artmedia at Parkhead.

In fifty years of European Cup competition, no team had ever overturned a 0–5 deficit in the second leg of a knockout tie. We would have to make history to stay in the Champions League and we came so very, very close to doing so.

To me, that night was the turning point of the whole season. We played with pace and passion and you could see the team starting to gel in front of your eyes. In the huddle, I called for everything we could give and more and then signalled to the supporters to get behind us. With our fans roaring us on, we just tore into attack after attack and goals were inevitable.

Alan Thompson got the first from the penalty spot and while Durica was off getting his jersey repaired – apparently they had no spares – big John Hartson forced home a second shortly before half-time.

Stephen McManus made it three when there was still more than half an hour to go. Craig Beattie came on for Magic and, after near things for big John and Shaun Maloney, Craig put us four up with a fine header in the eighty-third minute. We threw everything at them and Craig came agonizingly close to converting a cross from Shaun. At the final whistle, however, we had failed by a single goal to achieve that historic recovery. We were out of the Champions League and out of European competition entirely, but we had proven that we were far from finished as a team.

People then set out to discredit Artmedia. Some pundits

thought they were no more than a pub team – well, it must have been some pub as in the Champions League proper, they drew twice with Rangers and beat Porto 3–2 in Portugal.

The team was determined to bounce back and got a real boost when Nakamura made his debut in our home win over Dundee United. It was immediately clear he was a very fine footballer, good with both feet and full of silky skills. He is one of those players who can make something happen in a game and is always worth watching, so his extended contract is a real fillip for us.

As the first few matches progressed, you could see the players that the manager had brought in beginning to find their feet. Paul Telfer, for instance, had really been brought in as cover for Didier Agathe who was injured on the first day of pre-season, so it says a lot for Paul that Didier never really recovered his place and eventually left Celtic. However, he will never be forgotten for some of his vital contributions, in European matches in particular.

We had put a few results together, but as always, the commentators and the fans argued that the Old Firm game would be the acid test for the team.

We started the game really well and were passing the ball around when suddenly Alan Thompson caught Nacho Novo late. Referee Stuart Dougal immediately pulled out the red card. I just could not believe it and as I glanced over at the Rangers bench, I could see that they could not believe it either. I ran over to the referee and said, 'Come on, you can't send him off for that.' He replied curtly, 'I just did.' I was amazed at the decision because, frankly, there had already been tougher tackles than Alan's. It was a hot August day and with only ten men we struggled for a while. Rangers went 2–0 up through Dado Prso and Thomas Buffel but we pulled one back through Shaun Maloney's penalty and we were right back in the game with five minutes left. Three minutes later the referee gave a soft penalty against Stan Petrov and Nacho Novo converted for a 1–3 scoreline.

I had been exchanging views with the referee during the match and was eventually booked after seventy-one minutes. Straight after the final whistle I went up to Stuart Dougal and said, 'You were poor, you spoiled that game today.' My language was not the sort you would use in the diplomatic corps but it was no worse than a lot of players have used to referees over the years. I then shook Marvin Andrews' hand and the big fellow asked me if I would swap shirts for a charity event.

I said, 'Of course, happy to help', when I felt a hand on my shoulder and saw that the referee had produced the red card. I was furious – why could he not just have said 'get off' or 'I'll talk to you later' or even red-carded me in the tunnel?

Instead, he sent me off in full view of the main stand which heaved with gloating Rangers fans. It was the first time I had been sent off in a league match in Scotland and I was incensed.

I let rip at him verbally and got up close but I was never going to hit him. Assistant referee James Bee felt obliged to get in between us, which made it look as though he was intervening to stop me lashing out, but I would never, ever hit an official. At the most, I went shoulder to shoulder with the referee and tapped his assistant on the shoulder. Paul Telfer and Shaun Maloney were quickly on the scene and hustled me away.

I knew as I walked off that I would be in trouble. I also knew what was going to happen next in terms of publicity. Sure enough, my 'friends' among the broadcasting pundits and in the newspapers didn't miss the chance to have a pop at their favourite target. But the extent of the sheer abuse in the newspapers took me aback.

I have seen many much worse incidents but I would doubt if anyone has ever taken the level of personal criticism and abuse which I got from the media then. I know that what I did was wrong and I meant it when, the next day, I made a public apology to Stuart Dougal. I also knew that I had let down Celtic, the manager and the fans but in all honesty, I do not think my offence in any way deserved the kind of hysterical coverage which I received.

There were calls for me to get an eleven-game ban, to be stripped off the captaincy and to be kicked out of Scottish football, all in the sort of banner headlines normally reserved for a mass murderer. The Scottish FA had to react, of course, and announced that I would face a disciplinary hearing.

The annoying thing was the way that people kept comparing my case to that of Saulius Mikoliunas the season before. The Hearts player had been banned for eight matches, later reduced to five on appeal, for rushing over and barging into assistant referee Alan Davis. Even though I hadn't deliberately pushed or shoved any official, some commentators were predicting I would get a longer ban.

Even in the midst of all that turmoil, I could still laugh at one episode. It had really been Alan Thompson's red card which had sparked off the whole saga and that wasn't the end of him getting us into trouble that weekend. As we had the day after the Ibrox game off we arranged to play a round at Cadder Golf Club with a couple of pals. A road runs through the course and, at the second hole, a motorist waited in his car until we played. It was just bad luck that Alan shanked his seven-iron and the ball took off down the road, bouncing along until it smacked the car. You've guessed it – out got a Rangers fan. 'I might have guessed it would be a Celtic player that hit my car.' That time I let Tommo deal with the problem on his own . . .

Thankfully, when the Scottish FA held its hearing, common sense prevailed. I was accompanied by Fraser Wishart of the Scottish PFA, by Celtic's lawyer Rod McKenzie and by Gordon Strachan, whose presence I greatly appreciated. Stuart Dougal also attended the hearing and in an unprecedented move brought along his lawyer, which led to a long legal debate about just who was actually on trial. When that finished Rod McKenzie was able to put my case, which centred on the video evidence which showed that I had not assaulted anyone.

As we waited for the verdict, Fraser Wishart predicted that I would get a five-match ban but Rod correctly thought it would be three. Including the automatic one-match ban for the red card, in total I was banned for four games.

Of course, that sentence was just nowhere near harsh enough for some of my 'friends' in the press, who turned their ire on the Scottish FA. There was even some talk of a strike by referees because the sentence had been too lenient in their eyes. The fact that I had been judged fairly and had received a sentence entirely in keeping with the precedent set by the Mikoliunas case was neither here nor there to the press lynch mob. I just wondered why there had to be a special sort of 'justice' for me.

The irony was that Stuart Dougal, who, to be fair, had reported me only for my admittedly bad language towards him, had himself been fined £200 by the SFA in 2004 for swearing at Christian Nerlinger of Rangers – an offence picked up by 'lipreaders' watching the television. (By the way, those pesky lipreaders would have a field day on any training ground.)

Stuart Dougal has refereed several of our matches since then and there have been no recriminations whatsoever. He is a professional doing his job and so am I and that's the way it should be.

How I wish the press had similarly drawn a line under the matter on day one. Instead, the usual suspects queued up to give me a verbal kicking. One writer, Andy McInnes, a person I do not know, felt obliged to launch a most vicious personal attack on me, calling for me to be stripped of the captaincy, and accusing me of 'acting like a demented animal', showing 'all the ugly actions of a back-street thug' and so forth. 'Lennon was like a sewer emptying', he added, and called me 'the wee hard man you wouldn't want to meet in a dark close'.

I consulted my lawyers on that one, but decided it would be more trouble than it was worth, because McInnes, who I gather is not a household name, would only pen more abuse. Later, in another article, he tried to make me out to be paranoid about the press. As it happens, I'm not, but reading stuff like his you might consider I had every right to be. Here's the ironic thing – near the end of the season the same McInnes named me as one of four people that he had considered voting for as Player of the Year. He wrote that I had 'knuckled down to captaincy in the shadow of Roy Keane to produce great consistency' – rather more consistency than the journalist, I feel.

I normally shrug off such attacks, but their personal nature may explain why people think that it is perfectly all right to have a go at me in the street. Is it any coincidence that shortly after all the furore over the sending-off, when I was walking down Buchanan Street in Glasgow city centre a woman started shouting at me, 'You Fenian c***, you dirty f****** Fenian bastard'? A grown woman felt it was okay to scream abuse at me in full view of dozens of witnesses on a busy city street – why did she think that was permissible?

Another time at Motherwell, there were a bunch of kids – not even teenagers – in their colours who screamed and swore at me, calling me a Fenian this and that. I am not saying newspapers encourage sectarian abuse, but when they pillory a player in the manner in which I was subjected, I think they encourage people to believe that abusing someone is acceptable.

I consider myself to be pretty savvy about the media. I have a couple of friends who are journalists and so I am very aware of the pressures of the job. That is why I have tried to be helpful and cooperative over the years and have never shirked from doing my club duty to give interviews. I have great respect for a few writers, mostly in the broadsheets, but when you consider the treatment I have had over the years, from the Scottish tabloids in particular, you have to ask whether there is some sort of agenda at work. No other player seems to provoke such a reaction and I know that certain individuals are clearly acting out of bias. Until recently, however, I had no idea why some pundits have been trying to get me kicked out of the Celtic team for the last five-and-a-half years.

I have been criticized for everything under the sun. Some don't like my running action – they obviously don't know about my back – and some have taunted me over my weight, when my health records show that it has never varied more than a few pounds either way since I came to the club. Events that have happened off the field are supposed to have affected my game, but do you think for one second that Martin O'Neill or Gordon Strachan would have continued picking me if they thought that I couldn't do what they wanted on the pitch?

Some of those events away from football should not have made the papers. For example, I picked up a Sunday newspaper one morning a few years ago to read a lurid 'kiss and tell' description of a close encounter with a girl I thought was a friend. In fairly graphic terms, this girl told the world exactly what we had been up to in private. Now some of her descriptions were flattering, but I believe that what happens between consenting adults in their own bedroom should stay between them and not be paraded all over the press for the delectation of readers – which is why this book does not contain any such tales.

That was one episode where I was not responsible for the publicity that came my way, but there's no doubt I've done some wrong things over the years. Yet the way certain people in the media go on and on about me makes me think they have a personal axe to grind. But since I don't know them and they don't know me, it can't be personal, can it? After all, journalists are not supposed to exercise personal prejudices, are they?

Personal it is, however. I could name you all the pundits who have made serious personal attacks on me and I could get personal right back. I could tell you that they themselves are far from perfect – like the one whose love life is a standing joke in football and media circles – but I won't name them at all.

Only recently I worked out what these people are all about – ego. They spout their views, which, to be fair, are not always complete nonsense, in a manner which is calculated to get them more attention, attract more listeners or sell more newspapers. It has nothing to do with proper constructive views on football and its personalities and everything to do with massaging their own egos.

The media made me the story and the pundits have to keep outdoing each other in their verbiage – I almost said garbage – about me to remain at the top of the pile. That's why the criticism over the years has been so exaggerated. I cannot deny that I have been the most high-profile player in Scotland in recent years, but that was not my doing and certainly not my wish. Yet just because I have been the big story so many times, the pundits feel it is acceptable to intensify their criticism of me to the point where it becomes almost laughable.

Since they thrive on ego, on seeing their name in print, I won't name any of them at all . . .

I will make one exception though – Des McKeown, manager of Stenhousemuir FC, a fellow footballing professional with whom I had a real falling-out after he used his tabloid column to attack me. Journalists can write what they like as it's their job, and I do not mind criticism from former high-profile professionals, but I'm not taking it from someone still in the game who hasn't played at the top level – he was on Celtic's books as a youngster but didn't make the grade. Do something serious in football and you can have a pop at me with impunity, but McKeown does not come into that category, though I know that managing a small club can actually be pretty difficult as you have so few resources.

I just could not accept his criticism, however. The Scottish FA certainly didn't like it either and, after Celtic complained, he was fined for his remarks. The ironic thing is that, just like McInnes, McKeown later named me as one of his players of the year!

He called me once and I told him that his stuff had been offensive because it had nothing to do with football, that he was just trying to be smart and make a name for himself. I pointed out his conflict of interest, in that he was trying to manage a football club yet writing about a fellow professional. I also pointed out that I was captain of Celtic and had played for my country, whereas he had not done anything like that. I am glad to say he was more measured in his comments after that.

I just wish that more columnists and journalists would think about the possible consequences of their work. They have tremendous power and most do their jobs responsibly, but there are a few like McInnes and McKeown who occasionally go over the top with their criticism. Luckily I have been in the game long enough to take the brickbats and then turn them to my advantage.

For instance, in the days after my sending-off at Ibrox, I was incensed by some of the remarks, from former professionals in particular, so that match actually proved to be something of a watershed for me. I read their comments about me being finished and vowed to myself that I would show my critics just how wrong they were. I decided that I would have them eating humble pie by the end of the season. By and large, I think I succeeded and a few pundits were honest enough to acknowledge that they had got it wrong.

After the SFA hearing I sat out my sentence in the stand, but I also used the time out to do some extra fitness work with our coach Jim Henry. The result was that the break actually did me good in the long term – again, it was about using a step back to go two steps forward.

I went straight back into the team for the game against Hearts, who were flying high at that time under George Burley. It was a big call for our manager to make as the team had been doing well in my absence, but I'm glad to say I never looked back after that 1–1 draw which showed that Hearts really were our main, and indeed only, rivals. Indeed at that point they were unbeaten and topped the table.

Truly, it was turning out to be a strange season. Not only were Hearts doing so well, but Rangers were having a terrible time domestically. Things took several dramatic turns at Tynecastle such as the departure of George Burley and the arrival of Graham Rix, while Rangers' woes occupied much of the back pages. At Parkhead, we were actually quite pleased not to be the centre of attention and just went about our business of quietly accumulating points.

We were beginning to show real consistency, but the games which made people sit up and take notice were in the double header against Rangers in November.

In the CIS League Cup, we gave one of our best performances of the season to beat them 2–0. Shaun Maloney scored a magnificent goal that night, sparking a run of terrific form for him which culminated in Shaun being named both the Young Player of the Year and the Player of the Year at the end of the season. And he is only going to get better!

Rangers played well enough in the second part of that double header, a league game, but on a freezing day we still managed to win 3–0 with goals from John Hartson, Bobo Balde and Aiden McGeady. That win put us fifteen points clear of Rangers as early as 19 November, and I said afterwards that there would have to be a major disaster for them to catch us.

Back-to-back wins over the other half of the Old Firm are actually pretty rare, so we really felt that we could now go on and win the league as only Hearts seemed able to challenge us, and they were having their own much-publicized troubles.

The quiet period we had enjoyed media-wise promptly evaporated when Roy Keane announced his departure from Manchester United. From the start, his name was linked with Celtic as he had previously stated his wish to play for the club he had long supported.

I will admit that I was a bit apprehensive at the time that the arrival of Roy Keane at Parkhead might cause me some grief. We are similar in age, background and playing style, and it seemed likely that one of us would have to make way for the other. Some pundits suggested that we could never play together, but they had said the same thing about Paul Lambert and myself.

There was a lot of media hype about the money Roy was or wasn't going to get at Celtic, but I don't think any other player could tell you what he actually got. The fact is that he just wanted to come and sample life at Celtic and I don't think money was an issue.

There was much speculation that there would be a clash of egos, but it was purely speculative and was just the usual nonsense you get when you are associated with a big club like Celtic.

In fact he and I got on well from the start, as I liked his dry sense of humour and enjoyed his company straight away. Roy was really good for the dressing room and would sit with the lads and chat away at dinner times. He didn't talk that much about football, in fact, but discussed all sorts of other things. But when he did talk about football, perhaps to give a few pointers to a youngster, people always listened – he is a legend within the game, and his opinions count.

We already had a winning mentality, but Roy added a considerable presence of his own to the side and, when he played, he did very well for us. Unfortunately, he was injured on occasion and it was clear he had a long-term problem with his hip. Of course, we all now know that problem was insurmountable and Roy retired on medical advice at the end of the season. I wish him well in whatever he chooses to do in the future and I know he will remember well his all too brief time at Celtic.

When Shunsuke Nakamura arrived from Japan he brought with him a huge following of press and television cameras – some of them have never left and are on permanent Naka watch – but there was an even greater hullabaloo when Roy arrived at Parkhead. He was anxious for it all to die down so that he could get on with playing football, but we all understood that after the furore which surrounded his departure from Manchester United, there would be considerable interest in his presence for a number of weeks.

Most of the correspondents hung around for Roy's debut, a Scottish Cup tie against Clyde at Broadwood Stadium. As cup holders who were presently topping the league above Clyde, we were rightly the hot favourites, but sadly it was just one of those days when we were completely out of focus.

The previous week we had beaten Hearts at Tynecastle and had been quite brilliant in coming back from 0–2 down. Hearts had been the better side in the first half and led at the interval through a Ross Wallace own goal and a header from Steven Pressley. The Hearts players' body language seemed to indicate that they thought it was all over, but our manager told us to just keep playing our game and if we got a goal, we would win. He was proven absolutely correct with Stephen McManus scoring two late goals after Stephen Pearson had come on for an injured Stan Petrov and scored our first. That 3–2 win was a pivotal moment in the season as we had only just gained the league leadership from Hearts a couple of matches before, but now suddenly we had raced seven points clear. It must have been a psychological hammer blow to them and it certainly boosted us.

Yet the Clyde match brought us right back down to earth and ended any talk of a cakewalk in the league. It was nothing to do with Roy or anybody's position or the formation that day – we just did not perform, although we should have taken the chances we created.

That was the start of a short sticky patch for us. Chris Sutton left the club for his own good reasons, but I was sorry to see my friend leave. He had been a stalwart of the Martin O'Neill years, playing in a variety of positions and being both a terrific leader of the line and a real character in the dressing room. At the age of thirty-six – proving the manager's adage that age is no concern if you're good enough – Dion Dublin came in as cover. He too is a versatile type able to play in defence or up front. During that January transfer window there was even some speculation that I might leave and join Leicester City after Craig Levein was sacked, but I quickly put that to rest – I was too intent on captaining Celtic to the title to think of moving.

In the league we lost to Motherwell and drew with Dundee United, but then we went to Ibrox where Roy Keane made his Old Firm debut – he looked as though he had played in those games all his life, and his contribution was immense as we won by a single goal from Maciej Zurawski.

With Hearts falling further behind, we now looked certain to win the SPL, which would bring with it automatic entry into the Champions League, but that was not the way we approached things. Often it is at times like that, when everything seems to be going your way, that you need to be mentally strong, to force yourself to battle against complacency, and that was when the experience of players such as Roy, myself and Stan Petrov counted. The consistency of our two young 'home-grown' players, Stephen McManus and Shaun Maloney, was another big asset to what was a generally settled side. We just simply refused to lose – at Celtic, no other attitude is acceptable.

In the CIS League Cup we had progressed to the final by beating Motherwell 2–1 in the semi-final at Hampden. In that final we would meet Dunfermline, and what a dress rehearsal we had at East End Park.

I had always thought that one day our play would really click into the highest gear and it did that afternoon as we ran up the record score in SPL history, thrashing them 8–1. Magic

Zurawski scored four that day, but I'm sure he'll forgive me if I dwell on the penultimate goal, a magnificent strike of class and power from an attacking midfielder. Actually, I have no idea why I was so far forward and lurking around their box when I saw a bit of space and prodded one that just sneaked inside Bryn Halliwell's post. My celebrations were over the top, but that was surely understandable as I had notched only my third competitive goal at Celtic. Funnily enough, several years previously Martin O'Neill had predicted I would not score again until 2006 and he was not wrong. I called it a 'JFK moment' because every Celtic fan would remember where they were when I finally completed my 'hat-trick' in only five seasons.

No Celtic fan or indeed any lover of football will need reminding about what happened in the week before the CIS League Cup Final. After a long and brave battle against motor neurone disease, Jimmy Johnstone, the man voted by the fans as the Greatest Ever Celt, passed away at his home in Uddingston.

It was a very emotional time for everyone connected with Celtic Football Club. Jinky, the wee man who had electrified the footballing world with his dazzling wing play in the 1960s and 1970s, had come to embody the spirit of the club. I never saw him play in the flesh, but I saw enough film of him to realize he was a genius. In 2004, Henrik Larsson and I were at the launch of the tribute DVD *Lord of the Wing* which showcased his skills. I had never seen the footage of the night Celtic beat Real Madrid 1–0 in the Bernabeu Stadium in Alfredo di Stefano's testimonial back in 1967, but both Henrik and I just chuckled to ourselves at the sight of Jimmy single-handedly tearing their defence to shreds.

Like all the 'Lisbon Lions', he was always a welcome visitor to Parkhead. Whenever you saw him, you felt like smiling because he was just such a life-enhancing character who always had a good story to tell – to hear the stories of Jock Stein and the rest of the Lions from Jinky was a real treat. He had his fair share of troubles over the years even before he contracted his illness, but he always fought back and somehow people felt that, even though MND is always a terminal illness, Jinky might defy the odds.

In the end the disease won, though Jinky's courage in the face of it was absolutely awe-inspiring. The funeral at his local church was both emotional and dignified, with a lot of humour in the stories about Jimmy told by Bishop Joseph Devine, by Billy McNeill and former club director Willie Haughey, who had been his great friend and supporter. The scenes as the funeral cortege made its way to Celtic Park and then to the cemetery were simply stunning – to see so many thousands paying tribute to the hero they had lost made us all feel very humble.

As club captain, I was asked for my tribute and I can assure you my words came from the heart: 'When people here speak about playing the Celtic way, I think they are talking about Jimmy. He was entertaining, exciting and pretty fearless as well. We've lost a talismanic figure.'

After that, there was no way we could lose the final, and to their credit, everyone at Dunfermline Athletic agreed that it should be seen as a tribute to Jinky. That did not stop their players from competing fiercely on the day, and frankly we were nervous because our fans' expectations were so high. I was nervous personally, too, because I had the chance of lifting my first trophy as captain. I had also been injured in a freak accident at home just a few days before the final, slicing open my hand on a broken glass. The wound had been stitched and I needed to wear a protective bandage, but nothing was going to stop me lifting that trophy.

In the end we were too good for them, goals from Zurawski and Maloney putting us in easy street before big Dion Dublin came on and hit a third in injury-time.

Sadly Roy Keane was injured during the game, and for a while it looked as though he might not play enough matches to earn a league winner's medal, but in the end he made it safely enough.

With my family looking on, lifting that cup was one of the great moments of my life, and, yes, I milked it for all it was worth. Who wouldn't? I was just so delighted for Agnes Johnstone, Jimmy's widow, and all the family that we collectively donned a tribute shirt bearing Jinky's famous number seven.

There was an unpleasant moment afterwards when Dunfermline defender Greg Shields came out and said that I had boasted about my wealth on the pitch. What happened was that I was called a 'fat bastard' and I responded by saying 'If you're going to say that get it right, make it a rich fat bastard.' To me it was just part of the normal sledging that goes on all the time in football, and 999 times out 1,000 it stays on the pitch and is forgotten about.

Greg Shields hadn't heard the whole exchange and I'm afraid he rather made a fool of himself when he told the press his version. When the whole story came out, he looked like a schoolboy who'd got the story wrong, but I have no hard feelings about it.

However, I was less sanguine about the story which nearly ruined our championship-winning celebrations, a feat we duly accomplished a fortnight later against Hearts at Parkhead. It was a poor game, but big John Hartson's goal was all we needed to spark some riotous partying. Celtic had won the championship of Scotland for the fortieth time and we had done so in remarkable fashion. We had won the title with six matches remaining, a truly incredible turnaround from the beginning of the season. I am convinced that when the fans look back in five years or so, they will be amazed at what we did in going from the reverses at Bratislava and Ibrox to such an easy championship victory. Not only that, but we did it by playing some very fine attacking football, a trademark of Gordon Strachan's teams over the years.

The gaffer had to make some tough decisions in his first season with Celtic, but I have nothing but admiration for the way he has conducted himself, especially after the terrible start to the season in Bratislava. He is a winner who has always detested losing, both as a player and a manager, and he does not suffer fools gladly so I take it as a great compliment that we have worked well together.

I particularly appreciated his support after I was sent off by Stuart Dougal. He did not have to come out and back me but, even though he was rightly disappointed at my actions, he was beside me all the way and that was a real boon to me at a difficult time.

On the day we were presented with the trophy at Celtic Park against Hibs after our 1–1 draw, a newspaper broke the story that I was being taken to court by a former girlfriend who alleged that I was the father of her unborn baby. At the time of writing, I cannot say anything about this matter as it is the subject of forthcoming legal action, but the timing of the story was suspicious to say the least.

Thankfully my beautiful and wonderful Irene stood by me and showed incredible courage by walking onto Celtic Park that day with Gallagher in her arms. I was so proud to be seen with this strong and lovely woman – her courage is one of the many reasons I love her.

Though obviously the gloss was taken off my day as the captain lifting the trophy, nothing could spoil our celebrations. A lifelong Celtic fan, Billy Connolly, carried out the presentation and the Big Yin was very happy to do so and kept us all in stitches with his wisecracks.

The manager then arranged a wonderful gesture, in which all the backroom staff at Parkhead were introduced to the crowd. It was Gordon's way of emphasizing that Celtic are a family club and I know it was greatly appreciated by all the staff, such as John Clark, the Lisbon Lion who is our kitman and keeps us all neat and tidy, at least on the pitch. Clarky is a great character whose history at the club is unsurpassed, and he is always there to lend support when it's needed.

Tommy Burns is another Celtic legend and a mainstay of the club's coaching staff, but he has recently had to battle skin cancer. I was one of the first to know that Tommy was ill because I was in the doctor's room when he was being treated for the sore which was eventually diagnosed as being cancerous. I knew he had been operated on before and, being fair-skinned myself, I could tell he had a real problem, especially when he missed training. When the news broke that he was being treated for cancer, there was a real sense of shock, but at the time of writing it looks as though his treatment has been successful and the cancer was caught in time.

On a day-to-day basis there are a lot of people at the club who make our lives easier, such as the catering staff and the public relations crew. We may not always show it, but we players are grateful to them all.

We really don't have that much to do with the senior executives and directors, but I do, however, take a lot of time to deal with the fans. In return they have been very supportive of me, because I think they know I'm a fellow fan.

I particularly cherish the fact that the supporters named me as their Player of the Year in 2004, and I was truly honoured by the tribute dinner in Glasgow's Thistle Hotel which I received in November 2005, and which went ahead despite some moronic threats on the internet.

More than 900 people attended the dinner, superbly compered by broadcaster Rob McLean and featuring a side-splitting turn from my fellow Northern Irishman, comedian Frank Carson. We raised a lot of money that night for a cause dear to my heart – the spinal injuries unit at Glasgow's Southern General Hospital. I occasionally pop over there to see the patients and when I think of the courage of people like Tracy Ross, a young mother from Forfar who was in the unit for months after being partially paralysed in a car crash, I am truly humbled. I also always thank God for the fact that my own spinal condition was healed and did not prevent me playing football. Tracy, by the way, was able to leave the unit in her own special wheelchair designed in the colours of her favourite team, Celtic.

Later in the season I was guest of honour at the Celtic Supporters' Association's annual rally, where club chairman Brian Quinn gave me eloquent praise for which I will always be grateful. Then came the hard part – I had to reply! Unlike my sister Orla, I am not always at my best when speaking in public, but as captain it is something I have had to do and I have been working on it. Nor is my small talk always top quality. I tell the story against myself of how I met Ireland's Taioseach (Prime Minister) Bertie Ahern at a testimonial dinner for Jackie McNamara in Ireland. Bertie is a great Celtic fan and a quality guy, but I was a bit tongue-tied when I was introduced to him. I didn't know what to say so blurted out: 'So, Mr Ahern, how's work? Have you been busy?'

As soon as I said it I thought 'what an eejit' and could feel my face turning bright crimson. But he was obviously used to daft questions. 'Well,' he replied, 'apart from running the country and trying to avoid being shot every day, it's not been too hectic.' As I said, a class act.

Of course, the season did not end with that glorious trophy day at Parkhead. We fought out a goalless draw with Rangers the following week before going to Tynecastle where Hearts needed to win if they were to ensure they stayed on course to pip Rangers for the second place in the Champions League. The 3–0 result in their favour proved secondary to an incident involving myself and Rudi Skacel.

During the game I turned away and the next second all I saw was a huge wad of spit flying by my shoulder. To me, spitting at a fellow professional is the lowest of the low, and I just launched at Rudi Skacel.

Skacel ended up getting a free-kick, from which they nearly scored, and I got booked, which put me over the points limit and gained me a one-match suspension. After the game, I was asked what had sparked my anger, so I told the truth. I did not know then that Skacel had 'previous' as Stuart Duff of Dundee United had made a similar claim about the Hearts man in February.

But just like the Juanjo incident the previous season, the television cameras missed the incident. Hearts issued a statement backing their player. Steven Pressley as captain had every right to defend his colleague but I did not appreciate certain of his comments.

I was beginning to doubt my own sanity as everyone had lined up behind Rudi – club, captain, friends and fans. Fortunately, a photographer from the *Sun* newspaper double-checked his camera the following day and found the pictures which clearly showed Skacel's phlegm flying towards me. The *Sun* printed the pictures, and of course the reaction in some quarters was 'oh, they must have faked the photographs', while Hearts' response was to ban the newspaper from their premises.

But the pictures were not faked. Skacel had spat at me and there was the proof in full colour. A lot of people who had backed him suddenly felt very foolish but others said things like 'Rudi wouldn't mean it' – so Stuart Duff is a liar too?

Why can't people just accept that Rudi Skacel spat in my direction? As far as I'm concerned the matter is over and done with, but if I'm ever on the same pitch as Rudi Skacel, I'll make sure I'm carrying a spare handkerchief.

That was more or less the end of my season as captain, though we enjoyed a terrific night in Manchester at Roy Keane's testimonial.

So what now for me and Celtic? My long-term aim is to move into coaching and management and to that end I have begun my studies for my coaching licence.

Despite a generous and genuine offer from Crystal Palace, I have signed on for another year with Celtic and with the plans that Gordon Strachan has, I'm sure that we will prosper.

I am approaching the crossroads that every player must face but I am fit and well and will play on for as long as Celtic want me. In doing so, I have the support of everyone at the club and great people like my agents Martin Reilly and Mark Donaghy, my financial adviser Peter Kelsey and all the other friends who have stood by me through thick and thin over the years, such as Dessie Meginnis and Gary McCavigan in Lurgan and my mates at The Bear down in Leicester.

I have been fortunate to work under great managers and coaches, to play alongside some of the finest professionals and to take part in some of the best matches imaginable, latterly in front of the greatest fans in the world.

For their support in helping me do so, there are so many

people I wish to thank for their love and kindness that naming them would need another book. You know who you are and you know I appreciate you.

But I cannot end without thanking above all my parents and sisters, the rest of my family and Irene.

In time, Alisha and Gallagher may read this book, and will hopefully realize why I dedicated it to them as the best things ever to happen to me.

It is because – and perhaps despite some – of all the many things that have happened to me in thirty-five years on this planet that I look to the future with great hope, as I always do. My story is not finished yet, though I have no idea what chapters will be written in the years to come – none of us really do. In the meantime, I trust you have enjoyed this account of how a lad from Lurgan, via a circuitous route, became captain of Glasgow Celtic – the club I have loved, man and bhoy.

Career Statistics

NEIL FRANCIS LENNON

Date of birth: 25 June 1971

Place of birth: Portadown, Northern Ireland

Senior club matches played as at end of season 2005/06:

Club	**Dates**	**Appearances (as substitute in brackets)**	**Goals**
Glenavon	26 September 1987–4 October 1987	2	2
Manchester City	15 October 1987–9 August 1990	1	0
Crewe Alexandra	9 August 1990–22 February 1996	181 (6)	18

Club	Dates	Appearances (as substitute in brackets)	Goals
Leicester City	23 February 1996–8 December 2000	208 (1)	9
Celtic	9 December 2000–30 May 2006	257 (1)	3

INTERNATIONAL MATCHES:

Northern Ireland	11 June 1994 (v. Mexico in Miami) –13 February 2002 (v. Poland in Limassol, Cyprus)	40 (2)	2

PLAYING HONOURS:

Leicester City:
League Cup 1997, 2000

Celtic:
Scottish Premiership League 2000–1, 2001–2, 2003–4, 2005–6
Scottish Cup 2001, 2004, 2005
Scottish League Cup 2001, 2006
UEFA Cup Runners-Up 2003

Picture Credits

Page 13 (bottom) © Martin Reilly
Page 14 (top) © Ian Hodgson/Reuters; (middle) © Jeff Holmes/SNS Group; (bottom) © Jeff Mitchell/ Getty Images
Page 15 (top) © Empics; (bottom) © Alan Harvey/ SNS Group
Page 16 (top) © Alan Harvey/SNS Group; (bottom) © Empics

Index

Index

Index